RECORDS OF CIVILIZATION
SOURCES AND STUDIES

Edited under the auspices of the

DEPARTMENT OF HISTORY

COLUMBIA UNIVERSITY

✮

NEW YORK

COLUMBIA UNIVERSITY PRESS

1930

ROMAN THEATER AT ARLES

On the Government of God

A Treatise

wherein are shown by *Argument* and by *Examples* drawn from the *Abandoned Society* of the Times the Ways of GOD toward His Creatures

INDITED BY

S A L V I A N U S,

Presbyter of Marseilles
and Master of Bishops

as a WARNING *and* COUNSEL

This Fifth Century Polemic Done into English by

EVA M. SANFORD

Western Reserve University

NEW YORK
COLUMBIA UNIVERSITY PRESS
M·CM·XXX

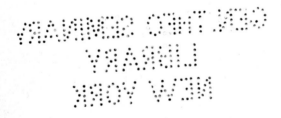
Printed in the United States of America
The Torch Press, Cedar Rapids, Iowa

TO MY FATHER

EDGAR LEWIS SANFORD

AND TO THE LEWISES AND SANFORDS BEFORE HIM
WHO LIKE SALVIAN HAVE PREACHED CONCERNING THE
GOVERNMENT OF GOD AND HIS PRESENT JUDGMENT

CONTENTS

   1. On the general belief in God's government. 2. That good Christians cannot be wretched. 3. Of the infirmities of the saints. 4. God's guidance and judgments of the world. 5. On the meaning of prayer. 6. The earliest instances of God's judgment. 7. God's judgment shown in the Flood. 8. The examples of Abraham, of Sodom and Gomorrah. 9. The Exodus. 10. Man's ingratitude for his present blessings. 11. Examples of God's mercy and of his severity. 12. God's judgments of the Hebrews.

   1. Of the presence of God. 2. God's watchful care. 3. His vengeance. 4. The punishment of David. 5. David's exile. 6. The immediacy of God's judgment.

   1. Divine authority and human reason. 2. Christian belief. 3. The obligations of the Christian life. 4. The apostle's imitation of Christ. 5. The services due to God. 6. How men follow Christ's precepts. 7. The necessity of impartial obedience. 8. The lesser commands of God. 9. The vices of Christians. 10. The guilt of rich men and nobles. 11. Their vain hope of salvation.

   1. The necessity of faith and good works. 2. Faith without works. 3. The sins of slaves compared with those of their masters. 4. The oppression of the nobles. 5. The enormity of their crimes. 6. The rich compared with their slaves; the burdens of taxation. 7. The penalties of conversion. 8. That men's crimes are the cause of their misfortunes. 9. The Father's love for his creatures. 10. The fulness

of God's love. 11. The ingratitude of man. 12. The guilt of Christians. 13. Comparison of Christians with barbarians. 14. The peculiar guilt of Christians. 15. Their oaths. 16. Their transgressions of the divine law. 17. Pagan ideas of the Christians. 18. Blasphemy. 19. The guilt of Christians compared with that of heathen.

INTRODUCTION

Salvus, incolumisque Salvianus,
Magnus Scriptor, Episcopus probatus,
Antiquum reparatus in decorem,
In lucem venit omine auspicato,
Vitae Regula, Episcopon Magister;
Dignus nomine, et hoc honore dignus.

Scriptorum decus elegantiorum;

Dignus, quem studiis, modisque cunctis
Mirentur, celebrent, legant frequentes
Quot sunt, aut aliis erunt in annis.
Hunc, lector, precor, accipe explicata
Fronte, hunc delicias tuas putabis.

Illum plus oculis tuis amabis,
Meras delicias, meros lepores,
Inscriptum simul, et tibi dicatum,
Salvum, incolumemque Salvianum.

—Brassicanus

INTRODUCTION

I. A FIFTH CENTURY TRACT FOR THE TIMES

"Be ashamed, ye Roman people everywhere, be ashamed of the lives you lead! . . . It is neither the strength of their bodies that makes the barbarians conquer, nor the weakness of our nature that makes us subject to defeat. Let no one think or persuade himself otherwise — it is our vicious lives alone that have conquered us."[1]

These are the words which Salvian would have made echo throughout the Roman world, had his human frailty permitted, the words which have earned him the title of the "Jeremiah of his times." The problem of the decline of the Roman power was not relegated to the historians at that time, but was the chief concern of all thinking men, and many solutions were proposed. Successive invasions and settlements of barbarian tribes had ended Rome's claim to rule the world, while at the same time the fiscal difficulties of the central administration had increased taxation beyond endurance. The world seemed to be dying of old age, and the Empire with it. The natural tendency to glorify the past was intensified by the poignant wretchedness of the present, and grave doubts arose in the minds even of faithful Christians. "The very people who, as pagans, conquered and ruled the world, are being conquered and enslaved now that they have become Christians. Is not this clear evidence of God's neglect of human affairs?"[2] The question did not of itself imply disbelief in God, but its implicit doubt of God's constant government and judgment of mankind endangered the foundations of the Christian faith. Salvian's answer was clear and uncompromising. "These words are harsh and austere,"

---

[1] Salvian *De gubernatione Dei* VII. 23.
[2] *Ibid.*, VII. 1.

3

he wrote elsewhere, "but what are we to do? We may not change the nature of things, and the truth cannot be pronounced otherwise than as the very essence of truth demands. Men think my words harsh. I know that well enough. But what are we to do? Except by hardship we do not make our way into the Kingdom." [3]

The treatise *On the Government of God*, which is Salvian's best known work, is essentially an exposition of this thesis: that the decline of the Roman power actually demonstrated God's government and judgment of human actions, since the sins of the Romans were such as had always, since the fall of Adam, been visited with instant punishment. Consequently the first two books of Salvian's discussion are chiefly devoted to demonstrations of God's judgment by examples drawn from the authority of the Old Testament. The third book builds on this foundation a clear exposition of the Christian obligation of an upright life in God's service. On this basis Salvian then proceeded to contrast the disgraceful actions of the Christian Romans of his time with their duty toward God, and with the virtues of the victorious barbarians. Yet the latter, being either heretics or pagans, were under less obligation to a godly life than the orthodox Romans. To the author himself, and to his fellow clergy, the first three books may well have seemed the essential portion of the argument: to us the great interest of the work lies in the picture of the times given in the last five. For here we have detailed accounts of the effects of the burden of taxation on the poor, whom it ruined; on the rich, who managed to shift their burden to weaker shoulders; and on the curials, who were forced into tyranny by their responsibility to the agents of the central government for the sums due. In this case as in others, reference to the imperial decrees collected in the *Codices* proves the essential truth of Salvian's account. Sidonius Apollinaris has given us in his letters charming descriptions of the life of the

---

[3] *Ad ecclesiam* IV. 8.

wealthy nobles of southern Gaul: Salvian showed the other side of the picture when he described the means by which some of these same nobles had acquired their neighbors' land, and when he inveighed against the corruption of domestic life in their villas. He has shown clearly the development of serfdom under pressure of taxation and patronage, and the other alternatives from which the poor might choose — flight to barbarian territory, or armed revolt against the Roman system. And he has described in graphic terms, in part as an eyewitness, the horrors that attended the capture and sack of wealthy Roman cities, even at the hands of barbarians whom he believed to be far less brutal and depraved than many Romans. He has pictured the triumphant progress of the Vandals, reckoned as the weakest of Rome's enemies, through the richest provinces of the West.

He showed, to be sure, only one side of life. The miseries of the time prompted the doubts that he undertook to resolve; with these alone he was directly concerned. He rarely admitted that there were exceptions to the prevailing corruption of his fellow Romans. It was hardly consistent with his thesis that he should do so, for his book was essentially a polemic. It is important, however, to note in this connection that his statements are very rarely in conflict with other contemporary evidence. Passages in the letters of Sidonius, in the sermons and letters of his friends at Lérins, and of other leaders of the church, as well as in the writings of pagans and in the laws of the empire, regularly corroborate his account of the times. And he, in turn, occasionally confirms their accounts of the beauty that still remained in life, by his glimpses of Provence, with its pleasant country life and rich harvests — "the one corner where the Roman power still lives."

II. The Life of Salvian

As we have seen, Salvian wrote "as one having authority." That he had earned the right to speak is fully proved by the chief

contemporary reference to his life and work. Gennadius wrote of
him, in his biographical dictionary of illustrious men:

> Salvian, presbyter of Marseilles, learned in human and divine letters,
> and, if I may apply the title to him, master of bishops, wrote many books
> in a clear and scholarly style. Of these I have read the following: four
> books addressed to Marcellus the presbyter, *On the Value of Virginity*,
> and four *Against Avarice*; five books *On the Present Judgment*, and one
> book *For the Satisfaction of These* [*Sins*], addressed to Salonius the
> bishop; one book in exposition of the last part of Ecclesiastes, addressed
> to Claudius, bishop of Vienne; one book of letters; one book composed in
> verse as a *Hexameron* after the Greek fashion, from the beginning of
> Genesis to the creation of man; many homilies written for bishops; and
> on the sacraments, books whose number I do not recall. He still lives today
> in a goodly old age.[4]

Salvian's other names we do not know, due chiefly to the fact
that fifth century etiquette forbade the use of more than one name
in friendly correspondence,[5] but the title "master of bishops"
which Gennadius bestowed on him has more than atoned for the
loss. The modest office of presbyter at Marseilles would seem sufficient to refute the early editors' claim of a bishop's mitre for him,
even without the negative evidence of the omission of his name from
the episcopal lists.[6] But the title "master of bishops," *magister
episcoporum*, is his by manifold right, and is inseparably connected
with his personality in the minds of all who have studied his work.
He lived and worked for some time at the very nursery of bishops,
Lérins, where he was chosen to teach the two sons of Eucherius,
both of whom were to become bishops later. At Marseilles he continued his teaching, composing many homilies for bishops, as Gennadius said. Although in his books *To the Church against Avarice* he
spoke of himself as "least of the servants of God," he spoke with

---

[4] Gennadius, *Catalogus virorum illustrium*, c.68; written about A.D. 490-495.

[5] See Symmachus *Ep.* II. 35.

[6] These unfounded claims have a curious echo in the statement of a recent
writer that Salvian was "priest and probably bishop." Holland, "The Crash
of Empire," *Dublin Review*, CLXXVII (1925), 2.

the voice of authority, and his words were chiefly addressed to the great lords of the church.

Many have called him by another title, which in its present meaning we cannot claim for him, but which he rightfully enjoyed in its fifth century use. *Sanctus* to him, as to all other Christians, before it seemed necessary to determine fixed categories for the communion of saints, meant a devout Christian. The word was applied to him by contemporaries, and recurs so often in his books that it is small wonder that many of his editors have informally canonized him, others have become involved in learned arguments to deprive him of sainthood,[7] and one university, at least, continues the good tradition in his honor.[8] Without doubt, as Baluze concludes, after disproving his claims to canonization, "there are many saints in heaven who are not so held by us in our catalogues."

Of his personal life we know little, though he contributes so much to our knowledge of the general circumstances of his time. Gennadius described him in the last decade of the fifth century as still living *bona senectute*. It is not possible for us to fix the exact date of his birth, but the wide experience and ripe wisdom shown in his treatise *On the Government of God* indicate at least that he had reached maturity some time before it was written. As this book was evidently composed between A.D. 439 and 450, it is natural to assume that he was born late in the fourth century or early in the fifth.[9] What we know of the events of his life belongs entirely to the period before the publication of his chief work. The forty years or more that followed must be filled in by the writing of some of those lost works of which Gennadius spoke, and the many activities of a priest and "master of bishops" in one of the chief centers of the Gallic church. Several years before Salvian settled in Mar-

---

[7] See, for example, the notes of Baluze, *Salviani opera* (1742), p. 356.

[8] He regularly appears as "Saint Salvianus" in the catalogue entries in the Harvard College Library.

[9] See Zschimmer, *Salvianus* (Halle, 1875), p. 6.

seilles, a poet beggared by the Gothic raids sought refuge there, and found "many saints my dear friends." [10] Such a haven from the storms that beset the rest of Gaul was sure to provide ample activity for its priests.

The place of Salvian's birth has been much disputed. Some early editors assumed that he was born in Africa — an assumption not unnatural in view of his graphic description of the sins and the ruin of that province.[11] The account of the capture of Trèves in his sixth book, however, makes it clear that his native district was near the Rhine frontier. The claims of both Trèves and Cologne have been supported by various authorities. Whether he lived in one of these cities, or on an estate in the countryside near by, his familiarity with the whole district is unmistakable.

Trèves was the place of all others in the western world where he could best have studied the fatal magnificence of the higher Roman officials in the face of the barbarian attacks. The praetorian prefect of the Gallic and Spanish provinces kept his official residence there in such state as Constantius the emperor had scarcely equalled when he fixed his capital in that city a century earlier. There Salvian must have watched with growing anxiety the increasing power of the Franks. The author of the twelfth century *Gesta Trevororum* tells us that they had conceived a special hostility for this most splendid of Gallic cities from the time of their first contact with it. This district also afforded excellent opportunities to observe the increasing ravages of Goths, Vandals and Burgundians. The great amphitheater of Trèves was the scene of many of those public spectacles against which Salvian inveighed so bitterly, and

---

[10] Paulinus of Pella, *Eucharisticos,* 11. 520-521.

[11] See Book VII. 12-13 and note 44, *infra.* His knowledge of Africa and his concern for it may be amply accounted for by its recent tragic history and also by the prominence of the African church. The Christian writers whose work chiefly influenced his were all connected with the African church except those whom he knew at Lérins and Marseilles. He may well have travelled in Africa.

when the Vandal Crocus captured the city in A.D. 406, the people were saved only by taking refuge within its strong walls.[12] Years later, Salvian wrote from Marseilles to the monks at Lérins, commending to their kindly offices a young kinsman, a refugee from the captured city of Cologne. He wrote to the brothers that the boy was "of a family not obscure, of which I might say something more, were he not related to me."[13] These words confirm the conclusions as to Salvian's family and position that we should naturally draw from his writings. His parents were clearly of the Gallo-Roman aristocracy: Salvian knew intimately the way of life of a man of position and substance, however much he disapproved of it. His examples indicate a considerable knowledge of life on the great estates, the masters' problems with slaves and tenants, the results of patronage, the various forms of cultivation employed, and at the same time a very real appreciation of the natural beauties of the country. For slaves and poor men, and all who suffered oppression, he had great sympathy. This, however, did not blind him to the probability that they would be as bad as their oppressors if the tables were turned. We do not need Gennadius' statement to prove that he had the full rhetorical education of his time. Despite the arguments of some scholars to the contrary, his works seem to indicate that he had continued to read widely in "human and divine letters." Greek he apparently did not read, and the works of philosophers he quoted only at second hand. He was fond of examples drawn from medical practice, but these are all of a sort with which any intelligent man would be familiar.

His knowledge of law was far more detailed, and his writings furnish a valuable commentary on the Roman *Codices*, which in their turn serve as a check on his statements. Rittershausen concluded that he had had regular legal training; certainly he had a legal mind, and legal phraseology recurs constantly in his dis-

---

[12] *Gesta Treverorum*, ed. Waitz, MGH, *Scriptores*, VIII, 157.
[13] *Ep.* 1.5.

cussions. But it seems equally probable, especially if his father held an imperial position, that his juristic knowledge merely represents the attainment of a Roman citizen concerned both in the complex management of a considerable estate and in affairs of government administration. That he belonged to an imperial official family is suggested by his attitude toward lesser officials. For the downtrodden poor his sympathy is great, but for clerks, soldiers and tax collectors, and for the curials who formed the miserable remnant of the local aristocracies, he seems to have felt only scorn and distaste. His aristocratic prejudices were tempered by Christian charity in other cases, but not in his attitude toward these men.[14]

It seems probable that he himself was brought up in the orthodox faith; at least he shows little of that bitterness toward pagans and heretics that recent converts are wont to feel. For those who called themselves Christians but continued heathen practices, however, his antipathy was very strong. His wife, Palladia, had been brought up in paganism, but her parents, Hypatius and Quieta, seem to have made no objection to the marriage. Later, however, they were alienated by the decision of Salvian and Palladia to follow a course which was being adopted by many other Christian couples. Unable either to endure Roman society as they found it, or to reform it from within, they determined to give their property to the church, and live no longer as man and wife, but as brother and sister in Christian fellowship. Paulinus of Nola, the one contemporary to whose example Salvian clearly alludes,[15] is the best known of those who sought that peace in Christian poverty which Roman wealth had failed to give. The anger of Ausonius at his friend's course reflects a situation that must have been many times repeated. In this case, however, it culminated in one of the most poignant expressions of friendship that man has ever written.[16]

---

[14] See Book III. 10.

[15] See Book VII. 3 and note 6.

[16] Paulinus of Nola *Carmen* XI. 11. 49-68, in CSEL, XXX. 2.

After an estrangement from their parents that lasted nearly seven years, Salvian, Palladia and the little daughter Auspiciola tried once more to effect a reconciliation. Their letter,[17] which has fortunately been preserved, seems far too mannered and artificial to be convincing, but this formality was a set convention in the letter-writing of the time. Their pleas are sincere and loving, though yielding not one jot as to the essential rightness of their course. The immediate occasion of the letter seems to have been the news of the parents' conversion to Christianity, which would seem indeed to work in favor of their case. Palladia followed her husband's arguments by memories of the days when they had called her "little starling, little mistress, little mother, birdling:" she pleaded tenderly, too, for little Auspiciola, who deserved her grandparents' love.

Of the issue of their suit we know nothing. They had withdrawn from the vicinity of Trèves, probably shortly after that destruction of the city which Salvian saw with his own eyes, and so graphically described.[18] About A.D. 418 the praetorian prefect of Gaul seems to have changed his seat from Trèves to Arles; perhaps Salvian's was one of the Roman families that withdrew soon after, either for official or private reasons.[19] We do not know whether it was before or after this move that their ascetic resolution was taken; in any case, they went soon to the islands of the Lérins, which offered monasteries, separate but not remote from each other, for families in such case as theirs. Nothing is known thereafter of Palladia and Auspiciola; Salvian's life apparently lay apart from theirs.

Lérins was that "earthly paradise"[20] which furnished a haven for many religious of the day, and was so powerful a stimulant to their faith that from it went forth a seemingly endless stream of

---

[17] *Ep.* IV.
[18] Book VI. 13.
[19] See Haemmerle, *Studia Salviana* I (Landshut, 1893), 7.
[20] *Vita S. Hilarii Arelatensis*, 5 (Migne, PL, L, col. 1226).

saintly men. Honoratus and Hilary, Caesarius and Virgilius went from Lérins to the archbishopric of Arles; Maximus and Faustus to the see of Riez; Lupus to Troyes. Eucherius came to Lérins with his wife Galla and his two sons. He himself left to become bishop of Lyons; his sons, Salonius and Veranus, were put under the successive tutelage of Honoratus, Hilary, Salvian and Vincent,[21] and became bishops of Geneva and Vence. Three bishops went from Lérins to Avignon, and many others might be named.[22]

Honoratus was abbot at Lérins in Salvian's time and was called by Eucherius "master of bishops, doctor of the churches," being thus the prototype of Salvian. Shortly after A.D. 429, Hilarius of Arles preached at Marseilles a sermon on the life of Honoratus, in which he quoted from the writings of "a man of not unmerited distinction, and most blessed in Christ, Salvian the presbyter, one of Honoratus' dear associates."[23] Thus he gives us not only a glimpse of the esteem in which Salvian was already held, but a *terminus ante quem* for his ordination. Just when Salvian moved to Marseilles we do not know, nor why. Certainly it was through no antagonism at Lérins, for his first letter, already mentioned, ex-presses the utmost affection for the brothers there. The initial para-graph, on the bitter-sweetness of love, which at times compels one to ask of beloved friends a favor that without love would be irk-

---

[21] Eucherius, in a letter to his son Salonius prefaced to his *Instructiones de quaestionibus difficilioribus veteris ac novi testamenti* (CSEL, XXXI. 1, pp. 65-66), recalling his sons' teaching, wrote: "When you had scarcely reached the age of ten, you entered the monastery and were not only given training among that sacred brotherhood, but were reared up under our father Honora-tus, first father of the islands and afterwards also master of the churches. There the teachings of the most blessed Hilarius, then a novice of the island, but now a most reverend bishop, formed you in all branches of spiritual study; a work completed by saints Salvian and Vincent, preëminent alike in eloquence and knowledge."

[22] Cooper-Marsdin, *The History of the Islands of the Lérins* (Cambridge, 1913), p. 49.

[23] Hilarius, *Sermo de vita S. Honorati Arelatensis* (Migne, PL, L, col. 1260): the passage which he quotes is not found in Salvian's extant works.

some, bears witness to the depth of his feeling for the monks. Its concluding words testify to his high esteem for them: "Surely, if there is any good character in this young man, his hope and salvation will not prove to be of great difficulty to you; even if he receives no actual teaching, it is enough for him to be with you."

The years at Lérins must have exerted great influence on the development of Salvian's thought and style. The close fellowship between the monks of the island is constantly demonstrated by likenesses of ideas and phrasing in the writings of the many great men who there received their early training. Parts of the homilies of Caesarius of Arles, of Valerius and Hilarius bear striking resemblances to passages in Salvian's work. Vincent's *Commonitorium* has been appropriately included in many editions of Salvian, thus continuing their ancient fellowship. The book *On the Government of God*, as well as a lost work, was dedicated to Salonius, whom Salvian addressed in his ninth letter as "master and most blessed pupil, father, and son, pupil by instruction, son by affection, and father by rank and honor."

The life of Caesarius of Arles throws some light on the statement that Salvian composed many homilies for bishops. We read of Caesarius that:

He composed also appropriate sermons for feast days and other occasions, and sermons against the evils of drunkenness and lust, against discord and hatred, against anger and pride, against sacrilegious men and soothsayers, against pagan rites, against augurs, the worshippers of woods and of springs, and against the vices of divers men. He so prepared these homilies that if any visitors asked, far from refusing to loan them, he offered them for copying at the slightest suggestion of a request, and himself corrected them. He sent copies by priests to men far distant in the Frankish land, in Gaul, Italy and Spain and divers provinces, to be preached in their churches, that, casting aside frivolous and transitory interests, they might, as the apostle preached, become followers of good works.[24]

---

[24] Cyprianus *Vita S. Caesarii* I. 5. 42 (Migne, PL, LXVII, col. 1021).

Gennadius' emphasis on the homilies of Salvian suggests that their composition may have been one of the major preoccupations of his life in Marseilles, and a chief ground for his title of "master of bishops." That many of his sermons took the form of invectives against the vices of his day may be assumed from the extant books *Against Avarice* and *On the Government of God*. Both of these, indeed, have the air of having been compiled from actual sermons. The congregation is clearly visualized, which may account for the frequent use of the second person, and of a vivid colloquial tone.

That his attacks on the weaknesses of his contemporaries caused him serious difficulties is indicated by his constant reiteration that his words are sure to give offence to many, but even so they must be said. Larinus Amatius said in his eulogy of Salvian: "For if wrath engenders hatred among all men, and begets it especially among the wicked, who was ever more hated for the truth than Salvian, since no one ever set forth more truths than he?" [25]

From the time of his removal to Marseilles, all that we know of Salvian's life is summed up in Gennadius' account. The few extant letters are chiefly of value for the glimpses they afford of his regard for the deference due to those of higher rank in the church, and their evidence of his continuing association with his former friends and pupils at Lérins. An example is his letter to Eucherius, thanking him for a copy of his *Instructions on the More Difficult Questions of the Old and New Testament*,[26] which the bishop had written for his sons, now themselves "masters of churches." Lacking any further evidence for the closing years of Salvian's life than the goodly old age with which Gennadius credited him, we can only hope that he gained fulfilment of the wish with which his letter to Eucherius ended: "May God in his mercy grant me throughout the days of my life, or at least when they are ended, that those who have been my pupils may daily pray for me."

---

[25] *Salviani opera* (Venice, 1696), p. 3.
[26] Ep. 8; cf. note 21, *supra*.

III. Salvian's Literary Work

Gennadius' list shows that, while much of Salvian's work has been lost, the books that remain are probably the most individual and the most interesting to us. The writings of several other early Christians present such titles as *On the Value of Virginity, A Book in Exposition of the Last Part of Ecclesiastes,* and books *On the Sacraments.* One title is obscure, the book to Salonius *Pro eorum merito satisfactionis,* or *Pro eorum praemio satisfaciendo.* The variants in the text of Gennadius indicate that the obscurity is of long standing in the manuscript tradition. In my translation I have followed Ebert's conjecture of *peccatorum* for *eorum,* which at least makes possible a conjectural translation of the title — *For the Satisfaction of These Sins,*[27] a book that might conceivably have been a companion volume to that *On the Government of God.*

Of the homilies written for bishops, and the influence of sermon writing on Salvian's general style, I have already spoken. It is possible, as Peter Allix suggested, that the anonymous poem on Genesis formerly ascribed to Tertullian may be part of the lost *Hexameron* of Salvian; the poem is, however, of slight importance, and its identification as the work of our author would be chiefly valuable as an indication of his wisdom in not publishing other verses.[28] Only nine of the letters are preserved; of these I have already spoken. The ninth, addressed to Salonius, is of special interest, since it explains both Salvian's purpose in writing his four books *Against Avarice,* and his reasons for publishing them anonymously. Salonius feared that since the work was issued as the

---

[27] Brakman suggests reading *Pro reorum merito satisfactionis librum unum,* which seems textually reasonable. He interprets this title as meaning a "book teaching how praiseworthy are sinners who atone for their sins to the satisfaction of God." Gennadius' account of Cassian's works contains one *De satisfactione paenitentiae,* which is a simpler statement of the same subject. *Mnemosyne,* LII (1924), p. 181.

[28] See Peter Allix, "Dissertatio de Tertulliani vita et scriptis," in Oehler, *Tertullianus,* III (Leipzig, 1853), 76.

Address of Timotheus to the Church against Avarice, it might be mistaken for an apocryphal work of the "Apostle" Timothy.

Like the *Government of God*, the invective *Against Avarice* was written because of Salvian's deep conviction of the dangers inherent in the persistent vices of men who called themselves Christians. Avarice was a besetting sin of many Romans, and had infected not only members of the church, but its clergy, even to the bishops themselves. The resultant neglect of the true service of God, and of the spiritual and material welfare of the church, led Salvian to "burst forth into words of lamentation" addressed to the church to which the offenders belonged. His failure to attach his own name to the book he explained not only by his desire to avoid vain glory in a service to God, but also by his conviction that the obscurity of his name might detract from the influence of his words. The pseudonym Timotheus ("Honoring God") was chosen to indicate the motive of the work: "Indeed, the writer thought it fitting that, writing his books for the honor of God, he should consecrate the title to his divine honor." [29]

In spite of this letter, and of Gennadius' ascription of the work to Salvian, its anonymity was preserved in modern times, for it was published by Sichardus at Fol near Basel in 1528 as the work of Bishop Timotheus, in a collection entitled *An Antidote against the Heresies of All Ages.*

While no one who reads the treatise *Against Avarice* can doubt the sincerity and depth of feeling with which it was written, the work is a curious document of the times. Avarice was considered one of the deadly sins. But it is hard now to avoid seeing some self-interest on the part of the church in the constant exhortations to the rich to give all their goods to the church in order to win remission of their sins. In its simplest form, this is the admonition of Christ to the rich young man: as it is elaborated to produce a surer conviction in the minds of fifth century Midases it is perilous-

---

[29] *Ep.* IX. 20.

ly close to the purchase of absolution. Some modern writers have thought the book more likely to encourage the avarice of the church than to discourage that of churchmen; others have seen in it an anticipation of the later satires against the greed of the clergy.[30] The irony that is never far from Salvian's writing is even more marked than usual in this indictment, but the unprejudiced reader is not likely to see in it an intention of actual satire. Nor is it sufficient to dismiss it, as Teuffel does, simply as a *ballon d'essai*.[31] It was clearly written in all seriousness, albeit in bitterness of heart, with the earnest hope of exerting a salutary influence against a chief evil of the times. The author employed the arguments that experience had taught him were most likely to be effective.

That this work was written before the completion of the treatise *On the Government of God* is shown by the quotation from it in the latter; it may with some probability be assigned to the years 435-439.[32] The words of Timothy to the church must have aroused much anger among ecclesiastical leaders, and apparently this antagonism made Salvian rather sensitive to criticism, though none the less determined to attack the vices of his day. That his later books would not be less fearless because of any hostility thus aroused, he showed in his concluding paragraphs, in which there is not a little of his own spiritual biography:

All human work is unworthy in comparison with the future glory. So nothing ought to seem hard and austere to Christians, because whatever they offer to Christ is in return for eternal blessings; what is given is vile when that which is received is so great. Nothing great is paid to God by men on earth, in comparison with the supreme gift of heaven. It is hard for misers to lavish their wealth. What is strange in this? Everything is hard that is demanded of the unwilling. Almost every divine word arouses animosity — there are as many hostile schools as there are teachers.

---

30 Zschimmer, pp. 77-79.

31 *Geschichte der römischen Literatur* (6th ed., Leipzig, 1913), III, 465.

32 See H. K. Messenger, *De temporum et modorum apud Salvianum usu*, Preface, p. 1. The quotation occurs in Book IV. 1. Valran, *Quare Salvianus magister episcoporum dictus sit* (Paris, 1899), p. 5, suggests that the two works may have been composed during the same period.

If the Lord orders men to be generous, the miser is angry; if he exacts parsimony, the prodigal curses. The wicked consider the sacred speeches their enemies; robbers shudder at what is written about justice, the proud at precepts of humility; the drunken oppose the request for sobriety and the shameless the command of chastity. So we must either say nothing, or expect that whatever is said will displease one man or another. Any wicked man would rather execrate the law than amend his character; he would rather hate precepts than vices.

Meanwhile, what do those men do who have been given by Christ the duty of speaking? They displease God if they are silent, men if they speak. But, as the apostles said to the Jews, it is better to obey God than man. This is the advice I offer to all to whom the law of God seems heavy and onerous, even if they do not entirely refuse to receive it, in order that those things may please them, which God ordains. All who hate the sacred commandments have the cause of their hatred within themselves. Every man's dislike of the law is due not to its precepts, but to his own life; the law indeed is good, but his habits are bad. So men should change their attitude and their point of view. If they make their habits worthy of approbation, nothing that the good law enjoins will displease them. For when a man has begun to be good, he cannot fail to love the law of God, which has within it that which holy men have in their lives.[33]

IV. ON THE GOVERNMENT OF GOD

The work on which for us the real interest of Salvian's life and thought depends, is that which Gennadius cited as five books *On the Present Judgment*, but which the manuscripts offer us as eight books *On the Government of God*. In this treatise Salvian discusses the defeat of Litorius in A.D. 439, but fails to mention the Vandal sack of Rome in 455, which must have profoundly impressed him. In view of the description he gives of the Vandal capture of Carthage, he would scarcely have omitted their raid on Rome. So we may reasonably suppose that the book was published between A.D. 439 and 455. We may probably limit the period somewhat more by the assumption that the great battle between the Romans and the Huns would have been mentioned if the treatise had been finished after 451. The argument from silence is less danger-

---

[33] *Ad ecclesiam* IV. 9.

ous in this instance, because of the general inclusiveness of Salvian's
allusions to contemporary matters germane to his purpose, as these
great events certainly would have been. Whatever the date of
publication, the book is the mature product of some years of preaching.

It is evident that only the third and fifth books mark distinct
developments in the argument. Some claim that elsewhere the
division into books is purely arbitrary and does not betray any
set intention on the part of the author. Since Gennadius speaks of
five, and not *eight* books it has been assumed that a new division
was made, perhaps as a matter of scribal convenience, after Gennadius wrote. Brakman, however, suggested with some plausibility
that Gennadius may actually have written VIII, and a scribe mis-
copied the letters as IIIII, which would be a natural error, if the
V were imperfect. And the length of the individual books varies
too much for a purely arbitrary division, whereas some case can be
made out for the logic of the present arrangement.[34]

For the modern reader the chief interest of Salvian's work lies
in the description of the life of the times in his later books. The
careful building up of the evidence of the sacred authorities for
God's judgment of the world seems tedious and repetitious. We
are inclined to rebel at the constant reference to authority in the
first three books. It is not unnatural to prefer the Old Testament
itself to Salvian's reworking of the same themes with abundance of
quotation. The cento is no longer a favored literary form, and
overabundant quotation, at least when openly acknowledged, is out
of favor. Few of us are likely to be in the position of the men of
the fifth century who found it difficult to choose among various
poor renderings of the Old Testament, since Jerome's version was
just beginning to make its way into Gaul, or to procure a complete
copy even if the initial obstacle of choice were overcome. The

---

[34] "Appendix de Gennadii capite lxviii," *Mnemosyne*, LII (1924), 180.

reader who wishes his interest readily aroused, who would read
the past in the light of his own experience, had best begin with the
fourth book. A generation ago it would have been natural to remark that in Salvian's tract for his own times in these later books
there is much that might be applied with little change to our own
day. Such a statement would be no less true now, were it the
present custom of historians to study past records as a source of
moral examples for the current age.

But to avoid the risk of tedium by omitting the first three books
is to lose much of the essence of the work, and of the fifth-century
manner of thought. Salvian wrote not for us, but for his contemporaries. Historically, therefore, it is of value to note how he built
up his demonstration of a fundamental principle — God's constant government and immediate judgment of his people. Not only
pagans, but men who called themselves Christians, were led by a
faulty reading of their times to question this tenet of the Christian
faith. The Christians must be made to realize that such doubts
were directly contradictory to the testimony of the Bible on which
their faith rested. Hence the full evidence of the Scriptures was
brought into court before the witness of contemporary life was
summoned. It is futile to say that Salvian was merely attempting
to prove God's judgment by reiterating his statement that God
constantly sees and judges his people, or, as some put it, that he
cites the authority of the Scriptures in support of that authority.
There is no indication that his opponents had questioned the authority of the Biblical narrative. They had, indeed, questioned a
fundamental doctrine of Christianity, having what would appear
to be good reason for such doubts in the distress into which they,
though a Christian people, had fallen. The validity of their estimate of God's injustice to themselves was a secondary matter to
Salvian. The first necessity was to remind them that their doubts
as to God's complete and immediate justice in the governance of
the world were constantly disproved by the scriptural authority.

Since they had shown themselves either ignorant or forgetful of the evidence of the Bible on this subject, it must be recapitulated for them. The foundation thus laid, they would be in a fit frame of mind to consider how the apparent injustice of their present misfortunes might be squared with the unvarying justice of the God they worshipped. We are too apt to forget that his words were addressed not to pagans or heretics but to orthodox Christians. For these the first essential was fulness of understanding of their own faith: its application to their transitory circumstances was secondary. To many of its first readers the latter part of the work may have seemed an irrelevant anticlimax to the real argument, since it depended less closely on scriptural authority for its substance and Lactantius for its structure, and dealt with matters of ephemeral interest.

Like Augustine, Salvian was distressed by the "false opinion held by many" in his time, that the contrast between the poverty and captivity of the Christian Roman Empire and the prosperous domination of pagan Rome proved that God neither cared for the world he had created nor governed and judged it, except by a judgment too far in the future to afford any present satisfaction to the just or fear to the wicked. Such attacks on Christianity Augustine had answered by his contrast, a generation earlier, between the ephemeral city of this world and the eternal City of God. Another portion of his answer had been assigned to Orosius, who undertook in his *History against the Pagans* to prove that the evils into which the Christian Roman Empire had fallen were less than those of past and pagan generations. He even dared to remind his readers that the most glorious conquests of Rome had afforded far greater misery, disgrace and suffering to her defeated enemies than the Romans themselves now suffered, and to prophesy that those who now seemed barbarous destroyers of a mighty empire would some day be honored as heroes of the nations they were founding. Orosius' minimizing of Rome's dangers was possible, though some-

what fantastic, even after the Gothic sack of the city in A.D. 410.
When Salvian wrote such an attitude was no longer reasonable.
Orosius had prophesied that new nations would take the place of
Rome; Salvian, while he conceived the Empire as still the great
cohesive force in the western world, saw the Teutonic nations
settled within its former borders. Goths, Vandals, Burgundians
and Franks had established their own kingdoms, and if any of them
lost ground, it was not because of the superiority of the Romans,
but of the other barbarians. Rome had long tried to suppress the
peasants' revolt of the Bagaudae, but without lasting success, and
this situation was rendered the more serious by the fact that the
cause of the rebellion was oppressive taxation for which no work-
able remedy was found. Britain was cut off from Rome by Saxon
raids and by her own dissensions. The Vandals were in possession
of the former province of Africa, the granary of Rome and the
great center of Christian teaching. Salvian's debt to Tertullian,
Cyprian, Lactantius and Augustine was so great that he recalled
with difficulty that many of his readers thought the home of these
Fathers remote from them, and were little concerned in its ruin.[35]

Salvian's own home in the Rhineland had been several times
ravaged by the Franks. The success of Aëtius in checking dis-
integration during the years of his leadership seemed due in no
small part to his shrewdness in alliances and his discretion in
granting favorable terms to the Goths and Vandals for security
against an aggression with which he might not be able to cope directly. His success was more than once endangered by the lack of
prudence and coöperation among his subordinates.[36]

> Rome herself opened her gates to fur-clad satellites,
> And was captive ere her capture.[37]

Everywhere the growing disproportion between the expenses
and the income of the Empire led to taxation that would have been

---

[35] See Book VI. 12-13.

[36] Book VII. 9-10.

[37] Rutilius Namatianus *De reditu suo* II. 11. 49-50.

heavy under the most favorable circumstances. With the opportunities for privilege and graft that the nobles in the imperial
hierarchy could always find, against which the more lowly could
only struggle impotently, this became unendurable. Salvian's
picture of the times does not stand alone: it is gloomy in comparison
with that of Sidonius Apollinaris in his letters, and yet Sidonius
gives ample evidence to confirm much of Salvian's detail. It is more
gloomy than that of Ausonius in his verses, but a man who had resigned all that he had to seek God's peace, could hardly be expected
to find the continuance of the elegant pleasures of society in southern Gaul a cause for light-heartedness. It must be remembered also
that matters had improved somewhat, though temporarily, in the
generation between Salvian's book and the letters of Sidonius.[38]

Salvian's sympathies for the poor and oppressed were very
great, the greater because he had himself become poor, though oppression could not touch him personally in any respect for which
he now cared. From his new point of view, the good men in the
upper orders at Rome were too few to count. The best of those who
still lived in the world were very far from following the teachings
of Christ. That poor men and slaves might be quite as wicked as
the rich, if a sudden access of fortune made it possible, did not
alter the reality of the oppression they suffered. That lack of a
sturdy middle class, the importance of which during the period of
decline of the Roman power Rostovtzeff has so vividly emphasized,
is abundantly illustrated in Salvian's curious picture of the society of his time.

He undertook, at a time when the task was as difficult as at any
period of the world's history, to justify the ways of God to man,
to prove his constant government of the world and his immediate
judgment. This involved the proof not only that the orthodox
Romans deserved their misfortunes, but that the pagan and heretic

---

[38] Heitland, *Agricola* (Cambridge, 1921), pp. 426-432.

barbarians merited their successes. It required also a satisfactory answer to the question why God had treated the Romans better when they were pagans than he did now that they were Christians. The latter question is never actually taken up, though Salvian promised at the beginning of the seventh book to answer it at the end of his work, if God should permit. But the end is missing.

It is inappropriate to judge the proofs that Salvian gives of the just judgment of God in the light of rational argument or historical criticism. He himself carefully defined his audience; his words were addressed to Christian Romans, not to pagans, heretics or barbarians. "For if I am addressing Christians, I do not doubt that I shall prove my case. But if I speak to pagans, I should scorn the attempt, not for any shortage of proofs, but because I despair of any profit in my discourse. Surely it is fruitless and lost labor, when a perverted listener is not open to conviction." [39]

Christianity and rationalism were to him inconsistent and mutually exclusive terms: "I am a man, I do not understand the secrets of God." [40] If his arguments seem at times to form a vicious circle, it is because he inevitably assumed as his basis the very points he was attempting to demonstrate. The great fact of the world, recognized by pagan philosophers and Christian theologians alike, was that God constantly governed and judged it; Lactantius had worked out philosophical and theological proofs of this in his *Divine Institutions.* Salvian deliberately adopted the groundwork furnished by his predecessor and made his indebtedness evident after the classical manner by direct though unacknowledged quotations. He was undertaking to reassure the Christian, not to instruct and convert the heathen or heretic; to enable the Christian to adjust his views of himself and of God to the dispensation under which he lived, and to effect such personal reformation as would take away the necessity of future punishment.[41]

---

[39] Book III. 1.

[40] *Ibid.*

[41] Bury, in his appendix to Gibbon (*The Decline and Fall of the Roman*

The first two books formed the foundation for the whole, following Lactantius closely in form and drawing most of their non-Biblical citations from him. This preliminary portion of the work is largely homiletic in character, demonstrating the government and judgment of God by examples drawn from the earlier books of the Old Testament, and by "testimonies" from the Bible as a whole. In the third book Salvian definitely undertook to answer the question "why we Christians, who believe in God, are more wretched than all other men." The answer in various forms occupied the rest of his work, which became more and more a study of contemporary society and events as he proceeded. For he saw the calamities and disasters of the world as God's judgments on the gross immorality of the Roman people. Not only were the triumphant barbarians less wicked than the Romans, but, being either pagans or heretics, they deserved indulgence for sins committed in ignorance, not in full knowledge of the Christian law. As Matter ably pointed out, Salvian's indictment of the Christians furnished plentiful material to the pagans for attacks on Christianity,[42] but Salvian might have countered that it was not the accusation but the crime that made such attacks possible. His ideal was that of ascetic Christianity, of poverty in this life for the sake of eternal salvation, but he was not one of those who looked for a speedy ending of the world, and the coming of the last judgment. He saw a

---

Empire [London, 1901], III, 490), says: "So far as Salvian's arguments are concerned, there is nothing to add to Gibbon's criticism (ch. xxxv, note 12) that 'Salvian has attempted to explain the moral government of the Deity; a task which may be readily performed by supposing that the calamities of the wicked are *judgments*, and those of the righteous *trials*.' " I cannot feel that this is a true summary of the case. Granted that Salvian wrote in complete acceptance of the Christian faith and of scriptural authority, he has accomplished his purpose very definitely; that we may not be convinced by the same means may be our loss or our gain, according to the point of view, but can hardly affect his success; it would seem likely that his discussion had a favorable effect in encouraging those for whom it was written. A full discussion of Salvian's theology will be found in G. Bruni, *Un apologista della Provvidenza* (Rome, 1925).

[42] *Histoire universelle de l'Église chrétienne*, I, 455.

continuing world, which God's immediate and constant judgment no longer suffered to continue as it had when the Empire was intact, in which a new and potentially better régime was gradually being formed. Among the ancient Romans to whom "everything unknown seemed glorious" it was an old tradition that barbarians were freer of vice than civilized men. If Salvian at times seems to exaggerate this view, he had some support not only in the readiness with which men in conquered territory adapted themselves to a régime less oppressive than the old, but also in the actual flight of many Romans to barbarian protection from the demands of Roman fiscal agents. He was not alone in feeling that there were compensations in the partial breakdown of the old system. Paulinus of Pella had been one of the luxurious, self-centered Aquitanians of the type that Salvian accused; his lapses from virtue were considerable, though not such as to occasion censure among his peers. When his great estates were lost and he was living in comparative poverty and full repentance, he wrote his autobiography in verse as a thanksgiving for God's mercies to him.[43] A like attitude is found in the poem of a husband to his wife, and also in a song on the divine providence, both formerly attributed to Prosper of Aquitaine.[44] Salvian was trying to bring others to a similar frame of mind.

Augustine had employed the same argument in his *Sermo de tempore barbarico*, a brief homily very closely akin to Salvian's book, and with the same conclusion: the calamities of the world were due to the wrath of God, warning us that we should not neglect atonement for our sins. The theme is not infrequent elsewhere.

In his books *Against Avarice* Salvian dwelt constantly on the need of repentance and charity because of the imminent danger

---

[43] Paulinus of Pella, *Eucharisticos.*

[44] *Poema coniugis ad uxorem* (Migne, PL, LI, coll. 611-615); *Carmen de providentia divina* (*Ibid.*, 617-638).

of death: in his treatise *On the Government of God* he was concerned instead with the amendment and reformation necessary for continued life. Of one thing he is sure, that the true Christian cannot be wretched, and therefore a fuller Christianity is the only real solution of the problem. His arguments are by no means free from inconsistencies of detail. On one occasion, for example, slaves are described as generally better than their masters, while on another we learn that the best masters usually have bad slaves. But there is no inconsistency in the fundamental thesis.

The violence of his feeling made him no respecter of persons; in spite of his avowed desire to consider the priests of God as above reproach, he is so bitter in his denunciations of wickedness within the church that Bellarmine said of him: "His exaggeration of the vices of Christians and especially of the clergy of his time would seem excessive, did his words not proceed from true zeal for the glory of God and the salvation of souls." [45] And Guillon found the indictment of the church in the ninth chapter of the third book so violent that he could scarcely bring himself to transcribe it, and finally effected a compromise between loyalty to his church and his scholarly conscience by copying the translation of Père Bonnet, and so gaining his pious sanction for the overbold words.[46]

Salvian's irony is very marked, especially in the treatise *Against Avarice*. The abbé de la Rue, in one of his Lenten sermons, followed a quotation from Salvian by the words: "*Voilà l'ironie de Salvien, mais discrète et charitable.*" [47] Salvian's friends, however, probably feared that it lacked discretion, and those against whom it was turned very likely felt it weak in charity; but it was seldom bitter. It is not inappropriate that the last sentence of the treatise *On the Government of God* that has come down to us displays an irony so

---

[45] *De scriptoribus ecclesiasticis* (Brussels, 1719), p. 168.

[46] *Bibliothèque choisie des Pères* (Louvain, 1832), XXIV, 118.

[47] Quoted by Guillon, *op. cit.*, p. 203, from de la Rue, *Carême*, II, 418.

pronounced that recent editors have destroyed it by inserting a negative.[48]

V. Style and Latinity

Salvian's style justifies the praise of Gennadius. While it is not altogether free from the faults of the rhetorical taste of his time, it is never obscure and rarely overburdened. In his preface he stressed the importance of subject matter as compared with style, and declared that his work was meant to be salutary rather than eloquent. This emphasis on content rather than form did not produce crudeness but served in general as a controlling element against the excesses of the rhetorician. He is fond of antithesis, of figures of speech and series of balanced phrases; he has a marked predilection for alliteration, assonance and rhyme, fostered by his love of plays on words.[49] His great fault is a wearisome repetition, a failing, however, that arises not so much from carelessness in style as from anxiety to hammer a point home. He runs out of words for his reiteration of a theme, and uses the same one till they are worn threadbare, yet this is a relief from the artificially varied phrases which the letter writers of his time would substitute. Indeed, his own letters are far more artificial than his other works. He was conscious of his wordiness, which may have been partly due to his preaching, and he speaks more than once of his fear that the prolixity of his style may arouse distaste in his readers.[50] It is at least, as Grégoire remarked, sufficient to terrify the most intrepid of translators, yet Joseph Scaliger could rightly exclaim of Salvian's work: "Le beau livre que c'est, et une belle simplicité!"[51]

Salvian's vocabulary was the source of much discussion among

---

[48] See H. K. Messenger, *op. cit.*, sec. 48, and Book VIII. 5.

[49] See Wölfflin, "Allitteration und Reim bei Salvian," *Archiv für lat. Lexikographie*, XIII (1902-4), 41-49.

[50] For example, Book VIII. 1.

[51] Grégoire et Collombet, *Oeuvres de Salvien* (Paris, 1833), Introd., p. lix: *Scaligerana* (Amsterdam, 1740), p. 544.

the earlier editors. Having in their introduction lauded him as a second Demosthenes or Cicero, and explored the history of rhetoric for phrases in his honor, they found themselves compelled, when they turned from the general to the particular, to account for his use of words which Cicero had never employed. Eventually they explained the considerable number of late Latin words by the influence of his subject and of his many Biblical quotations. Most of the late Latin and ecclesiastical words in his vocabulary are found also in Tertullian, Lactantius, Hilarius, Cyprian and Sidonius Apollinaris; others reflect the language of the jurists. In common with the other writers of his day, he shows a noticeable but not excessive fluidity of word formation, a fondness for negative adjectives and for diminutives, the latter usually to give a sense of humility or of sympathy and pity. A few of them are rather sesquipedalian formations, as the *excusatiuncula* and *deprecatiuncula* of the second chapter of the third book *Against Avarice.*

A recent thorough study of his use of moods and tenses resulted in the conclusion that, in spite of frequent departures from the pure classical norm, Salvian cannot be accused of negligence or lack of skill; that he followed fixed rules, though not always those of the best classical Latinity.[52]

A very large proportion of his material is drawn from the Bible or from his own and contemporary experience. Aside from his direct and purposed use of Lactantius in the first two books [53] and from natural reminiscences of both Lactantius and Tertullian when writing of a subject which they had considered from the same point of view as his (e.g., on the games), he seems deliberately to avoid obvious citations and quotations other than those from the Bible. Yet there is ample evidence that his memory was well stocked with pagan and earlier patristic literature. His reticence in quotation from secular authors is distinctly at variance with the

---

[52] H. K. Messenger, *op. cit.*

[53] Zschimmer, pp. 61 ff.

habit of his times, and corresponds to his general strictures on the
rhetorical ideal of literary composition. He cites Vergil and Cicero
as the authors of quotations only when the latter are drawn from
Lactantius, although elsewhere there are clear reminiscences of
both. His acquaintance with the works of Seneca is indicated by
several passages in which the resemblance between the thought and
ideas of the two authors is unusually striking. Rittershausen cites
parallels from Minucius Felix almost as often as from Seneca, but
for most of these equally close parallels may be found in Lactantius, so that no other source need be considered. The obvious extent of Salvian's education makes it an unnecessary strain on one's
credulity to believe with some commentators that all the similarities
to known passages in the works of pagan authors are due to chance,
and none to his personal knowledge of the books concerned.

The result of his method of allusion is very satisfactory; classical reminiscences are readily apparent to the reader with a well
stocked mind, but do not intrude themselves on the less informed,
to distract his attention from the argument. Nor was there any
risk of seeming to set pagan writers on a level with biblical authority. The frequent biblical quotations are drawn most commonly
from the old *Itala* versions, but Salvian also used the translation of
Jerome occasionally; indeed, with his friend Eucherius he was
among the first of the Christian writers in Gaul to employ the new
text.[54] His citations are rather loose, and where the same passage is
quoted more than once, there are sometimes variations in the word-
ing. The translation of his numerous biblical quotations presents
some difficulty. It is, of course, natural and almost inevitable to use
the familiar and beautiful text of the King James Version, and in
general I have done this, even in some cases where Salvian's word-
ing might suggest a slightly different rendering. In several pas-

---

[54] Fr. Kaulen, *Geschichte der Vulgata* (Mayence, 1868), p. 197. The paper
of Ulrich, *De Salviani scripturae sacrae versionibus*, Neostadii ad H., 1892, I
have not been able to consult.

sages, however, either marked differences between Salvian's text of
the Bible and that on which the King James Version is based, or
his rather free adaptations of the text to its setting in his argument,
have required corresponding changes in the English rendering.

VI. THE EDITIONS OF SALVIAN'S WORKS

Schoenemann distinguished three ages in the editions of Salvian; [55] the first, from 1528 to 1580, is that in which the two major
works were published. The treatise *Against Avarice* was issued by
Sichardus at Fol near Basle in 1528: two years later Brassicanus
published in the same city his *editio princeps* of the books *On the
Government of God*, based apparently on the extant Vienna manuscript of the fifteenth century (MS Vindobonensis 826). The next
period, from 1580 to 1663, was dominated by the editions of Pierre
Pithou, the first of which, published at Paris in 1580, was so much
in demand that it soon came, as Baluze said, to have almost the
rarity of a manuscript. This was the more unfortunate, as the
several reprints were inferior.[56] In 1611 Conrad Rittershausen
published an edition at Altdorf, with far more copious notes than
those of previous editors. He seems to have been the first to find
much space for commentary on other points than the establishment
of the text, and included literary and juristic references of considerable interest and value. His edition, however, was little used
outside of Germany.

In the third period, as Schoenemann says, *solus regnat Baluzius.*
Stephen Baluze published his first edition of Salvian's works together with the *Commonitorium* of Vincent of Lérins in 1663, and
this rapidly superseded the earlier editions. Using the tenth century manuscript of Corbie (Paris, Bibl. Nat. MS Lat. 13385), by

---

[55] *Bibliotheca historico-literaria Patrum*, II (Leipzig 1794), 826.

[56] Yet such is the infrequency of the present demand for editions of Salvian,
that Pithou's original edition could be had recently at a lower price than
obscure editions with better bindings.

far the best of existing manuscripts, he was able to construct a text superior to any previously published. The commentary of Baluze has formed the basis, often unacknowledged, of many notes on Salvian since, a source of information which one could not afford to overlook. His work is chiefly cited now in the fourth edition, published in 1742 at Stadtamhof.

Here end Schoenemann's three ages; but as far as the text is concerned, Baluze has been dethroned in our present age, first by Halm in 1877 and then by Pauly in 1883.[57] Since notes in these modern editions are limited to the *apparatus criticus*, Baluze still reigns in the field of commentary. Meanwhile, from the sixteenth century to the early nineteenth, there have been numerous lesser editions, frequently pirated from those more famous.[58]

VII. Estimates of Salvian's Work

When Brassicanus published his first edition of Salvian's treatise *On the Government of God*, he found ready applause for his achievement in rescuing so great a work from the dust and spider webs of a thousand years; the occasion was a fitting one for those

---

[57] C. Halm, *Salviani presbyteri Massiliensis libri qui supersunt*, MGH, *Auctores Antiquissimi*, I, 1, Berlin, 1877: Fr. Pauly, *Salviani presbyteri Massiliensis opera quae supersunt*, CSEL, VIII, Vienna 1883. I have used Pauly's text throughout, except for occasional emendations proposed by H. K. Messenger, *De temporum et modorum apud Salvianum usu*.

[58] For additions to the editions cited above, see G. Bruni, *Un apologista della Provvidenza* (Rome, 1925), 68-79, or Schoenemann, *op. cit.*, pp. 825-833, reprinted in Migne, PL, LIII, cols. 13-24. For translations see also Ceillier, *Histoire générale des auteurs sacrés*, XV (Paris, 1748), p. 81, and Grégoire et Collombet, Introd. pp. lxiii-lxvii. The most useful of the translations are: S. Carlo Borromeo, *Libro di Salviano Vescovo di Marsiglia contra gli Spettacoli ed altre Vanità del Mondo*, Milan, 1579; Père Bonnet, *Nouvelle Traduction des Oeuvres de Salvien, et du Traité de Vincent de Lérins contre les Hérésies*, Paris, 1700; P. F. Grégoire et F. Z. Collombet, *Oeuvres de Salvien*, Paris, 1833; A. Helf, *Des Salvianus acht Bücher über die göttliche Regierung*, Kempten, 1877. In English, a part of the sixth book appeared in 1580 as ''a second blast of retrait from places and theaters''; a translation of the whole work which I have been unable to consult, was published at London in 1700.

odes which his contemporaries so loved to write. Perhaps his romantic tale of the manuscripts he had found at Buda in the library of his friend Matthew Corvinus, king of Bohemia, just before its destruction by the Turks, absorbed his friends' interest so far th·.. they forgot the scribes who had made this edition possible b·, their earlier copies of the book. While we have no other evidence for the reading of Salvian's books between the date of Gennadius' account, which seems to be the source of the scanty later mentions, and Sichardus' publication of *Against Avarice* in 1528, the manuscripts lend their testimony that copies were made, corrected, and presumably read, in the tenth century, and in the twelfth, thirteenth and fifteenth as well. The scholars of th· sixteenth century were not unlike some of our own days in con·idering those ages dark of which they knew little.

Once printed, however, Salvian's works enjoyed great popularity. Jurists, including Sirmond, Cujas, Godefroi and Rittershausen, whose notes on Salvian are packed with legal references, consulted his books and cited them extensively in their studies of the Roman codes. The French clergy during four centuries found that he furnished material so appropriate to the personal vices and social disorders of their own times that they emulated the earlier bishops of Gaul in preaching Salvian's sermons instead of writing their own.[59] When Bossuet called him *"le saint et éloquent prêtre de Marseille"* his clerical readers must have assented with due gratitude. A German translator also praises his usefulness for the clergy in furnishing them so rich a source of *Schönheiten* and practical suggestions, that they should never let his works leave their hands.[60] Historians found his work of great value, espe-

---

[59] Guillon, *op. cit.*, cites Bossuet, Le Jeune, Joli, Massillon, Saurin, Cheminais, de la Rue and others as having made extensive use of Salvian. Grégoire and Collombet in their notes cite long passages from the sermons of de la Rue which are taken bodily from Salvian's works. Indeed, Guillon says he "has transported them almost entire into his sermons" (p. 143).

[60] A. Helf, *Des Salvianus acht Bücher über die Göttliche Regierung* (Kempten, 1877), p. 13.

cially when the current interpretation of history was most sympathetic to his constant reiteration: "It is only our vicious lives that have conquered us." So Johannes Jovianus Pontanus pointed out Salvian's special distinction in that, while writing of Christ and Christian topics, he had yet joined with these "very many histories and events of his own age, and commented sagely on them in the course of his account." [61] Zschimmer cites a long list of historians who have made extensive use of him; of these Guizot and Gibbon are the best known to us now, but many not named by Zschimmer would need to be added to bring the list up-to-date.[62] Indeed of late years Salvian seems to have been cited more than read. It is difficult to find a history of the period that does not refer to him, or a source book of ancient or medieval history that does not quote at least one of half-a-dozen famous passages, but the text itself is little read.

That this neglect has been a distinct loss to students of the later days of the Roman power in the west, will, I trust, be apparent even to those who make their acquaintance with Salvian through the medium of a translation. Since, however, a study of his works inevitably engenders the habit of reference to "authority," I shall not leave our author without this support. Know, then, that Pierre Pithou called Salvian "a most excellent author," Joseph Scaliger named him "the most Christian writer." Rittershausen, one of the most enthusiastic of editors, considered his opinions not only wholesome and holy,[63] but fully apostolic, and judged, therefore, that Salvian should be deemed master not only of bishops, but of the whole Christian world as well.

---

[61] Cited among the *elogia* in Rittershausen's edition.

[62] *Salvianus*, p. 54, note 1.

[63] *Sanas et sanctas*, the alliteration lawfully born of much reading of Salvian.

ON THE GOVERNMENT OF GOD

PREFACE

To the holy bishop Salonius, Salvian sends greetings
in the Lord.

Practically all men who have chosen some form of literary composition as a fitting expression of their native genius have taken
especial pains, whether they were writing of useful and worthy
matters, or of useless and unworthy, to lighten the order of their
discourse by the brilliance of their language and to illumine by
their style the questions under discussion. It is to style therefore
that the majority of writers on secular topics, whether in prose or
verse, have paid most attention, not considering sufficiently the
necessity of choosing subjects worthy of approbation, provided that
whatever they said was either chanted in smooth and elegant verse,
or narrated in distinguished prose.[1]

These authors have sought their own ends, and looking toward
their individual praise rather than the benefit of others have not
tried to be considered salutary and helpful, but rhetorical and
eloquent. Therefore their writings are swollen with vanity, infamous for their falsehood, smeared with filth, or vicious because
of their obscene subjects. Trafficking in such unworthy fashion to
purchase praise for ingenuity seems to me less a glorification than
a condemnation of one's genius. Since we, on the other hand, are
lovers of deeds rather than words,[2] we seek utility rather than
applause.

---

[1] As is usually the case with writers trained in the later Roman rhetorical
schools, Salvian's disclaimer of any interest in rhetorical style leads him to
use an elaborate phraseology in his preface, somewhat at variance with his
usual simpler and more colloquial style.

[2] See Seneca *De tranquillitate vitae* I. 1, and IV. 1, *infra*. In these notes,
references without title are to Salvian, *De gubernatione Dei (On the Govern-*

It is not, then, for vain and worldly adornments that we solicit praise, but for salutary prescriptions. Our writings, trifling though they are, shall present no vain lures but actual remedies, calculated not to please idle ears but to benefit the minds of the sick. So do we hope to gain our full reward from heaven.

Now if this healing grace of ours cures the unfavorable opinion of our God held by certain men, it will be no small reward that I have thus aided many. But if no such benefit accrues, the very fact that I have tried to be of service may not be unfruitful. For a mind devoted to a good work and a charitable aim, though it has not achieved full success in its undertaking, is still rewarded for its good intent. At this point then I shall begin.

---

ment of God): Ad ecclesiam refers to the treatise *To the Church against Avarice; Ep.* to the *Letters.*

THE FIRST BOOK

1. By certain men God is said to be careless and neglectful of human actions, on the ground that he neither protects good men nor restrains the wicked; and they claim that this is why at the present time the good are generally wretched and the wicked happy. Since we are dealing with Christians the Holy Scriptures alone should be sufficient to refute this charge. The many who are still somewhat infected by pagan unbelief may perhaps be convinced by the testimony of the greatest pagan philosophers. Let us, then, prove that not even these men had any conception of a God careless and neglectful of the world, though they had no means of really knowing God, since they were outside the true faith and were ignorant of the law through which he is apprehended.

Pythagoras the philosopher, whom Philosophy herself regarded as her master, said in his discourse on the nature and beneficent works of God: ''The Soul moves to and fro and is diffused through all parts of the world, and from it all living creatures receive their life. . . .''[1]

How then can God be said to neglect the world for which he so far shows his love that he extends his own being through its whole mass? Plato and all the Platonic school confess that God is the controller of all things. The Stoics testify that he remains always as steersman within that which he guides. What truer or more religious conception could they have had of the loving care of God than this comparison with a helmsman? For they clearly understood that as the helmsman never takes his hand from the tiller, so God

---

[1] See Cicero *De natura deorum* I. 11. 27. Salvian, however, cited the passage from Lactantius *Institutiones divinae* I. 5. 17. The best discussion of Salvian's borrowings from Lactantius will be found in Zschimmer, *Salvianus und seine Schriften*, p. 62.

never in the slightest degree withdraws his care from the world;
and as the pilot catching the breezes, avoiding rocks, watching the
stars, is completely absorbed, body and soul, in his task, so our
God never turns his most gracious eyes from the whole extent of
the world, nor takes away the guiding power of his providence, nor
removes the indulgence of his most kindly love. Whence comes also
that ancient mystic saying by which Maro wished to prove himself
no less philosopher than poet: "For God makes his way through
all lands and the paths of the sea and the high heavens." [2] Tully
also says: "Nor indeed can God himself, who is known by us, be
known in any other way than as a mind loosed and free and sep
arated from all mortal matter, understanding all things and mov
ing them." [3] Elsewhere he states that nothing is more immediately
present than God; [4] by him the world is necessarily ruled. God,
therefore, is neither subject nor obedient to any natural force; he
himself rules all nature. Unless forsooth we are led by our great
wisdom to believe that he, by whom we say all things are ruled, at
the same time both rules and neglects them! Since even men outside our faith have been compelled by sheer necessity to say that all
things are known by God and are moved and ruled by him, how
is it that some now think him careless and neglectful of the world?
Is it not he who comprehends all creation by the fineness of his
perception, moves it by his strength, rules it by his power, and
protects it by his kindness?

I have told you what men preëminent alike in philosophy and
eloquence have thought of the majesty and government of the most
high God. Moreover, I have cited the noblest masters of both these
supreme arts expressly to facilitate my proof that all others have
either agreed, or, if they have disagreed, have done so without any
authority. And, in fact, I can find none who have differed from this

---

[2] Quoted by Lactantius *op. cit.* I. 5. 12 from Vergil *Georgics* IV. 221-222.

[3] *Ibid.* I. 5. 25, quoted from Cicero *Disputationes Tusculanae* I. 27. 66.

[4] Cited by Lactantius *op. cit.* I. 5. 24 as from Cicero *De natura deorum*, but
the passage is not found there.

judgment, except for the delirious ravings of the Epicureans and certain of their imitators.[5] These last have associated God with carelessness and sloth, just as they have linked pleasure with virtue — so it appears that those who entertain this idea are likely to follow the vices of the Epicureans along with their opinion and doctrine.

2. I do not think that we need also use the divine word to prove so obvious a case, especially since the sacred writings furnish such abundant and open refutation of all the claims of ungodly men that, in meeting those of their vile charges which follow, we shall be able to refute more fully those already mentioned. They say that God neglects us entirely, since he neither restrains the wicked nor protects the good, and therefore in this world the condition of the better men is substantially the worse. They contrast the poverty of good men with the wealth of the wicked, their weakness with the strength of the wicked, their constant grief with the others' perpetual joy, their misery and mean estate with the honors and prosperity of sinners.

I wish at the outset to ask those who mourn this state of affairs, or base their accusations on it, this one question: is their grief for the saints, that is, the true and faithful Christians, or for the false impostors? If for the false, it is a needless grief that mourns for the unhappiness of the wicked, since, to be sure, all evil men are made worse by success in their undertakings, and rejoice at the lucky turn of their folly. Yet they ought to be most wretched in order that they may cease to be wicked, that they may cease to apply the name of religion to their most evil gains and to bestow the title of sanctity on their sordid traffickings; in such a case, indeed, a comparison of the misfortunes of sinners with their misdeeds

---

[5] The early Christian attitude toward the Epicureans was regularly hostile, in striking contrast to their ready recognition of the kinship between the Stoic philosophy and Christianity. The Epicurean denial of any divine government of the world was in itself sufficient to lead Salvian to condemn their doctrines.

shows that they are less unfortunate than they deserve, for the utmost misfortunes they can suffer leave them still less wretched than they are wicked. It is foolish to grieve for their lack of wealth and happiness. Far less should we lament in the case of the saints, for however unhappy they may seem to men who do not understand their condition, it is impossible for them to be otherwise than happy. Moreover, it is superfluous to think them wretched because of sickness or poverty or any like misfortune, in the midst of which they count themselves happy; for no man is wretched because of other men's judgment, but only in his own.[6]

So those who are truly happy in their own estimation cannot be unhappy through the false conception of any man; for none, I think, are more fortunate than those who live and act according to their own determination and vows. Religious men are lowly — they wish to be so; poor — they delight in poverty; without ambition — they spurn it; unesteemed — they flee from honors; they mourn — but they seek out occasion for mourning; they are weak — nay, they rejoice in weakness. For the apostle said, "When I am weak, then am I strong."[7] Nor was this opinion held undeservedly by the man to whom God himself spoke thus: "My grace is sufficient for thee: for my strength is made perfect in weakness."[8]

It is useless for us to bemoan this affliction of bodily illness, which we know is the mother of strength. Therefore, whatever their sorrows may have been, any who are truly religious should be called happy, since amid any hardships or difficulties whatsoever none are happier than those who are what they wish to be. Although we all know individuals whose aims are vile and shameful, who think themselves happy in gaining their desires, yet in actual fact such men are not happy, because they ought not to desire what

---

6 See Seneca *De remediis fortuitorum* XVI, end: "The happy man is not he who seems such to others, but to himself."

7 II Corinthians 12. 10.

8 *Ibid.* 12. 9.

they do. Moreover, the religious are happier than all others in this, that they have what they wish and at the same time cannot possibly wish for anything better than they have.[9] So toil, fasting, poverty, humility and weakness are not burdensome to all who suffer them but only to those who are unwilling to bear them. For the mind of the sufferer determines whether his troubles are heavy or light to endure. Just as no task is so light that it is not heavy to the man who performs it unwillingly, none is so heavy that it does not seem light to him who performs it gladly.[10]

Or are we perhaps to think that it was a burden to those ancient patterns of virtue, the Fabii, Fabricii and Cincinnati, that they, who did not wish riches, were poor?[11] Remember that they directed all their efforts, all their labor, to the common good, and by their individual poverty contributed to the growing wealth of the state. Surely you do not think that it was with groans and sadness that they endured their famous life of rustic economy, when they ate their cheap country fare before the very fire over which they had cooked it, and delayed even this poor meal until evening? Did they take it ill that they were not piling up talents of gold in the pursuit of miserly wealth, when they were passing laws to restrict the circulation even of silver? Could men who judged a patrician unworthy of the senate because he had wished to increase his wealth

---

[9] A conception of the religious life common throughout the Middle Ages, and mirroring for the saints in this life the future joys of paradise. Compare the familiar line from the hymn of Peter Damiani:

"Avidi et semper pleni, quod habent desiderant."

[10] See Salvian *Ad ecclesiam* IV. 9. 49: "Every command is hard that is given to unwilling men."

[11] These were among the best-known examples of early Roman virtue; cf. H. W. Litchfield, "National *Exempla Virtutis* in Roman Literature," *Harvard Studies in Classical Philology*, XXV (1914), 1-71. All these are cited in Valerius Maximus IV. 3-4, as examples of abstinence, continence and poverty, and were used by Christian writers from Augustine and Orosius to modern times to illustrate the same virtues. The contrast between Roman and Greek ambition which follows was also a commonplace before Salvian's time, and has been since.

to the sum of ten pounds of silver possibly think it a penalty for
their illicit greed that they had not their purses stuffed with
gold? [12]

In those days, I think, men did not despise humble ways of life,
when they wore only one short and shaggy garment, when they
were summoned from the plow to the dictator's *fasces*, and, on the
point of winning fame in the consular robes, very likely wiped off
their dusty sweat on those same imperial togas that they were about
to don. In their time the magistrates were poor, but the state
wealthy, whereas now the wealth of officials makes the state poor.
What madness, I ask you, or what blindness, leads men to think
that private fortunes can survive in the midst of the need and
beggary of the state? Such were the ancient Romans; so they in
their day scorned riches, though they knew not God, just as in ours
men who follow the Lord still scorn them.

But why do I speak of those men who in their desire to extend
the Roman power turned their scorn of private means to the public
enrichment, and while individually poor still had abundance in the
common wealth of the state? Even Greek philosophers without any
interest in public gain, through sheer greed of glory have been
known to strip themselves of almost all articles of common use, and,
not content with this, have exalted their creed to the lofty pinnacle
of contempt of suffering and death, saying that even in chains and
punishment a wise man still is happy.[13] They would have it that
the power of virtue is so great that a good man can never fail to be
content. If, then, certain wise men now think that those men were
not unhappy, though they received no reward for their efforts but
transient praise, how much more must religious and saintly men
cease to be thought wretched, who both enjoy at this present time

---

[12] See the story of Cornelius Rufinus in Valerius Maximus II. 9. 4; Tertullian
Apologeticum 6.

[13] A stock characteristic of the Stoic and the Epicurean sage: cf. Seneca
Epistulae morales lxvi. 18; Cicero *Disputationes Tusculanae* II. 7. 17, *De finibus*
II. 27.

the delights of their faith, and are to attain as well the reward of eternal blessedness?

3. One of those of whom we complain said to a certain holy man who followed the true doctrine, that is, that God rules all things and tempers his governance and guidance according to his knowledge of human necessities: "Why then, I ask, are you yourself infirm?" His line of reasoning, I suppose, was as follows: "If God, as you think, rules everything in this present life, if he dispenses all fortunes, then how is it that a man whom I know to be a sinner is strong and healthy, whereas you, whose sanctity I do not question, are infirm?"

Who does not marvel at the depth of feeling of one who considers the merits and virtues of a godly man worthy of such great recompense that he thinks they should be rewarded in this present life by the fleshly strength of the body? I answer, therefore, not in the name of any one saint but of them all: "Do you ask, then, whoever you are, how it is that holy men come to be weak? My answer is brief: they make themselves infirm for the express reason that if they are strong, they can hardly be holy." [14] I think that men gain strength entirely through their food and drink, and are weak through abstinence, thirst and fasting. Therefore it is not strange that those are weak who scorn the use of the means by which others are made strong. And there is good reason for such scorn, according to the words of the apostle Paul, when he said: "I keep under my body and bring it into subjection; lest that by any means, when I have preached to others, I myself should be a castaway." [15] If the apostle himself considered the weakness of the body an end to be sought, who acts wisely in avoiding it? If the apostle feared the strength of the flesh, who rightly presumes to

---

[14] See Salvian *Ep.* V. 3: "Although I do not think that even this infirmity of your earthly vessel has been harmful to you, for its strength, as you know, is always hostile to the mind; so that I am right in thinking you as much stronger now in spirit, as you have begun to be weaker in the flesh."

[15] I Corinthians 9. 27.

be strong? This, then, is the reason why men who have given themselves over to Christ both are and wish to be weak. Far be it from
us to think that holy men are neglected by God for the very reason
for which, we trust, they are the more loved by him. We read that
the apostle Timothy was most weak in the flesh.[16] Was this a sign
of God's neglect, or did Timothy through his weakness fail to
please Christ, willing as he was to be weak in order to please him?
Even so the apostle Paul, though Timothy was suffering from
serious infirmities, yet permitted him to take and sip only a very
little wine; that is, he wished him to have regard for his weakness
but not so far as to attain full vigor.[17] And why was this? What
other reason could there be but that which he himself has given?
"For the flesh lusteth against the spirit, and the spirit against
the flesh; and these are contrary," he says, "the one to the other,
so that ye cannot do the things that ye would."[18]

It was not without insight that a certain author [19] said in this
connection that if the strength of the body prevents us from doing
what we wish, the flesh must be weakened in order that we may
achieve our desires. For he says: "The weakness of our flesh
sharpens the vigor of the mind, and when our limbs are weakened
bodily strength is transformed into spiritual virtue. Then our
inmost parts no longer seethe with disgraceful passions, and secret
desires no longer kindle a diseased mind; our senses do not roam
wantonly over various enticements, but the soul alone exults, re-
joicing in the weakness of the body as over a defeated adversary."

---

[16] In common with others of his time, Salvian used the term "apostle" more
loosely than we do now.

[17] See I Timothy 5. 23. An excellent example of Salvian's occasional readiness to distort Scripture for his purpose, perhaps justifiable in this case because of the frequent misuse of the same text by other authors, to support
both sides of the same argument.

[18] Galatians 5. 17.

[19] Salvian, in *Ep.* V. 4, his letter to "sister Cattura," in which he con-
gratulates her not only on recovery from an illness but also on the illness
itself, which had strengthened her soul at the expense of her body. See also
note 14.

This, as I said, is the cause to which religious men ascribe their infirmities, and you, I think, can no longer deny its validity.

4. But perhaps they have, you say, other and greater sufferings, that is, they endure many hard and bitter trials in this life; they are captured, tortured and butchered. That is true, but what are we to make of the fact that the prophets were led away into captivity and that the apostles also suffered torments? Surely we cannot doubt that God had the greatest concern for them, since it was for God that they bore these afflictions. But perhaps you claim this as an additional proof that God neglects everything that happens in this life and reserves his whole care for the judgment to come, since the good have always suffered, as the wicked have performed, all things evil. This idea does not seem to be that of an unbeliever, especially as it admits the future judgment of God. But we say that the human race is to be judged by Christ, while yet maintaining that now also God rules and ordains all things in accordance with his reason. While we declare that he will judge in the future, we also teach that he always has judged us in this life. As God always governs, so too he always judges, for his government is itself judgment.

In how many ways do you wish this proved, by reason, or by examples, or by authorities? If you wish it proved by reason, who is so lacking in ordinary human intelligence and so utterly averse to the truth of which we speak, that he does not recognize and see that the surpassing beauty of the created world, the inestimable grandeur of the heavens above and of the regions below are ruled by the same power that created them? He who devised their elements will himself be their governor. He will guide all things by a providence and reason consistent with the majestic power by which he founded them. And certainly, since even in those matters that are conducted by human activity, absolutely nothing exists without reason, and all things derive their security from providence, even as the body derives its life from the soul; so in this world not only empires and provinces, civil and military affairs, but also the lesser offices and private homes, the very sheep and the smaller sorts of domestic animals are controlled by no other means than human ordinance and wisdom, as by a guiding hand on the tiller. All this beyond a doubt is in accordance with the will and judgment of the most high God, that the whole human race should govern the lesser parts, or limbs of the world, following the example of God's government of the whole body of the universe.

But, you suggest, in the beginning the governance of his creatures was so determined and arranged by God; yet after he had formed and perfected the whole scheme of things, he abdicated, and renounced the administration of earthly matters. I suppose you mean to imply that he fled from the idea of toil and repudiated it, that he sought to avoid the annoyance of constant effort. Or was it that, occupied with other business, he abandoned a part of his affairs, since he could not attend to the whole?

5. God then puts far from himself, you say, all thought of mortal men. In that case what rational ground is there for our belief in his divinity? What reason is there for worshipping Christ, or what hope of winning his favor? For if God in this life neglects the human race, why do we daily stretch out our hands toward heaven? Why do we pray so often for the mercy of God? Why do we hasten to the churches? Why kneel in prayer before the altars? There is no reason for praying if the hope of an answer to prayer is taken from us. You see what vain folly lies in the urging of this idea; truly, if it is accepted, nothing at all remains of our religion. But perhaps you take refuge in the argument that we honor God in the fear of a future judgment, and perform all the ritual of our daily worship to gain absolution on the judgment day hereafter. In that case, what was the meaning of the daily preaching of Paul the apostle in the church, and his command that we offer constantly to God our prayers, our entreaties, our requests and our thanksgivings?

What is the purpose of all this? What else than, as he himself says, "that we may live a quiet and peaceable life in all chastity?" [20] For our present needs, as we see, he orders us to pray and beseech the Lord. Surely he would not command this if he were not sure that God hearkens to prayer. How can any one suppose that the ears of God are open for the granting of boons at some future time, but deaf and blocked against immediate petitions? Or what leads us when praying in the church to ask God for present safety, if we think that he does not listen at all to our prayers? In that case we should make no vows for our safety and prosperity.

Perhaps, to the end that the modesty of the request may win favor for the voice of the petitioner, we should rather pray thus: "Lord, we do not seek prosperity in this life, nor beseech you for immediate favors, for we know that your ears are closed to such petitions and that you do not listen to such prayers, but we ask only for those favors that shall be granted us after our death."

Granted that such a petition is not without value, on what rational basis does it rest? For if God is without interest in this life, and closes his ears to the prayers of his suppliants, then doubtless he who does not hear our present pleas is deaf also to our prayers for the future. Are we to believe that Christ listens or denies his attention according to the diverse nature of our prayers, that he closes his ears when we ask for present boons, and opens them when we ask for blessings to come? But enough of this. The arguments are so stupid and frivolous that one needs to beware lest what is said for the honor of God seem injurious to him. For so great and terrible is the reverence due to his sacred majesty that we should not only shudder at the arguments of our opponents, but should also make our defence of religion with due fear and circumspection.

If, therefore, it is stupid and impious to believe that the divine love despises the care of human affairs, then God does not despise

---

[20] I Timothy 2. 2.

it; moreover, if he does not scorn it, he governs; if he governs, he judges by the very exercise of his government, since there can be no rule without the constant exercise of judgment on the part of the ruler.

6. Perhaps some one may think a proof too insecure that rests on reason alone without the support of authority. Let us see how God has ruled the world from the beginning; for by demonstrating that he has always ruled the universe, we shall prove that he has at the same time exercised judgment.

What is the testimony of the Scriptures? "Therefore God formed man of clay and breathed into him the breath of life." And what followed? "He placed him in a paradise of pleasure." [21] What next? What else than that he gave him law, filled him with his commands, formed him by his instruction? But what happened then? Man transgressed the sacred ordinance, underwent judgment, lost paradise and suffered the penalty of damnation. Who can fail to see God as both governor and judge in this whole account? For he placed Adam in paradise in innocence; he expelled him in guilt. In Adam's establishment we see the divine ordinance; in his expulsion, the divine judgment. For when God set man in a place of delight, he ordained his way of life; but when he expelled him in guilt from that realm, he exercised judgment. This then is the story of the first man, that is, of the father.

What of the second, the son? "In process of time it came to pass," say the Holy Scriptures, "that Cain brought of the fruit of the ground an offering unto the Lord. And Abel, he also brought of the firstlings of his flock and of the fat thereof. And the Lord had respect unto Abel and to his offering: but unto Cain and his offering he had not respect." [22]

Before I speak of the more obvious judgment of God, I think that even in the account just given there is a certain indication of

---

[21] Genesis 2. 7-8.

[22] *Ibid.* 4. 3-5.

judgment; for in the act of receiving one brother's sacrifice and
rejecting the other God gave a most open verdict as to the justice
of the one and the injustice of the other. But this was not enough.
Thereafter Cain paved the way for his later crimes by leading his
brother into the wilderness; in the friendly protection of the
desert he committed his murder. He proved himself at once the
most wicked and most stupid of men, since he thought he had sufficient secrecy for the most evil and abhorrent act if he avoided the
sight of men when about to commit fratricide with God as his
witness.

Whence I think he had this same idea that is now so prevalent,
that God does not behold things done on earth and does not see
any of the acts of wicked men. Nor is there any doubt of this, since,
when he was admitted to speech with God after the commission of
his crime, he answered that he knew nothing of his brother's death.
He was so sure of God's ignorance of his deed, that he thought the
most deadly wrong could be hidden by a mere lie.

But the event proved other than he anticipated. For though
he thought his fratricide unseen by God, his condemnation taught
him that God had seen. I now have one question to ask of those who
deny that human affairs are regarded by God or ruled or judged
by him: are all the circumstances different in these accounts that
we have given? For I think that he is present who is concerned in
the sacrifice; he rules who rebukes Cain after his sacrifice; he is
anxious who requires the victim of the murderer; he judges who
condemns the wicked slayer by a just verdict.

In this incident, indeed, there is yet another point convenient
to our argument. Surely we are not to wonder that holy men are
now suffering certain hardships, since we see that God even at that
time permitted the first of his saints to be most wickedly slain. As
to the reason why he permits such actions, it is not within the
power of human weakness to discover fully, nor is this a fit occasion
for such discussion. For the present it is enough to prove that deeds

of this sort do not occur because of the negligence or inattention of God, but are permitted by the dispensation of his wisdom. Moreover, we can by no means call him unjust, for the will of God is the highest justice; nor does a divine action cease to be righteous because man is incapable of grasping the workings of the divine justice. But let us return to the main argument.

7. We have seen in the accounts already given that nothing is done without the care of God, but that some of these actions were so arranged by his divine wisdom, some endured by his forbearance, some punished by his sentence. Certain people, perhaps, think that these few cases do not sufficiently establish our contention; let us see if we can make it completely clear through the experience of all men.

When, therefore, the human race had increased and multiplied alike in numbers and in wickedness, as the Holy Scripture says: "God seeing that the wickedness of man was great in the earth, and that every imagination of the thoughts of his heart was only evil continually, repented that he had made man on the earth, and it grieved him at his heart, and he said: 'I will destroy man whom I have created, from the face of the earth.' " [23]

Let us consider how both the care of God and his severity are equally shown in the whole account. For first we read, "moreover God seeing"; secondly, "it grieved him at his heart"; and thirdly, "he said, 'I will destroy man whom I have created.' " In the first statement, that God sees all things, his care is shown; in the statement that he grieves is shown the terror of his wrath; that he punishes, his severity as a judge. "God therefore repented," says the Holy Scripture, "that he had made man on the earth"; this does not indicate that God is subject to repentance or any other emotion, but rather that the divine word, to further our understanding of the true meaning of the Scriptures, speaks to us in terms of human feeling and shows the force of God's anger under

---

[23] *Ibid.* 6. 5-7.

the name of repentance; moreover, the divine wrath is the punishment of the sinner.

What followed then? When God saw that the earth was corrupt he said to Noah: "The end of all flesh is come before me; for the earth is filled with violence through them: and behold, I will destroy them with the earth." [24] What happened next? "All the fountains of the great deep were broken up, and the flood-gates of heaven were opened and the rain was upon the earth forty days and forty nights." [25] And a little later: "All flesh died that moved upon the earth." And again: "And Noah only remained alive, and they that were with him in the ark." [26]

Now I wish to ask those who say that God neglects human fortunes whether they believe that at this time he cared for earthly matters and judged them? I think he not merely judged but gave a twofold judgment; for in preserving the good he proved himself a generous giver of rewards, and in destroying the wicked, a severe judge.

Perhaps these instances may seem to stupid wits to lack authority, since they happened before the Flood — in another age, as it were. As if we could assume that God was different at that time, and afterwards ceased to desire to exercise the same care for the world! Indeed, by the divine grace I could prove my statements by examples from all generations since the Flood, but their great number forbids. However, certain of the more important instances will suffice, for since God is undoubtedly the same in the greater and the lesser cases, the lesser may be inferred from the greater.

8. After the Flood God blessed the generation of men, and when this blessing had brought forth an immeasurable host of men, God spoke to Abraham from heaven, ordering him to leave his own land and go to a strange country. He was called, he followed; he

---

[24] *Ibid.* 6. 13.

[25] *Ibid.* 7. 11-12.

[26] *Ibid.* 7. 21, 23.

was guided and established; from a poor man he became rich; from an obscure man, powerful. Though reduced by his journeyings to the lowest estate, he came to be most high in honor. Yet in order that the previous gifts of God to him should not seem undeserved generosity, he who rejoiced in prosperity was tested in adversity. Then came toil, danger and fear; he was vexed by travelling, worn out by exile, visited with shame, and deprived of his wife. God ordered him to sacrifice his son; the father offered his child, and so far as the resolution of his heart was concerned, performed the sacrifice. Again came periods of exile, again fear, the hatred of the Philistines, the rapine of Abimelech — many evils, yet compensated by equal consolations, for though he was afflicted in many things, yet was he rewarded for them all.

What conclusion are we to draw? In all the events which we have recounted, is not God seen examining Abraham, inviting and leading him, anxious for him, his sponsor, protector, benefactor, testing and exalting him, at once his avenger and his judge? Surely he examined him, for he chose him as the one best man of them all; he invited him, for he called him; he was his guide, leading him through in safety to unknown lands; anxious for him, for he visited him by the oak tree; his sponsor, in promises of things to come; his protector, guarding him among barbarous races; his benefactor, in that he enriched him; his examiner, in that he wished to test him by harsh trials; his exalter, for he made him powerful beyond all men; his avenger, for he avenged him on his adversaries; his judge, for in avenging him he exercised judgment.

Moreover, God at once added another item to this history when he said: "The cry of Sodom and Gomorrah is grown great, and their sin is increased overmuch." [27] The cry of Sodom and Gomorrah, he said, is grown great. He said well that sins cry out, for without doubt the cry of sinners is great, as it ascends from earth to heaven. Why does he speak of men's sins as crying out? Cer-

---

[27] *Ibid.* 18. 20.

tainly because he means that his ears are smitten by the cries of
our sins, that the punishment of sinners may not be delayed. Truly,
it is a cry, and a great cry, when the fatherly love of God is overcome by the cries of sin, so that he is compelled to punish the
sinners.[28]

God showed how unwillingly he punishes even the worst of sinners, when he said that the cry of Sodom ascended to him. That is
to say: "My mercy indeed persuades me to spare them; nevertheless
the cry of their sins compels me to punish." When he had said this,
what resulted? Angels were sent to Sodom; they set out, and entered the city; they were treated hospitably by the good and
injuriously by the wicked; the wicked were blinded and the good
saved. Lot, with his dear ones who honored God, was led out of
the city; Sodom itself was burned with its wicked inhabitants.

I ask at this point whether it was in accordance with justice or
contrary to it that God burned these wicked men? He who says
that the Sodomites were unjustly punished by God accuses him of
injustice; if, on the other hand, God justly destroyed those evil
men, he judged them.

Surely he judged them, and indeed his judgment clearly fore-
shadowed that which is to come. For it is well known that in time
to come Gehenna will be in flames for the punishment of the wicked,
just as flames from heaven then consumed the city of Sodom and
its neighbors. Moreover, God wished his immediate action to pre-
figure that coming judgment, when he sent Gehenna down out of
heaven upon an impious people. So the apostle also says that God
condemned the cities of Sodom and Gomorrah by their overthrow,
making them an example to those that hereafter should live ungodly lives,[29] although his action on that occasion had in it more

---

[28] Rittershausen, *Salviani opera* (Altdorf 1611), *ad loc.*, cites a verse listing
the five sins that were proverbially said to cry for justice to heaven:

"Clamitat in caelum vox sanguinis, et Sodomorum,
  vox oppressorum, viduae, pretium famulorum."

[29] II Peter 2. 6.

of mercy than of severity. For that he so long delayed their punishment was due to his mercy; that he finally punished them, to his justice. So when God sent his angels to Sodom, he wished to prove to us that he is loath to punish even wicked men; to the end that when we should read what insults the angels endured from the people of Sodom, and see plainly the enormity of their crimes, the disgraceful character of their vices and the obscenity of their lusts, he might prove to us that he did not wish to destroy them, but they themselves forced their destruction on him.

9. I might mention countless further examples, but I am afraid that in my effort to give adequate proof I may seem to have composed a whole history. Moses pasturing his sheep in the desert saw a bush burning, heard God from the midst of the bush and received his commands. He was exalted in power and was sent to Pharaoh; he spoke with him, was scorned, but conquered. The Egyptian was struck down, Pharaoh's disobedience was smitten, and not in one way alone, but many, to the end that he should be tortured by a diversity of punishments in consideration of the greatness of his sacrilege. What was the outcome? Ten times he rebelled; ten times he was smitten. What is our conclusion? I think you must recognize that in all these cases God shows equally his care for human affairs and his judgment of them.

In Egypt, indeed, the judgment of God at that time was evidently not single but manifold. For as often as he smote the rebellious Egyptians, so often he judged them. But after the events already told, what happened? Israel was dismissed; after celebrating the Passover they despoiled the Egyptians and departed in wealth. Pharaoh repented, gathered his army, overtook the fugitives, encamped beside them, was separated from them by the darkness; the sea was dried up, Israel crossed over and by the friendly withdrawal of the waves was set free. Pharaoh followed, the sea rolled over him, and he was drowned by the engulfing waves.

I think that the judgment of God has been made clear in these events, and indeed not merely his judgment but also his moderation and patience. For it was due to his patience that the Egyptians in their rebellion were often smitten, to his judgment that for their persistent stubbornness they were condemned to death. Therefore, after this series of adventures the race of the Hebrews, victorious without warfare, entered the desert. They followed an uncharted course, pathless wanderers, with God to lead the way, honored by his divine comradeship, powerful through their heavenly leader, following a moving column of cloud by day, of fire by night, which took on shifting changes of color to suit the changing skies, that its dull obscurity might stand out in contrast to the strong light of day and its flaming splendor illumine by its clear glow the mists of night.

Add to this the springs that suddenly gushed forth, add the bitter waters given and changed, keeping their old appearance but changing their character. Add mountain peaks cleft open by streams gushing forth, dusty fields foaming with new torrents. Add flocks of birds sent into the camp of the wanderers, since God in his most indulgent love catered not only to the needs but also to the palates of his people; the food granted throughout forty years by the daily ministry of the stars, the dew of sweet morsels shed from the poles, offering abundance not merely for nourishment but for delight. Add that the men experienced in no part of their bodies the growth or losses natural to human beings, their nails did not grow, nor their teeth decay, their hair stayed always of one length, their feet were not worn by the march, their clothing was not tattered, their shoes not broken, and thus the honor granted to the men themselves was even sufficient to dignify their mean garments.[30] Add to all this God descending to earth to instruct his

---

[30] Another instance of details added without scriptural authority: in fact the instances of leprosy and death among the Israelites during the march seem directly contradictory to Salvian's statements.

people, lending himself, God the Son,[31] to earthly sight, the countless throngs of people admitted to familiar intercourse with him,
waxing strong in the power of his sacred intimacy.

Add to this the thunders, the lightnings, the terrifying blasts of
celestial trumpets, the fearful crashing over the whole sky, the
poles rumbling with a holy sound, the fires, mists and clouds filled
with the very presence of God, God speaking to man face to face,
the law resounding from his holy lips, the letters inscribed in
minutest accuracy on the stone page by the finger of God, the stone
become a written scroll, the people learning and God teaching in a
school of heaven and earth commingled, almost a union of men and
angels.

For it is written that when Moses had taken the words of the
people to the Lord, the Lord said to him: "Lo, now I come to thee
in a thick cloud, that the people may hear when I speak with
thee." [32] And a little later: "Lo, there were thunders and lightnings, and a thick cloud upon the mount." [33] Again: "And the
Lord came down upon Mount Sinai, on the top of the mount." [34]
Again: "And the Lord talked with Moses. And all the people saw
the cloudy pillar stand at the tabernacle door: and all the people
rose up and worshipped, every man at his tent door. And the Lord
spake unto Moses, face to face, as a man speaketh unto his
friend." [35]

In view of all this, does God seem to take any thought for men,
giving them such great gifts, helping them so much, sharing his
speech with a vile mortal, as if admitting him to converse in his

---

[31] Again an addition not justified by the words of the Old Testament.
Salvian, in common with other early Christian writers, not infrequently names
Christ when we should expect the name of God instead. And the "throngs of
people" were expressly excluded from familiar intercourse with God; cf.
Exodus 19. 21-24; 24. 1-2.

[32] Exodus 19. 9.

[33] *Ibid.* 19. 16.

[34] *Ibid.* 19. 20.

[35] *Ibid.* 33. 9-11.

sacred fellowship, opening before him his hands filled with immortal riches, nourishing him with a cup of nectar, feeding him with celestial food? What greater care, I ask, could his guidance afford, what greater love could he show, than possession in the course of this present life of such a mirror of future blessedness?

10. Perhaps at this juncture you may answer that God did once exercise such care for men, but now does not at all. Why should we believe this? Because we do not now eat manna daily as the Israelites did? But we reap fields full of grain at the harvest. Because we do not catch quails that fly into our hands? But we devour all kinds of birds, cattle and beasts. Because we are not granted waters gushing from clefts opened in the rocks? But we pour the fruits of our vines into our wine cellars. I have more to add: we ourselves, who say that the children of Israel at that time were cared for by God but that we are neglected by him, would absolutely reject the choice of their condition if we could receive their past favors in exchange for our present benefits. For we should not be willing to lose what we now have in order to gain what they then enjoyed, not that we are better off than the Israelites were, but that they too, who were then daily fed by the ministry of the stars and of God, preferred the old accustomed fodder for their bellies to the favors they enjoyed. They were actually sad at their vile recollections of carnal foods, pining away with a vulgar yearning for onions and garlic, not because their former diet was more wholesome, but because they acted just as we do now. They loathed what they had and longed for what they lacked. We would rather praise bygone days than the present, not that we should prefer to revive the past if the choice were given us, but because it is a well-known failing of the human mind always to desire what it lacks, and, as the proverb says, "Another's goods please us, and ours please others more." [36]

---

[36] Publilius Syrus, verse 28. Salvian's text here is influenced by Seneca *De ira* 3. 31. 1.

To this may be added a trait shared by almost all, of being forever ungrateful to God, and all in turn are bound by the deep-
rooted and inborn vice of belittling the blessings God gives, in
order that they may not feel obliged to look on themselves as his
debtors.

But enough of this: let us at last return to our original proposition. I think we have made no slight progress toward proving the
point; still let me add one instance more, if you please, since it is
better to prove a matter more fully than is necessary than to risk
falling short of conviction.[37]

11. Freed from Pharaoh's yoke the people of the Hebrews
transgressed near Mount Sinai, and were at once smitten by the
Lord for their transgression. For it is written: "And the Lord
plagued the people for their delusion concerning the calf which
Aaron made."[38] What greater and clearer judgment could God
give concerning sinners than that punishment should overtake them
forthwith in the midst of their sin? Yet since all the people were
guilty, why was not destruction visited on all alike? Surely because
the Lord, loving them, smote some with the sword of his sentence, in
order to correct the others by their example, and to prove to all at
one time his censure in chastising their sin and his affection in
pardoning them. For his censure was shown in the punishment,
his mercy in the pardon, though disproportionately, for on that
occasion he yielded more to mercy than to severity.

Surely then, since our most indulgent Lord shows himself always
more prone to mercy than to punishment, even though in punishing
a part of the Jewish host by his divine censure he gave some scope
to judgment and severity, yet his love claimed the greater portion
of the people — a special and peculiar act of mercy to countless

---

[37] Rittershausen, *ad loc.*, cites the proverb: *Superflua non nocent*. The phrasing suggests a legal connotation, in connection with which he cites Paulus and
Ulpian on the value of more than the required number of witnesses to a will,
or more written evidence than is actually needed to prove a case.

[38] Exodus 32. 35.

men that the punishment might not destroy all who were implicated in the guilt. But toward certain individuals and families, as
we read, the censure of God was inexorable. Such an instance is
that of the man who, when the people rested on the Sabbath day,
presumed to gather wood and was killed. For although his action
seemed harmless in itself, yet the observance of the day made it
sinful. Or the time when two men were contesting with each other,
and one, since he had blasphemed, was punished by death. For it is
written: "Lo the son of an Israelitish woman, whose father was an
Egyptian, went out among the children of Israel; and this son of
an Israelitish woman and a man of Israel strove together in the
camp; and the Israelitish woman's son blasphemed the name of the
Lord, and cursed. And they brought him to Moses." And a little
later: "And they put him in ward, that the mind of the Lord might
be showed them. And the Lord spake unto Moses, saying, 'Bring
forth him that hath cursed without the camp; and let all that heard
him lay their hands upon his head, and let all the congregation
stone him.' " [39]

Was not God's judgment immediate and manifest and his sentence pronounced as if the heavenly decision followed the forms of
our legal procedure? First the man who had sinned was arrested,
then he was led, so to speak, before the judge's seat, thirdly accused and then put into prison, lastly punished by the authority
of the divine judgment; furthermore he was not only punished
but punished in accordance with evidence given, so that God's
justice and not merely his power was seen to condemn his guilt.
This truly was meant as an example working toward the correction
of all men, so that none should commit thereafter the deed which
all the people had punished in one person. For this reason and by
this judgment the Lord does all things now and has always done
them, that whatever penalties individuals have to bear should work
toward the correction of all.

---

[39] Leviticus 24. 10-14.

So it was also when Abihu and Nadab, men of priestly blood, were consumed by fire from heaven; in whose case, to be sure, the Lord wished to show not merely judgment but judgment immediately impending. For it is written that when the fire sent by the Lord had consumed the burnt offering: "Nadab and Abihu, the sons of Aaron, took either of them his censer, and put fire therein and put incense thereon, and offered strange fire before the Lord, which he commanded them not. And there went out fire from the Lord and devoured them and they died before the Lord." [40] What else did he wish than to show his right hand stretched over us, and his sword ever threatening? For he punished the errors of the aforesaid men at once, in their very act, and the crime of the sinners was scarcely committed before punishment was exacted for their misdeeds.

Yet not only this was accomplished in their case, but much else besides. For, as in these men not a wicked intention but only a misguided impulse was punished, the Lord surely made clear what punishment any one would deserve who committed a sin through contempt of the divine power, since even those who had sinned only through thoughtlessness were struck down by God — or how guilty they would be who acted contrary to his command, when those who merely acted without his command were thus stricken. God also wished to further our correction by a salutary example, that all laymen should understand how much they ought to fear the wrath of God, since neither did the high priest's merits rescue his sons from instant punishment, nor did the privilege of the sacred ministry redeem them.

But why do I speak of men whose ill-advised action really did in some measure affect God and work injury to his divinity? Mary spoke against Moses and was punished; she was not only punished, but punished in due course of trial. For first she was called to justice, then accused, and thirdly chastised. In the accusation she

---

[40] *Ibid.* 10. 1-2.

learned the full force of her sentence, and in her leprosy she paid full atonement for her crime — yet this punishment humbled not Mary alone, but Aaron as well. For, though it was unsuitable for the high priest to be deformed by leprosy, yet the correction of the Lord plagued him also. Nor was this all. In the punishment that Mary suffered, Aaron too was involved, as sharer in her guilt; Mary indeed was punished that Aaron might be put to confusion.

Furthermore, that we might recognize in the individual cases that the form of the divine judgment is inexorable, God did not even yield to the intercession of the injured party. For we read that the Lord spoke thus to Aaron and Mary:

"Wherefore then were ye not afraid to speak against my servant Moses?" And the anger of the Lord was kindled against them, and he departed. And behold, Mary became leprous, and white as snow: and Moses cried unto the Lord, saying: "Heal her now, O God, I beseech thee." And the Lord said unto Moses: "If her father had but spit in her face, should she not be ashamed seven days? Let her be shut out from the camp seven days, and after that let her be received in again." [41]

These things that we have told should be sufficient for this division of the argument and for this part of our work; for it is an endless task to discuss all the cases; indeed, it would be overlong merely to enumerate them without any discussion. But let me add one more instance.

12. The people of the Hebrews repented having gone out of Egypt; they were struck down: then they grieved at the weariness and toil of the journey, and were afflicted: they desired flesh-meat, and were smitten. And because, eating manna daily, they desired to satiate the cravings of their bellies with illicit foods, they were sated indeed in their passionate greed, but tortured in that very satiety. "For while their food was still in their mouths," says the Scripture, "the wrath of God came upon them, and slew very many of them and smote down the chosen men of Israel." [42]

[41] Numbers 12. 8-15, condensed. Note that Salvian uses the name Mary for the Biblical Miriam.
[42] Psalms 78. 30-31.

Og rebelled against Moses: he was blotted out. Korah taunted him: he was overwhelmed. Dathan and Abiram murmured against him: they were swallowed up. "For the earth opened and swallowed Dathan, and covered the company of Abiram." [43] Two hundred and fifty leaders of the people also, as the sacred narrative testifies, who were called upon by name to speak at the time of the council, rose against Moses. "And they gathered themselves together against Moses and against Aaron, and said to them: 'Ye take too much upon you, seeing all the congregation are holy, every one of them, and the Lord is among them; wherefore then lift ye up yourselves above the congregation of the Lord?'" And what happened after this? "There came out a fire from the Lord, and consumed the two hundred and fifty men that offered incense." [44]

When such deeds were committed, heavenly mercy was of no avail. Correction was administered again and again, yet improvement did not follow. For just as we are chastised again and again, and do not improve, so they too, though constantly struck down, did not mend their ways. For what is written? "But on the morrow all the congregation of the children of Israel murmured against Moses and Aaron, saying, 'Ye have killed the people of the Lord.'" [45]

What happened then? Fourteen thousand seven hundred men were struck down at once and consumed by divine fire. Since all the multitude of the people sinned, why did not the punishment fall on all alike? Especially since, as I said before, no one escaped from Korah's sedition. Why did God on the former occasion wish all the assemblage of sinners to be killed, but at this time a portion only? Surely because the Lord is full of justice and mercy and therefore his indulgence causes many concessions to his love, and his discipline to his severity. And so on the one occasion he gave first place

---

[43] *Ibid.* 106. 17.

[44] Numbers 16. 3, 35.

[45] *Ibid.* 16. 41.

to discipline that the punishment of all the guilty might redound to the general betterment; on the other he yielded precedence to mercy, that the whole people might not perish. Although he acted with such mercy, yet because the punishment so often repeated for a part of the people did not profit them, finally he condemned them all to death. This example should contribute to our fear and our correction alike, that we, failing to be improved by their example, may not come to be punished by a destruction like theirs.

There is no doubt what their end was. Although the whole race of the Hebrews went out of Egypt to enter the promised land, yet not one of them entered it save two holy men alone. For it is written: "The Lord spake unto Moses and unto Aaron, saying: 'How long shall I bear with this evil congregation, which murmur against me? As truly as I live, saith the Lord, as ye have spoken in mine ears this day, so will I do to you: your carcasses shall fall in this wilderness!'" What followed? "Your little ones," he said, "which you said would be a prey, them will I bring in, and they shall know the land which ye have despised. But as for you, your carcasses, they shall fall in this wilderness." And what then? "All died and were struck down in the sight of the Lord." [46]

What detail is lacking in this whole account? Would you see a ruler? Behold him, correcting present sins and disposing the future. Would you see a severe judge? Behold, he punishes the guilty. Would you see a just and loving judge? Behold, he spares the innocent. Would you see the judge of the whole world? Behold, his judgment is in all places. For as judge he accuses and as judge he rules; as judge he pronounces sentence; as judge he destroys the guilty, and as judge he rewards the innocent.

---

[46] *Ibid.* 14. 26-29, 31-32, 37.

THE SECOND BOOK

1. The examples given above are sufficient proof, therefore, that our God acts constantly as a most anxious watcher, a most tender ruler, and a most just judge. But perhaps one of my less enlightened readers is thinking: "If all things are now conducted by God as they were in those days, why is it that the evil prevail while the good are afflicted; and whereas in the past the evil felt God's wrath, and the good his mercy, now by some strange reversal the good appear to experience his wrath and the evil his favor?" These questions I shall answer presently, but now since I have promised to prove three points, namely, God's presence, his government and his judgment, by three methods, that is, by reason, by examples and by authority; and since I have already given sufficient proof of them by reason and examples, it remains for me to verify them by authority. Yet the examples I have given should rank as authority, since that term is rightly applied to the means by which the truth of matters under discussion is established.

Which then of the above-mentioned points should first be proved by sacred authority — his presence, his government, or his judgment? His presence, I think, because he who is to rule or judge must surely be present, in order to be able to rule or judge anything whatever.

Speaking through the Sacred Books, the Divine Word says: "The eyes of the Lord are in every place, beholding the evil and the good." [1] Here you find God present, looking upon us, his eyes watching us wherever we may be. If the Divine Word assures us that God observes the good and the wicked, it is expressly to prove that nothing escapes his watchful scrutiny. For your fuller comprehension, hear the testimony of the Holy Spirit in another part

---

[1] Proverbs 15. 3.

of the Scriptures, when it says: "Behold, the eye of the Lord is upon them that fear him, to deliver their soul from death, and to keep them alive in famine." [2] This is why God is said to watch over the just, that he may preserve and protect them. For the propitious oversight of his divinity is the safeguard of our mortal life.[3] Elsewhere the Holy Spirit speaks in the same fashion: "The eyes of the Lord are upon the righteous, and his ears are open unto their cry." [4]

See with what gentle kindness the Scripture says the Lord treats his people. For when it says the eyes of the Lord are on the righteous, his watchful love is shown; when it says that his ears are always open to their prayers, his readiness to hear is indicated. That his ears are always open to the prayers of the righteous proves not merely God's attention, but one might almost say his obedience. For how are the ears of the Lord open to the prayers of the righteous? How, save that he always hears, always hears clearly, always grants readily the pleas he has heard, bestows on men at once what he has clearly heard them ask? So the ears of our Lord are always ready to listen to the prayers of his saints, always attentive. How happy should we all be if we ourselves were as ready to hearken to God as he is to hear us!

But perhaps you say that the proof of God's guardianship of the just is useless to our argument, since this is not a general watchfulness of the divine power but merely a special favor granted to the righteous. Note, however, that the Sacred Word testified above that the eyes of the Lord watch over both good and evil. If you still wish to argue the point, consider this, for it follows in the text: "Moreover the face of the Lord is against them that do evil, to cut off the remembrance of them from the earth." [5]

---

[2] Psalms 33. 18-19.

[3] Note the converse of this statement already given in I. 7 *supra*: "The divine wrath is the punishment of the sinner."

[4] *Ibid.* 34. 15.

[5] *Ibid.* 34. 16.

You see that you have no ground for complaint that God does not look upon the unjust also, since you know that he watches all men, but with different effect because of the inequality of their merits. The good indeed are watched by him that they may be preserved, the evil that they may be destroyed. You yourself, who deny that God watches men, have your place with these last; know then that you are not only clearly seen by God, but are without doubt in imminent peril. For since the face of the Lord is upon them that do evil, to cut off remembrance of them from the earth, you, who wickedly say that the eyes of the Lord do not see you, must learn by your destruction the wrath of an all-seeing God. These arguments, then, are sufficient to prove the presence and watchfulness of God.

2. Let us now see whether he who watches us also rules us, although, forsooth, his watchfulness in itself implies governance as its motive, unless he looks upon us in order to neglect us thereafter. Surely the fact that he deigns to look upon us is itself an indication of his care for us, especially since the Sacred Word has borne witness, as I have shown above, that the wicked are observed by God to their destruction, the good to their salvation. Certainly this very fact shows the divine guidance, for this is actually ruling by just government and dealing with men individually according to their several merits.

Listen, however, to fuller testimony on this point. The Holy Spirit spoke thus to God the Father in a psalm: "Give ear, O Shepherd of Israel." [6] Israel means "Seeing God," since indeed Christians who believe faithfully see him with faith in their hearts. Though God is the governor of all things, still his governance is spoken of as being chiefly assigned to those who especially deserve divine guidance. Therefore you also, whoever you are, if you are a Christian, must of necessity believe in God's government. If, however, you refuse utterly to believe that you, together with other

---

[6] *Ibid.* 80. 1.

Christians, are ruled by God, you must recognize that you belong outside the whole body of Christians.

But if, as we suggested earlier, you are more interested in the case of men in general, than of Christians alone, see how clearly the Holy Book says that all things are daily ruled by the divine will and the whole world incessantly guided by God, for it says: "He himself loves counsel and discipline." [7] "For neither is there any other God beside thee that careth for all, but being righteous thou rulest all things righteously and with great reverence dost dispose us." [8]

Here you have God constantly arranging, constantly governing; yet in the passage cited not only his divine governance but also the high honor of man is declared. For the words, "thou dost dispose us," show the power of his divine government, but the words, "with great reverence," show the culmination of human honor. Elsewhere also we read in the words of the prophet: "Do I not fill heaven and earth?" [9] And he himself tells us why he fills all things: "Because I am with you to save you." [10] Obviously then God shows us not merely his rule and the fulness of his power but also the might and benefits that result from its plenitude. For the fulness of divinity bears within it this fruit, that it saves all things that it fills. Thus in the Acts of the Apostles the most blessed Paul said: "In him we live and move and have our being." [11] Doubtless he is more than the controller of our lives, in whom is the very source of life. For Paul did not say that we are moved by God but in him, teaching us, to be sure, that our real substance is rooted within his sacred attributes, since we truly live in him from whom we receive our being.

[7] Ecclesiasticus 39.10; Salvian has *diligit* for the *diriget* of the Vulgate, though the latter reading would express his idea better than the verb he uses.
[8] Wisdom 12.13, 15, 18.
[9] Jeremiah 23.24.
[10] *Ibid.* 42.11.
[11] Acts 17.28.

The Savior himself said also in the Gospel: "Lo, I am with you alway, even unto the end of the world." [12] He not only said that he is with us, but that he is with us all our days. Do you then, most thankless of men, say that he who is constantly with us has no care or thought for us? What then does he do in our company? Can you possibly think that he is with us in order to neglect and overlook us? And how can he consistently grant his presence to our virtue and neglect our vice? "For lo," he says, "I am with you alway, even unto the end of the world." Truly we have a marvelous comprehension of God's love if we say falsely that he is constantly neglectful of us while he says that he is constantly with us. Through this he wishes to show that his love and protection are constantly with us, since his very presence does not leave us. But we turn the divine charity into contempt; we change the indications of his love into proofs of hatred. For we try to see evidence of hatred rather than of love in his saying that he is with us. If the Lord had said that he would remain apart from us, we might perhaps have less occasion to gossip about his lack of care, in his absence. Constant neglect is a proof of greater contempt and scorn from one who never leaves us. There is the more odium in staying with us always if, while never depriving us of his presence, he continually shuts us out from his loving care.

But far be it from us to believe that our most loving and merciful God would have wished to be always near us for the sake of increasing by his presence the apparent contempt of his neglect: far be it from us even to say such a wicked thing. For I think there is no one in the whole human race who is so evil that he wishes to be with any man on account of his dislike of him, or wishes to employ his presence solely to achieve greater satisfaction of his hatred by scorning him face to face. Let human nature itself teach and convince us that we wish to be with one man or another because we love the one whose company we desire. And just because we

---

[12] Matthew 28. 20.

love a man, we wish our presence to be of benefit to him whom we love. So what we cannot deny even to a criminal, we deny to God, and make him seem worse than the worst of men, if we think that he promised to be with us in order to show greater contempt for us by his subsequent neglect. But enough of this.

3. We have already proved by sacred testimony that all things are both watched and ruled by God; it remains now to show that the greater part are also judged by his divine power in this world.

When the blessed David had suffered the insulting scorn of Nabal the Carmelite, since he himself postponed vengeance, he received his revenge at once at the hand of God. So when, shortly after, his enemy had been overwhelmed and killed by the hand of the Lord, he spoke thus: "Blessed be the Lord, that hath pleaded the cause of my reproach from the hand of Nabal." [13] Likewise when his rebellious son had driven him from his kingdom the Lord as his judge in a brief space requited him, and more abundantly than he himself desired.

God wished to show that the affliction of those who suffered injustice was greater in his eyes than in their own. For when a man takes vengeance beyond the wish of the injured person, what else can he mean than that he is acting on his own behalf also? So when, for his attempted parricide, David's son was being hung on a cross not made with hands, the Divine Word tells us that the punishment divinely brought upon him was thus reported: "I bring thee good tidings, my lord king; for the Lord hath avenged thee this day of all them that rose up against thee." [14]

4. You see how the sacred books prove through divine witnesses that God judges not only by deeds, as we said above, and by examples, but by the very name and terms of judgment, even in our present age. Perhaps you think that it was as a special favor granted by God to a holy man, that he wrought judgment forthwith on David's enemies. The day will not suffice if I would tell of

[13] I Samuel 25. 39.
[14] II Samuel 18. 31.

his immediate sentences and judgments in this world. Yet, that you may clearly understand that it is not so much in consideration of the persons concerned as of their actions that he exercises his sacred censure, hear how God our judge, who constantly gave his unmistakable verdict on behalf of his servant David, many times passed judgment on David himself. And indeed this occurred not in a matter affecting many men, nor — which would perhaps naturally have aroused God the more — affecting holy men, but in the case of a single individual, a barbarian,[15] a case in which it was not the person concerned that demanded vengeance, but the action. For when David had killed Uriah the Hittite, a man belonging to an impious people and a hostile nation, he was at once charged thus by the divine voice: ''Thou hast killed Uriah the Hittite with the sword and hast taken his wife to be thy wife, and hast slain him with the sword of the children of Ammon. Now therefore the sword shall never depart from thine house. Therefore thus saith the Lord, 'Behold, I will raise up evil against thee out of thine own house, and I will take thy wives before thine eyes and give them unto thy neighbor. For thou didst it secretly; but I will do this thing before all Israel and before the sun.' ''[16]

What answer have you to this, you who believe that God not only fails to judge our every action but does not regard us at all? Do you see that the eyes of the Lord were in no wise withdrawn from the single secret sin which David once committed? Wherefore do you also, who — as a consolation I suppose for your sins — think that our acts are not observed by God, learn from this same instance that you are always seen by Christ, and know that you must receive punishment, perhaps very shortly. For you see that even the blessed David was unable to hide his own misdeed in the secret places of his innermost chambers, and to claim exemption from instant punishment by the undoubted merit of his great deeds. For what did the Lord say to him? ''I will take thy wives before

---

[15] That is, not a Hebrew.
[16] II Samuel 12. 9-12.

thine eyes, and the sword shall never depart from thine house.'' You see what immediate judgment so great a man suffered at once for one sin. Condemnation followed close on the heels of the fault, a condemnation punishing immediately without reservations and arresting the wrongdoer on the spot, not putting off the charge to a later time.

Therefore he did not say: ''Because you have done this, know that the judgment of the Lord shall come and you shall be tortured hereafter by the flames of Gehenna.'' No; he said: ''You shall suffer torture at once, and shall feel the sword of divine justice already at your throat.''

And what followed? The guilty man acknowledged his fault, was humbled, stung by remorse, confessed and mourned his sin. He repented and implored pardon, gave up his royal jewels, laid aside his gold-wrought robes, put off the purple, resigned the glory of his crown, changed his whole bodily habit, cast off every aspect of kingship with its trappings, and put on the guise of a penitent fugitive, eagerly assuming a squalor that should plead in his defence; he was wasted by fasting, withered by thirst, exhausted by weeping, self-imprisoned in loneliness. And yet this king of so great repute, greater in holiness than in mere temporal power, surpassing all men in the favors earned by his former merits, although he sought pardon so earnestly, did not escape punishment. The fruit of such great penitence was indeed sufficient to win remission from eternal expiation, but not to earn pardon at the moment. Finally, what did the prophet say to the penitent? ''Because thou hast made the enemies of the Lord blaspheme, the son that is born to thee shall die.'' [17] In addition to the bitter loss of his son, God wished the loving father to suffer also the knowledge of the full extent of his punishment, that he himself had caused the death of the dearly loved son for whom he mourned, when the boy born of his father's crime was slain for the very crime that had begotten him.

---

[17] *Ibid.* 12. 14.

5. This is the first instance of the divine punishment; the first, to be sure, but not the only one, for a long series of great griefs followed and an almost unending succession of misfortunes haunted his household. Thamar was seduced by the mad act of Amnon, and Amnon slain by Absalom. A great crime indeed was committed by the first brother, but its retribution by the other was worse. In these actions David the father was punished alike by both sons' crimes. Two children sinned, but three were ruined by the sin of two; for Thamar suffered the loss of her virginity, while in Amnon also the destruction of Absalom was mourned. And verily you cannot tell for which of the two sons so loving a father mourned the more grievously, the one slain in this world by his brother's hand, or the other who by his own hand was doomed forever.[18] From this time indeed ills were piled up beyond reckoning, according to the word of God. The father long endured the treachery of his son, was driven from his kingdom, and sought in exile an escape from murder. Which was worse, the vice or the bloodthirstiness of his son? By incest he disgraced his father when his attempted parricide failed, and by his diligent heaping up of crime achieved an incest passing the bounds of incest, committing in public, to his father's greater shame, a crime abominable even in secret. It was a mortal sin that he performed against his exiled father, but worse still was the injury wrought by his public incest before the eyes of the whole world.

Must we add to this the spectacle of David's actual flight? Picture this mighty king, so greatly renowned, higher in honor than all others, greater than the world itself, fleeing his whole people with a tiny band of slaves. In comparison with his former state he was needy indeed; in comparison with his wonted train [19] he went

---

[18] Here Salvian seems to overlook II Samuel 13. 39: "And the soul of King David longed to go forth unto Absalom: for he was comforted concerning Amnon, seeing he was dead."

[19] I have followed here Pauly's conjecture: *in comparatione comitatus sui soliti solus.*

alone. He fled in fear, disgrace and sorrow — "walking," the Scripture says, "with covered head, and barefoot." [20] He had out-lived his former state, exiled from himself, almost, one might say, surviving his own death. He sank so low as to merit the scorn of his own servants, or — which is harder yet to bear — their pity. So Ziba was fain to feed him, and Shimei did not fear to curse him publicly. God's judgment so changed him from his former self that he endured the open insults of a single enemy — he who had made the world to tremble!

6. Who now denies that God watches over human actions? Be-hold how often the Scriptures have shown in the case of one man that God not only observed, but also judged his acts! And why? Why indeed, except that we should understand that the Lord's ver-dict and coercion are always to be exercised in this world as they were then? So we read that even holy men were punished afore-time by God's judgment, to teach us that we too must always be judged in our present life by God. For as God always is, so is his justice eternal. As God's omnipotence is never-failing, so is his ver-dict unchangeable. As long as his law endures, so long also shall his justice remain. Therefore all his saints in their sacred books, amid the imminent fear of martyrdom and the swords of the perse-cutors, demand that the immediate judgment of God be established. For thus said the just man in a psalm: "Judge me, O God, and plead my cause against an ungodly nation." And that this might not be construed as a reference to some future judgment of God, he added at once: "Deliver me from the deceitful and unjust man." [21]

Certainly it is the immediate judgment of God that he demands who begs to be freed from the hands of the persecutor. In his con-sciousness of a just cause the psalmist did well to pray for God's justice rather than for his favor, for the best verdict is always given to the righteous cause if the case is conducted with justice.

[20] II Samuel 15. 30.
[21] Psalms 43. 1.

Elsewhere also the psalmist spoke most clearly, saying: "Judge, O Lord, them that injure me; fight against them that fight against me; seize arms and shield and stand up for mine help." [22] You see in this case that he does not demand the severity of a future trial, but the verdict of immediate justice.

For what are his words? "Take up the shield and seize the sword" — the shield, of course, for protection and the sword for vengeance — not that God's judgment needs such weapons, but because in this world the names of dreaded arms are the instruments of dread judgments. Speaking to human intelligence in figures drawn from human life, since he was praying for judgment and for vengeance on his adversaries, he expressed the power of God's punishment in terms of the instruments of earthly vengeance.

Lastly, the same prophet showed elsewhere the great difference between the present and the future judgments of God. For what did he say to the Lord about his verdict in the present trial? "Thou sittest on the throne and judgest." And what about the future and everlasting judgment of God? "He shall judge the world in righteousness;" and again: "He shall minister judgment to the people in uprightness." [23] By these words surely he made a clear distinction in time between the present and the future judgments of God. For to indicate the present he wrote, "thou judgest," and to distinguish the future from the present he added, "he shall judge."

Sufficient proof of God's care for us and of his government and judgment has now been given by reason, by examples and by authority,[24] especially since the books to follow are all to be concerned with the same proof. Now if we receive from God, whose work we are performing, strength to complete our task, we shall attempt to bring to light and to refute the customary arguments opposed by our adversaries to these essential doctrines.

---

[22] *Ibid.* 35. 1-2.

[23] *Ibid.* 9. 4, 8.

[24] See II. 1 *supra.*

THE THIRD BOOK

1. It is well: the foundations have been laid [1] for a work undertaken from pious motives and from love of a sacred duty; they have not been laid in marshy ground or built of perishable stone, but are strengthened by the sacred treasures used in their building and by the skill of their divine architect. These foundations, as God himself says in his Gospel, cannot be shaken by raging winds, undermined by river floods, or washed away by the rains.[2] Since the divine writings in some fashion lent their aid to the erection of this structure, and the Holy Scriptures performed the joiner's task, the work itself must, through the help of the Lord Jesus Christ, be as strong as its makers. So this edifice receives its character from its parent stock and cannot be shaken while the builders remain sound.

As no one can tear down the walls of earthly houses without tearing apart their stones and mortar, so none can destroy this structure of ours unless he first destroys the materials of which it is composed. Since these certainly can in no way be weakened, we may safely assume the permanence of a building whose strength is insured by immortal aid.

The question is raised why, if everything in this world is controlled by the care and governance and judgment of God, the condition of the barbarians is so much better than ours, why among us the fortune of good men is harder than that of the wicked. Why should upright men fall ill and reprobates recover? Why does the whole world fall prey to powers for the most part unjust? Perhaps a rational and fairly consistent answer would be: "I do not know." For I do not know the secrets of God. The oracle of

---

[1] See Lactantius *op. cit.* VII. 1. 1: *Bene habet, iacta sunt fundamenta, ut ait eximius orator* . . . ; where Lactantius is quoting Cicero *Pro Murena* 6. 14.
[2] Matthew 7. 25.

his heavenly word is sufficient proof for me in this case. God says, as I have already proved in my earlier books, that all things are subject to his oversight, his rule and his judgment. If you wish to know what doctrines you must accept, you have the sacred writings: the perfect course is to hold fast what you have read in them.

Moreover, I would not have you ask me to account for God's actions in the cases of which I speak. I am a man; I do not understand the secrets of God,[3] I do not dare search them out, I am afraid to pry into them, for to seek to know more than is permitted is in itself a kind of rash sacrilege.[4] God says that he moves and ordains all things: let that suffice. Do you ask me why one man is greater and another less, one wretched and another happy, one strong and another weak? Why indeed God does such things I do not know, but the proof that he is the source of all actions should convince you fully. As God is greater than the sum total of human reason, our knowledge that everything is done by him ought to have more weight with us than reason alone. You do not need, therefore, to hear any new argument on this point; let God's authority be set over against all reason from any source whatever.

We are not at liberty to say that of the actions of the divine will one is just and another unjust, because whatever you see is done by God, whatever you are sure is done by him, you must confess is more than just. So much can be said of God's government and justice without further discussion and without uncertainty. I need not prove by arguments what is proved by his very words. When we read that God says he constantly sees all the earth, we have proof that he sees it, since he says so. When we read that he

---

[3] The much quoted words of Terence (*Heauton Timoroumenos* 77) here take on a new significance, from the Christian connotation. ''I am a man, nothing human is alien to me''— Salvian's wide sympathies echo the spirit of these words many times, but the secrets of God, he says, pass man's understanding. Salvian's acquaintance with Terence is indicated by his use of a line from the *Andria* in *Ad ecclesiam* III. 12.

[4] See Lactantius *op. cit.* II. 5. 2-3; 8. 69, 71.

rules all creation, we have proof that he rules it, because he so affirms. When we read that he orders all things by his immediate judgment, his judgment is clearly proved by his own testimony. All other statements, made in human terms, need proofs and witnesses, whereas God's speech is its own witness, since the words of perfect truth must be perfect testimony to the truth. Yet since our God willed that we should through the Sacred Scriptures know certain things, as if from the archives of his spirit and mind — since the pronouncements of the Holy Scriptures are themselves in a way the mind of God — I shall not conceal anything that God has wished his people to know and preach.

One thing, however, I should like to know before I begin — whether I am to address my words to Christians or to pagans. If to Christians, I do not doubt that I shall prove my case. But if I speak to pagans, I should scorn the attempt, not for any lack of proofs, but because I despair of profit from my discourse. Surely it is fruitless and lost labor when a perverse listener is not open to conviction. Yet because I think there is no one belonging to the Christian name who does not at least wish to seem a Christian, I shall address my words to Christians. However many pagans still adhere to their impious unbelief, it is enough for me to prove my contentions to a Christian audience.

2. So you keep airing the question why we Christians who believe in God are more wretched than all other men. The words of the apostle to the churches might have furnished me with a sufficient answer to this: "That no man should be moved by these afflictions; for you yourself know that we are appointed thereunto." [5] Since the apostle says we are meant to endure hardships, miseries and sorrows, why is it strange that we suffer every evil, who are fighting for the sake of enduring all adversities? Since, however, many do not appreciate this, but think that Christians should receive from God, as the wages due to their faith, greater

[5] I Thessalonians 3. 3.

strength than all other races, because they are more religious than all others, let us agree to their opinion and argument.

Let us see what it means to believe firmly in God. We who wish our reward for belief and faith in this life to be so great must consider what sort of belief and faith we should have. What is belief and what is faith? I think it is that a man believe in Christ faithfully, that he be faithful to God, that is, that he faithfully keep God's commandments.[6] For as the slaves of rich men or of government officials, to whom expensive furnishings and valuable stores are entrusted, cannot be called faithful if they have swallowed up the goods entrusted to them; so Christians also are proved unfaithful if they have corrupted the good things granted them by God.

Perhaps you ask what the good is that God grants to Christian men? What else but all the substance of our faith, all those things through which we are Christians? First the law, then the prophets, thirdly the Gospels, fourthly the reading of the apostles, finally the gift of fresh regeneration, the grace of holy baptism, the unction of the divine chrism. You remember that of old among the Hebrews, the people especially chosen of God, when the office of the judges had passed over into the power of kings, God called the most approved and excellent men to reign through the royal unction. So every Christian, having performed all God's commands after receiving the chrism of the church, shall be called to heaven to receive the reward of his labors. Since these are the elements of our faith, let us see who keeps these great sacraments in such a way as to be judged faithful, for, as I said, the unfaithful must be those who do not keep their trust. And indeed I do not ask that a man perform all the commands of the Old and New Testaments: I exempt him from the censorial power of the old law, the threats of the prophets, even from the strictest interpretation of the apostolic books or the full doctrine of the Gospels in their complete perfection, though these last admit no exception. I only ask who lives in

---

6 The definition is repeated in **IV. 1** *infra.*

accordance with the least number of God's commands. I do not mean those which so many avoid that they are almost accursed. God's honor and reverence have advanced so far among us that those things which our lack of devotion leads us to neglect, we consider worthy even of hatred.

For instance, who would deign even to listen to our Savior's bidding not to take thought for the morrow? Who obeys his order to be content with a single tunic? Who thinks the command to walk unshod possible or even tolerable to follow? These precepts then I pass over. For here our faith, in which we trust, falls short, so that we judge superfluous the precepts the Lord intended for our benefit. "Love your enemies," said the Savior, "do good to them that hate you, and pray for them which despitefully use you and persecute you." [7] Who could keep all these commandments? Who would deign to follow God's commands in respect to his enemies, I do not say in wishes, but even in words? Even if a man compels himself to do so, still it is his lips alone that act, and not his mind; he lends the service of his voice to the action without changing the feeling of his heart. Therefore, even if he forces himself to say a prayer for his adversary, his lips move, but he does not really pray.

To discuss all such cases would take too long; but one point I add, that we may know that not only do we fail to accede to all God's commands, but we actually obey almost none of them. This is why the apostle cried: "For if a man think himself to be something when he is nothing, he deceiveth himself." [8] We add this to our sins, that although we are guilty in every respect, we still believe ourselves to be pure and holy. Thus the offences of our iniquity are piled high by a false assumption of righteousness. "Whosoever hateth his brother," says the apostle, "is a murderer." [9] We may know from this that there are many murderers who

---

[7] Matthew 5. 44.

[8] Galatians 6. 3.

[9] I John 3. 15.

think themselves innocent, because, as we see, murder is committed not only by the hand of him that kills, but also by the heart of him that hates. For this reason the Savior added to this precept a still harsher decree, saying: "Whosoever is angry with his brother without a cause shall be in danger of the judgment." [10] Anger is the mother of hatred. Hence the Savior wished to shut out wrath, that hatred might not spring from it. If then not only hatred but even wrath makes us guilty in God's judgment, we clearly see that as no one in the world is free from anger, so no one can be free from conviction of sin. Moreover, God seems to trace every fiber of that precept to its end, and cut off all its fruits and branches, when he says: "But whosoever shall say, 'Thou fool,' shall be in danger of hell fire; whosoever shall say to his brother, '*Racha*,' shall be in danger of the council." Many do not know what kind of danger is involved in *racha*, but they know very well with what slanderous intent men are charged with folly.[11] So, using their knowledge rather than their ignorance, they prefer to expiate in the divine fires the guilt incurred by a form of abuse they understand, rather than to atone before human councils for one that they do not know.

3. Since this is true, and since these commands of the Lord not only fail of being carried out by us, but are practically all reversed, when shall we come to obey his greater precepts? The Savior said: "Whosoever forsaketh not all that he hath, he cannot be my disciple. . . . And he that taketh not his cross and followeth after me, is not worthy of me." [12] He who calls himself a Christian ought to walk as Christ walked. Certainly not only those who follow the delights and pomps of the world, but even those who abandon worldly interests fail to meet these requirements. Those who

---

[10] Matthew 5. 22.

[11] *Ibid.* 5. 22. See also Gregory *Moralia* 21. 5: "*Racha* indeed in the Hebrew tongue is the exclamation of the angry man, which shows his intention without fully expressing his wrath in words." For other contemporary discussions cf. Baluze *ad loc.*

[12] Luke 14. 33; Matthew 10. 38.

make a show of renouncing their wealth do not appear to make their renunciation complete, and those who are thought to be carrying their cross so carry it that they gain more honor in the name of the cross than suffering in its passion. Even though all those men should in good faith accomplish these precepts in some measure, still it is certain that none of them could succeed in walking along the paths of this life as the Savior walked. For the apostle says: "He that saith he abideth in him ought himself also so to walk, even as he walked." [13]

4. Perhaps certain men think the commands of the apostle are hard. Clearly they must be considered difficult, if the apostles exacted from others the performance of duties they did not lay upon themselves. But if, on the other hand, they enjoined upon others much lighter duties than on themselves, instead of being considered harsh teachers, they must be thought most indulgent parents, who, through their religious zeal, themselves in loving indulgence take the burdens their sons should bear.

What was it that one of them said to the people of the church? "My little children, of whom I travail in birth again until Christ be formed in you." And again: "Be ye followers of me, even as I also am of Christ." [14] This is his command, that we imitate him who gave himself over to the imitation of Christ. Indeed, none can doubt that he himself imitated Christ. As Christ for our sake subjected himself to the world, so did Paul for Christ's sake. As Christ for us endured the heaviest pains and labors, so did Paul for Christ. As Christ for us suffered scorn and mockery, so did Paul for Christ. As Christ for us endured his passion and death, so did Paul for Christ. Therefore not without cause, conscious of his own merits, he said: "I have fought a good fight, I have kept the faith; henceforth there is laid up for me a crown of righteousness." [15]

---

[13] I John 2. 6.

[14] Galatians 4.19; I Corinthians 11.1.

[15] II Timothy 4. 7-8.

Since he so followed Christ, let us consider which of us seems to be a true follower of the apostle. He writes of himself first of all that he never gave offence to any, but in all things showed himself the minister of God, in much patience, in affliction, in necessities, in blows, in imprisonments, in stripes.[16] Elsewhere, comparing himself with others, he says: "Howbeit, whereinsoever any is bold (I speak foolishly) I am bold also: I speak as a fool, I am more; in labors more abundant, in prisons more frequent, in stripes above measure, in deaths oft. Of the Jews five times received I forty stripes save one. Thrice was I beaten with rods, once was I stoned, thrice I suffered shipwreck."[17]

Surely, even if we leave out of account the other apostolic virtues that he lists, when the apostle says that he has suffered shipwreck three times, in this at least we can outdo him. We have not merely been wrecked three times, but our whole life is one continuous shipwreck; indeed all men are living such vicious lives that there seems to be no Christian who is not wrecked constantly.[18]

5. Some one may object that it does not befit our present time to endure for Christ such sufferings as did the apostles of old. It is true that there are no longer heathen princes, nor tyrannous persecutors; the blood of the saints is not shed now nor their faith tried by tortures. Our God is content with the service of our peace, that we please him simply by the purity of our spotless acts and the holiness of an unstained life. Our faith and devotion are the more due him because he demands lesser services from us and has foregone the greater exactions. Since even our princes are Christians, there is no persecution and religion is not disturbed, we who are not forced to test our faith by harsher trials ought certainly to

---

[16] II Corinthians 6. 4-5.

[17] *Ibid.* 11. 21, 23-25.

[18] Here Salvian makes use of his fundamental thesis, that the disasters of the Romans are due to their sins. The first part of this sentence would suggest to his readers the losses due to the barbarian invasions; in the conclusion he reminds them of the real danger they face.

seek the more to please God in small ways. For he by whom trifles are duly performed proves that if occasion arises he will be capable of greater things.

6. Let us then pass over the trials of the most blessed Paul, let us even omit the accounts we read in the books later written about our faith, of the sufferings endured by almost all Christians, who, mounting to the doors of the heavenly palaces by their tortures, contrived steps for their ascent from the very racks and scaffolds. Let us see whether in those lesser and ordinary observances of religious devotion which we all as Christians can perform in utter peace at all times, we are really trying to accede to the Lord's commands.

Christ orders us not to quarrel. Who obeys this order? He not only gives the command, but insists on it so far that he bids us renounce those things about which a dispute has arisen, provided we may thus end the suit. "For," he says, "if any man will sue thee at the law, and take away thy coat, let him have thy cloak also." [19] I ask who there are who yield to the attempts of their adversaries to despoil them; further, who there are who do not try to rob their opponents in turn? For we are so far from leaving them other property in addition to our coats, that if we can find any way to do it we take away coats and cloaks as well from our enemies. Indeed, so eagerly do we obey the Lord's commands that it does not satisfy us to refuse our adversaries even the least part of our garments, unless we rob them of everything we possibly can, as far as the circumstances permit.

Moreover, there is a second similar commandment joined with this one, in which the Lord says: "Whosoever shall smite thee on thy right cheek, turn to him the other also." [20] How many men do we think there are who would listen politely to such words, or agree to them in their hearts, even if they pretended to listen? How

---

[19] Matthew 5. 40.
[20] *Ibid.* 5. 39.

often do you find a man who does not return many blows for the one that he has received? He is so far from turning his other cheek to the man who strikes him that he thinks that he is winning when he has outdone his adversary, not in being struck, but in striking.

The Savior said: "What you wish that men should do unto you, do ye even so to them." [21] A part of this saying we know so well that we never overlook it — a part we omit so constantly that we do not know it at all. For we know very well what we wish others to do for us, but we do not know what we ourselves ought to do for them. Would that we really did not know! For our guilt would be less if due to ignorance, according to the saying: "He who does not know his lord's will shall be beaten with few stripes; but he who knows and does not do according to his lord's will, shall be beaten with many stripes." [22] But now our offence is the greater because we cherish a part of this sacred command on account of its usefulness to our convenience, and pass over a part of it in injury to God. Paul the apostle also adds to this word of the Lord in his preaching, saying: "Let no man seek his own, but every man another's wealth." And again: "Look not every man on his own things, but every man also on the things of others." [23]

You see then how faithfully he performed the precepts of Christ when, as the Savior bade us take thought for others just as we do for ourselves, he ordered us to consult the welfare of others more than our own, proving himself, to be sure, a good servant of a good master, and a glorious disciple of an exemplary teacher. He so followed in the steps of the Lord, that his own footprints somehow made those of his Master more evident and more clearly formed.

Which of these do we Christians obey, the command of Christ or that of his apostle? I think we obey neither one. For we are so far from doing anything that inconveniences ourselves, that we choose

---

[21] *Ibid.* 7. 12.

[22] See Luke 2. 47-48.

[23] I Corinthians 10. 24; Philippians 2. 4.

instead to provide first of all for our own convenience, whatever discomfort this involves for others.

7. Perhaps you may think we are choosing only the greater commandments, which no one follows, and which, as Christians themselves think, cannot be followed in any case, and are passing over others which can be and indeed are followed by all. But this point must be considered first, that no slave is allowed to choose according to his own wishes which of his master's commands he will carry out and which he will not, nor by a most insolent abuse to assume the task that pleases him and reject the rest. Certainly human masters think it impossible to tolerate calmly slaves who hear part of their orders and despise the rest, who, according to their own desires, carry out the commands they think should be performed and trample under foot those they think deserve such treatment. If slaves obey their masters according to their own free will alone, they are not rendering true obedience even when they seem to obey. When a slave obeys only such of his master's orders as he pleases, he is no longer doing his master's will but his own. If then we, who are but weak little men, are still utterly unwilling that our slaves, who are equal to us in their common humanity, though our inferiors in their condition of servitude, should despise us, how unjustly, forsooth, do we scorn our heavenly Master, since we, being ourselves men, yet think we ought not to be despised by men of our own condition! [24] Unless perhaps we have such great wisdom and deep intelligence that we who are unwilling to hear any insults from our slaves wish God to be subject to insults from us,

---

[24] See Cyprian *Ad Demetrianum* 8: "You yourself exact servitude from your slave and, yourself a man, compel a man to obey you, though you share in the same lot of birth, the same condition of death, like bodily substance, the same mental frame, and by equal right and the same rule come into this world and later leave it. Yet unless he serves you according to your will, unless he is subservient to your whim, you act the imperious and over-exacting master, afflicting and torturing him often with stripes, lashes, hunger, thirst, nakedness and the sword, with chains and imprisonment. And do you not recognize your God and master, who yourself exercise mastery in this fashion?"

and believe that he deserves to endure from us such treatment as we consider unfit for human endurance.

For this reason, to return to our former topic, any who think that I am talking of the greater commands of God and omitting the lesser, must recognize the unreasonableness of their complaint. There is no just reason for preferring some commands, when all must be performed. As I have already said, just as the servants of carnal masters are by no means permitted to choose which of their master's precepts they are to perform and which they are not, so we, who are the servants of our Lord, ought not to think it in any way permissible to humor ourselves by choosing those commands that please us, or by an abusive indulgence of our pride to trample under foot those that displease us.

8. Let us, however, come to an agreement with those who do not wish us to tell of the greater commands of the Lord, for the reason perhaps that they think they are fulfilling his lesser precepts, though it is not sufficient for salvation to perform the lesser commandments while scorning the greater. It is written: "For whosoever shall keep the whole law, and yet offend in one point, he is guilty of all." [25] Although for this reason it is not sufficient for us to obey all God's small and least commands, yet I agree to speak only of these, in order to show that most Christians have not performed even the least and slightest of their duties.

Our Savior ordered that Christian men should not swear. The men who perjure themselves daily are more numerous than those who do not swear at all. He commanded that no one should curse. Whose speech is not cursing? For curses are always the first instrument of wrath; whatever in our weakness we cannot perform we ardently desire in our anger, and thus in every impulse of our wrathful hearts we use evil wishes as our weapons.[26] Hence every

---

[25] James 2. 10.

[26] Rittershausen, commenting on the "elegant phrasing" of this sentence, cites Petronius *Carmen de bello civili* 228: *Absentem votis interficit hostem.*

man shows plainly that whatever he wishes may happen to his adversaries he would do to them if he could. Since we all put our tongues to this wicked use on the slightest provocation, our disregard of the Lord's will shows that we think it will be held of small account by God, who gave these commands. But the Holy Scripture says: "Revilers shall not inherit the kingdom of God." [27] From this we may judge how serious and deadly a crime evil-speaking is, which by itself shuts a man out of heaven, even though the rest of his life may have been good.

Christ ordered that envy be far from us, but we, contrary to his teaching, envy not merely outsiders but even our friends. This is the ruling vice in the hearts of almost all: our greed for eating has its limits, but our greed for slandering others has no end; our appetite for food becomes sated, but our appetite for spite does not. Perchance the punishment for this fault is a slight one? "The slanderous man," says the Holy Scripture, "shall be rooted out." [28] Surely that is a serious and fearful punishment, yet it does not serve to reform us. Every one of us thinks it worth while to endanger himself as long as he may continue to injure others. The retribution for this vice is clearly a suitable one, as it attacks the doer only; it does no injury at all to the person slandered, but only punishes the man from whose lips the libel comes.

I suppose I seem to be out of my mind in repeating these words, and I can easily bear the appearance of madness in such a case. For the Lord was not speaking senselessly when he enjoined us through his apostle: "Let all clamor be put away from you, with all malice." [29] Both of these evils indeed are ever present with us, but malice more than clamor. Clamor indeed is not always on our lips, but malice is always in our hearts. So I think that if clamor should cease among us, yet malice would remain to the end.

---

[27] I Corinthians 6. 10.

[28] See Romans 1. 30-32; Psalms 140. 11; Proverbs 21. 28.

[29] Ephesians 4. 31.

Our God orders us also to live without murmuring and without complaints.[30] When in the history of the human race have these been unknown? In hot weather we complain of drought, in rainy weather of floods; if it is a bad season for the crops we complain of scarcity, in a good season, of low prices. We long for plenty, and when we get it we object to it. What could be more wicked or more disgraceful than this? We complain of God's mercy even in this, that he gives us what we ask.

God bade his servants keep all scandal from their sight altogether, and so he said: "Whosoever looketh on a woman to lust after her hath committed adultery with her already in his heart."[31] From this we can fully understand how chaste our Savior wished us to be, who even shut out licentiousness from our eyes. Knowing that our eyes are in a way the windows of our souls,[32] and that all evil desires make their way into the heart through the eyes as their natural passageways, he wished us to destroy such desires utterly while they were still outside that they might not spring up within us and put forth their deadly shoots within the soul, if they once germinated in our eyesight.[33] Therefore the Lord said that the wanton glances of lustful men are adulterous, meaning that a man who truly wishes to shun adultery must keep a watch on his eyes. The Savior, indeed, wishing to cultivate a most genuine and perfect sanctity in his worshippers, ordered them to avoid scrupulously even the least offences, on the ground that according to the cleanness of his eyesight, so also is the purity of a Christian's life. Just as a man's eye could not receive a mote of dust without impairing his sight, so our life should not permit any stain of dishonor

---

[30] Philippians 2. 14-15.

[31] Matthew 5. 28.

[32] See Lactantius *De opificio Dei* 8. 11: "The mind is that which sees through the eyes, placed in front of it, as if through windows covered with translucent glass or mica."

[33] Among the parallels quoted by Rittershausen *ad loc.*, note especially Seneca *De remediis fortuitorum* 12.

to find a place in it. Whence come the following words of the Lord:
"If thine eye offend thee, pluck it out, and if thy hand offend thee,
cut it off; it is better for thee, that one of thy members perish, than
that thy whole body be cast into hell." [34] If, therefore, according
to the word of God, we are dragged down into hell by scandalous
actions, surely it is right to sacrifice our eyes and hands in order
to escape this punishment. No man should deprive himself of his
members, but in the case of certain domestic relationships so necessary to us that we have come to consider them as eyes or hands, it
is right to deprive ourselves of their present service in order to
escape the torture of eternal fire. When the choice lies between
comfort and life, it is certainly better for the Christian to forfeit
his convenience and gain life.

9. In all the points of which we have spoken our Lord has ordered us to obey him, but where are those who obey all his ordinances or even a very few of them? Where are those who love their
enemies or do good to those that persecute them, or overcome evil
by doing good, who turn their cheeks to those that strike them,
who yield their property without a lawsuit to those that rob them?
Who is there that permits himself no slander whatever, that injures
no man by evil speaking, that keeps his lips silent that they may
not break out in bitter curses? Who is there that keeps these least
commandments, not to speak of those greater ones which I mentioned a short time ago?

Since this is the case and since we keep none of the Lord's commands, why do we complain of God, who has far more right to
complain of us? Why should we grieve that he does not hear us,
when we ourselves do not hear him? What right have we to whisper
that God does not look upon the earth, when we ourselves do not
look up to the heavens? What reason have we to be vexed that our
prayers are despised by the Lord, whose commands we despise?

---

[34] See Mark 9. 43-47; Matthew 18. 8-9.

Suppose that we were equal to our Lord; what chance is there for just complaint when each side receives the same treatment it gives? And this entirely overlooks a point easily proved, that we are very far from receiving what we give, since God really treats us much more kindly than we do him. For the moment, however, let us act on the assumption that I proposed. The Lord himself spoke thus: "I cried unto you and ye did not hear me: you too shall cry unto me and I shall not hear you." [35] What is more fair and just than this? We have not hearkened, therefore he does not hear us. We have not been mindful of him, therefore he does not consider us. What mortal master, I ask, is content to treat his underlings according to this rule, that he will scorn them only in proportion to their contempt of him? And yet we do not stop with such injurious scorn of God as mortal masters receive from their slaves, since the greatest contempt a slave can show is in not doing what he has been ordered. We, however, bend all our efforts and energy not only to neglecting our orders, but even to acting directly contrary to them. For God commands us all to love one another, but we rend each other in mutual hatred. God enjoins us all to give our goods to the poor, but we plunder other men's goods instead. God orders every Christian to keep his eyes pure; how many men are there who do not wallow in the filth of fornication?

What more can I say? It is a heavy and sorrowful charge that I must bring: the church itself, which should strive to appease God in all things — what else does it do but arouse him to anger? Except a very few individuals who shun evil, what else is the whole congregation of Christians but the very dregs of vice? How often will you find a man in the church who is not a drunkard or glutton or adulterer or fornicator or robber or wastrel or brigand or homicide? And what is worst of all, they commit these crimes endlessly. I appeal to the conscience of all Christians; of these crimes and

---

[35] See Proverbs 1. 24; Micah 3. 4; Psalms 18. 41; Jeremiah 11. 11; Zechariah 7. 13.

misdeeds that I have just named, who is not guilty of some part, who is not guilty of the whole? You would more easily find a man guilty of them all than of none. And because what I have said may perhaps seem too severe an accusation I shall go much farther and say that you could more easily find men guilty of all evils than of a few, more easily find men guilty of the greater faults than of the less. That is, it is easier to find men who have committed the greater sins along with the less than the less without the greater. For almost the whole body of the church has been reduced to such moral depravity that among all Christian people the standard of holiness is merely to be less sinful than others. Some hold the churches, which are the temples and altars of God, in less reverence than the houses of the least important municipal magistrates. The common run of men indeed do not presume to enter the doors, I shall not say of illustrious potentates, but even of governors or presiding officials, unless the official has called them or contracted business with them, or unless the honor due their individual position permits their entrance. If anyone enters without due occasion he is flogged or roughly put out or punished by some humiliation or personal indignity.[36] But to the temples, or rather the altars and sacred shrines of God, all mean and evil men resort violently, entirely without reverence for his sacred honor. I do not mean to deny that all should hasten thither to pray to God, but he who enters to win God's favor should not go out to arouse his anger. The same action should not demand his indulgence and provoke his wrath. It is a monstrous thing for men to keep committing the same sins which they lament having committed, and for those who enter the church to weep for their old misdeeds to go out [to commit new ones].[37]

---

[36] Rittershausen cites this as a passage used by Cujas and other jurists in their commentaries on the *Corpus Juris*. Cf. Cod. Just. XII. 19 on those who have the right of access to the officials of the highest grade.

[37] The slight lacuna in the MSS is here supplied according to Pauly's conjecture.

Go out, did I say? They are usually planning fresh crimes in the very midst of their prayers and supplications. While men's voices do one thing, their hearts do another; while their words lament their past misdeeds their minds plan further wrongs, and thus their prayers increase their guilt instead of winning pardon for it. So the scriptural curse is truly fulfilled upon them, that from their very prayers they go out condemned and their petition is turned into sin.[38]

Finally, if any one wishes to know what men of this sort are thinking in church, let him consider this. When their religious duties are accomplished they all hurry off at once to their accustomed pursuits — some, for instance, to steal, others to get drunk, others to commit fornication, others to commit highway robbery — so that it is perfectly clear that they have spent their time inside the temple in planning what they will do after leaving it.

10. Undoubtedly some men think that all these evils and all the infamous vice of which I have spoken above may be properly ascribed to slaves or to the lowest of men, whereas the freeman's reputation is not spotted by the stain of such disgraceful deeds. Yet what else is the life of all business men but fraud and perjury, of the curials but injustice,[39] of petty officials but slander, of all soldiers but rapine?

Perhaps you think that one need not object to such a charge against characters of this sort. For, you say, their actions fit their professions, so it is no wonder that they act according to their

---

[38] See Psalms 109. 7.

[39] On the curials cf. V. 4 *infra*. The curials, once honored as the local aristocracy, making up the chief governing body of the municipalities of the Empire, the *curia*, had now, through the financial stringencies of the administration, become a class as much oppressed by the imperial financial agents as they were hated by those from whom they themselves exacted payments. The requirement that the curials of a district must make up from their own fortunes any deficit in the payments due had made it increasingly difficult to keep up the required number, and the injustice of which Salvian spoke worked in more than one direction. The burdens and difficulties of the office are best illustrated by the 192 sections of Cod. Theod. XII. 1.

business in life; as if, indeed, God wishes any man to do or profess evil. Or is it no offence whatever to His Divine Majesty that the lower classes are known to commit the greatest crimes, especially when by far the greater part of the human race belongs to this group? Without doubt, the insult that his divinity suffers is proportionate to the number of sinners.

Do you say that the nobles are free from these crimes? At best that is but a small gain, for all the nobles in the world would seem no more than one man in a great crowd of people. Is even this small group free from guilt? First let us consider what the Divine Word says of men of this sort. You remember that the apostle, addressing the people of God, spoke thus: "Hearken, my beloved brethren. Hath God not chosen the poor of this world rich in faith, and heirs of the kingdom which he hath promised to them that love him? But ye have despised the poor. Do not rich men oppress you by their power? Do they not blaspheme that worthy name by the which ye are called?" [40]

The testimony of the apostle is potent, unless perhaps the nobles think that they are exempt from his accusation because he named only the rich. The nobles, however, are either identical with the rich, or, if there are rich men who are not counted in their number, they are practically in the same category, for so great is the misery of our times that no one is considered of higher rank than he who has the greatest riches. It makes little difference which of these the apostle meant, or if he was talking of both; since his words certainly apply to both the rich and the noble, it does not signify which of the two he had in mind. What noble or what rich man ever had any horror of crime? Yet my query was mistaken — many indeed do fear it, but few avoid it. They fear in others the crimes they themselves constantly commit, being in a strange manner both the accusers and doers of the same evils. They denounce in public what

[40] James 2. 5-7.

they do in secret, and for that reason, when they think they are passing judgment on others they condemn themselves even more by their censure.

Let us overlook those men who have the greater guilt, and ask what single rich man or noble there is who preserves his innocence and keeps his hands clean of every sort of crime? It was foolish for me to say of every sort — would God they were clean of the greatest! Great men seem to consider it their personal prerogative to commit the lesser crimes as a matter of course. So I shall say nothing of their more ordinary misdoings. Let us see if any one of them is free from the two which we consider capital offences, that is, homicide and sexual vice. Which of them is not either reeking with human blood or smeared with the filth of an impure life? Either one of these is enough to render him liable to eternal punishment, but there is hardly a wealthy man who has not committed both.

11. Perhaps one of this number is thinking to himself: "I am not doing such things now." I commend you if you are not, yet probably you did in the past, and to have stopped is not equivalent to never having done them at all. But if it were, what value would there be in one man's desisting from wickedness when so many persist in their crime? The conversion of one man does not atone for the sins of the many, nor is it enough to appease God that one man should leave off sinning, while the whole human race offends him. Consider too that he who is converted for the sake of escaping eternal death certainly gains a great reward for his conversion in this escape. By no means could he succeed in turning away the punishment of damnation from others. It is a mark of intolerable presumption, and an enormous wickedness, for a man to think himself so holy that he even supposes wicked men can find salvation through him. God spoke thus of a certain land and a sinful people: "Though these three men, Noah, Daniel and Job, were in

it, they shall deliver neither sons nor daughters, they only shall be delivered.''[41]

No one, I think, will be so shameless as to dare compare himself with such men as these. However much a man may now try to please God, yet to assert one's own morality is an example of the greatest unrighteousness. Thus is destroyed our confidence in the false notion that an innumerable host of sinners can be saved from the evils that threaten them by the intercession of a few good men. For since no one is equal to the three men named above, what hope can any have that countless wicked men unrelated to them can be saved by a very few good men, when those saints, who were close to God, did not deserve of the Lord that their very members, in the persons of their children, should be saved? It is right that this should be so. Though all sons seem to be members of their parents, yet they must not be considered members of those whose love they have begun to cast aside, inasmuch as the wickedness of their degenerate lives has degraded their natural endowments. So it happens that even we who are said to be Christians lose the virtue of so great a name by our evil vices. It is of no possible benefit to have a holy name without morality, for a life that denies our Christian profession cancels the honor of a glorious rank by the baseness of unworthy actions.

Since then we see practically no group among all the Christians, no corner in all the churches, that is not full of all manner of offence and stained with every deadly sin, why should we beguile ourselves with the name of Christian? Assuredly our guilt is made the greater by this most sacred name, if we belie it by our conduct. The name of Christian aggravates our offences against God, since we continue our sins in the very bosom of the church.

―――――――
41 Ezekiel 14. 14, 16.

THE FOURTH BOOK

1. Let us then give up that prerogative of the Christian name, of which I spoke above, by which we consider that because we are more religious than other people, we ought also to be stronger. For since, as I have said, the faith of a Christian is to believe faithfully in Christ,[1] to keep Christ's commandments, it surely follows that the man who is unfaithful has no faith, that he who crushes under foot Christ's commandments does not believe in Christ. The whole question centers on this point, that he who does not perform the work of a Christian does not appear to be one, for the name without its proper acts and function is nothing. A certain man[2] says in his writings: "What else is high office without lofty merits but an honorable title without the man honored, or what is lofty rank without worth but an ornament in the midst of filth?"

So, to use the same phrase ourselves, what else is a sacred name without merit but an ornament in the midst of filth? The sacred word bore witness to this in the divine writings, saying: "As a jewel of gold in a swine's snout, so is a fair woman which is without discretion."[3] Thus among us also the name of Christian is like a golden ornament; if we use it unworthily, we make ourselves seem like swine wearing jewels.

Finally, whoever wishes fuller proof that mere words are nothing without actions should consider how countless peoples, by failing in

---

[1] See III. 2, *supra*.

[2] Salvian *Ad ecclesiam* II. 37; a work issued anonymously as the address of Timothy to the church on avarice, but accepted by Salvian as his in *Ep.* IX, to Salonius. The anonymous publication explains the manner of his reference in this case. On this passage cf. also *Ep.* IX. 9: "The names of things are of no avail without the substance, and the words for virtues are nothing without their active strength."

[3] Proverbs 11. 22.

good works, have lost the names given them. The twelve tribes of
the Hebrews, when they were of old chosen by God, received two
holy names, for they were called the people of God, and Israel.
We read: "Hear, O my people, and I will speak; O Israel, and I
will testify against thee."[4] Once the Jews bore both these titles,
now they have neither. They who long since left off the worship of
God cannot be called God's people, nor can they who denied his Son
be given a name that means "Seeing God." So it is written: "But
Israel does not know, my people doth not consider."[5]

For this reason on another occasion our God spoke of the people
of the Hebrews to the prophet, saying: "Call his name, Not Beloved." And speaking to the Jews themselves: "You are not my
people and I am not your God."[6] Moreover, he himself showed
clearly why he spoke thus about them, for he said: "They have
forsaken the Lord, the fountain of living waters."[7] And again:
"They have rejected the word of the Lord and there is no wisdom
in them."[8]

But indeed I am afraid that this is true of us now no less than
it was of them, since we do not obey the words of the Lord, and
our disobedience certainly shows that there is no wisdom in us.
Unless perhaps we believe that we act wisely in scorning God, and
consider it as a sign of the greatest prudence that we despise
Christ's commandments. There is some reason why we should be
thought to hold this opinion, for we all sin with as much accord as
if we were doing it in pursuit of an elaborately planned policy.

Since this is the case, what logical reason have we for deluding
ourselves by a false notion into the belief that the good name of
Christian can be of any possible help to us in the evils we commit?
The Holy Spirit says that not even faith, without good works, can

---

4 Psalms 50. 7; cf. Psalms 81. 8.
5 Isaiah 1. 3.
6 Hosea 1. 9; Romans 9. 25.
7 Jeremiah 17. 13.
8 *Ibid.* 8. 9.

benefit Christian men. Yet surely to have faith requires much more than the name alone, for the name is the mere instrument by which a man is addressed, whereas faith is the fruit of the spirit. That this same fruit of faith is profitless without good works, the apostle testifies when he says: "Faith without good works is dead." And again he says: "For as the body without the spirit is dead, so faith without works is dead also." [9] He adds also certain harder sayings for the confusion of those who delude themselves by their false claims to the Christian faith.

2. "Yea, a man may say: 'Thou hast faith and I have works; show me thy faith without thy works, and I will show thee my faith by my works.'" [10] By this, indeed, he shows that good acts serve also as witnesses of the Christian faith, because unless a Christian has performed good works, he cannot prove his faith at all, and since he cannot prove that it exists, it must be considered as altogether non-existent.[11] For he shows at once that it must be considered as nothing, in his additional words to the Christian: "Thou believest that there is one God; thou doest well: the devils also believe, and tremble." [12] Consider what the apostle meant by this. Let us not be angry at the divine testimony but assent to it; let us not speak against it but profit by it. "Thou believest," says the Divine Word to the Christian, "that there is one God; thou doest well: the devils also believe, and tremble." Was not the apostle in error when he compared the faith of a Christian to that of a devil? Surely not, but wishing to demonstrate what was said above, that without good works a man should claim no merit through pride in his faith, for this reason he says that the devils also believe in God. The intent is, of course, that as the devils, though they believe in

---

[9] James 2. 20, 26.

[10] *Ibid.* 2. 18.

[11] Rittershausen suggests that Salvian here alluded to the saying of the jurisconsults: "Not to be, and not to appear, or not to be susceptible of proof, are one and the same thing."

[12] James 2. 19.

God, still persist in their wickedness, the sort of faith that they
hold is like that of certain men who, while they assert their belief
in God, still do not cease to do evil. Moreover, the apostle adds, for
the confusion and condemnation of sinful men, that the devils not
only believe in the name of God, but fear and tremble before it.
Which is as much as to say: "Why do you flatter yourself, O man,
whoever you are, for your belief, which without fear and obedience
to God is as nothing? The devils have some advantage over you in
this. For you have but one thing alone, and they have two: you
have your belief, but not fear; they have belief and fear alike."
Why do you wonder that we are chastised, that we are given over
into the hands of the enemy, that we are weaker than all other men?
Our miseries, our infirmities, our overthrow, our captivities and the
punishments of our evil slavery are the proof that we are bad servants of a good master. How are we bad servants? Because, to be
sure, our sufferings are only in proportion to our deserts. How are
we the servants of a good master? Because he shows what we deserve, even though he does not inflict on us the punishment due,
for he would rather correct us by the most kind and merciful
chastisement than permit us to perish. As far as our misdoings are
concerned, we deserve the penalty of death, but he, attaching more
importance to mercy than to severity, prefers to better us by merci-
fully tempering his censure, than to slay us by the infliction of a
just chastisement.

I know only too well that we are ungrateful for the blows we
receive. But why do we wonder that God strikes us for our sins,
when we ourselves strike our slaves for theirs? Like unjust judges
we petty men are unwilling to be scourged by God, though we
scourge men of our own condition. I am not surprised that we are
so unjust in this case, for our very nature and wickedness are of a
servile sort. We wish to do wrong and not be beaten for it. In this
we have the same characteristics as our poor slaves. We all wish to
sin without punishment. I call all men to witness whether I lie: I

declare that there is no one, however great his guilt, who admits
that he deserves torture. From this we may observe how unjust
and how exceedingly wicked a thing it is that we are most severe to
others, but most indulgent to ourselves; harsh to others, but lax
with ourselves. For the same crimes we punish others and let ourselves go free; truly a mark of intolerable indulgence [13] and presumption. We do not wish to recognize any guilt in ourselves, but
we dare to claim the right to judge others. What can be more unjust or more perverse than we show ourselves in this? We think
that very crime justifiable in our own case that we condemn most
severely in others. So it is not without cause that the apostle cries
out to us: "Therefore thou art inexcusable, O man, whoever thou
art, that judgest; for wherein thou judgest another, thou condemnest thyself; for thou that judgest doest the same things." [14]

3. But some rich man may say: "We do not do the same things,
not at all the same things, that slaves do; for slaves turn into
thieves and runaways; slaves live only for their greedy appetites."
It is true that these are vices characteristic of slaves, but their masters, though not all of them, have more and greater faults. Certain
of them must indeed be excepted, though very few, whom I do not
name for fear that in so doing I may appear less to praise them than
to libel those whom I do not name.

First then, slaves, if they are thieves, are usually forced into
robbery by need, since even though the customary allowances are
furnished them, these conform better to custom than to sufficiency
and so fulfill the canon [15] without satisfying the needs of those who
receive them. Their necessity makes the fault itself less blameworthy, since a convicted thief who seems compelled to robbery

---

[13] The MS reading *incontumaciae*, the single occurrence of this word, was
formerly questioned, but Pauly now accepts it, following Hartel, as equivalent
to *obsequium*.

[14] Romans 2. 1.

[15] That is, the usual slave allowance. The language seems to be borrowed
from Cod. Just. XII. 23: *De canone frumentario urbis Romae.* Cf. Grégoire
et Collombet *ad. loc.*

against his will deserves pardon. The Scripture itself seems to palliate the wrongdoing of needy men when it says: "Men do not despise a thief, if he steal to satisfy his soul when he is hungry." [16] He steals to satisfy his soul; it is for this reason that we think we cannot accuse strongly enough those who are pardoned by the Divine Word. Regarding the running away of slaves we speak in the same way as about their thefts; but with even more justification, forsooth, in this case, since not only their wretched condition but also their punishments drive them to try to escape. They fear their overseers, they fear those set to keep silence among them, they fear their masters' agents. Among all these there are scarcely any to whom they seem to belong less than to their owners; they are beaten and broken down by them all. What more can be said? Many slaves take refuge with their masters from fear of their fellow-slaves. We ought not to hold responsible the slaves who try to escape, but those who force them to make the attempt. Our slaves labor under a most unhappy compulsion; longing to serve, they have no choice but to flee. They have no desire whatever to leave their masters' service, but the cruelty of their fellows does not allow them to continue in it.

They are called liars also. None the less, they are driven to falsehood by the brutality of the impending punishment — they lie in the hope of escaping torture. Why is it strange that a terrified slave would rather lie than be flogged? They are charged with having greedy mouths and stomachs, but this is nothing new; the man who has often endured hunger has the greater desire for satiety. Even supposing that he does not lack dry bread, he still hungers for delicacies, and so must be pardoned if he seeks more greedily that which is constantly lacking.

But you who are noble, you who are rich, who have an abundance of all good things, who ought to honor God the more because you enjoy his benefits endlessly, let us see whether your actions are, I

---

[16] Proverbs 6. 30.

shall not say holy, but even harmless. What rich man, to repeat my former question, save only a few, is not stained by every sort of evil deed? And when I except a few, would that I might include many more in the exception! for then the innocence of the majority might be the salvation of all. I am speaking about none now save the man who recognizes that my words apply to him. If what I say lies outside his conscience my charge will do him no discredit. If, on the other hand, his heart admits the truth of my words, he should realize that it is not my tongue that is accusing him but his own conscience.

To recount first the vices characteristic of slaves: if a slave is a runaway, so are you also, rich and noble though you are; for all men who abandon the law of the Lord are running away from their master. What fault can you rightly find in the slave? You are doing as he does. He flees from his master, and you from yours; but in this you incur more blame than he, for in all likelihood he is running away from a bad master, while you flee from a good one. In the slave you criticize incontinent greed. This is a rare fault in him, for want of means to satisfy it, but a daily one in you because of your abundance. Hence you see that the words of the apostle censure you more than him; nay, they censure you alone, for "wherein thou judgest another, thou condemnest thyself; for thou that judgest doest the same things"; [17] nay, not the same, but far greater and more wicked. In the slave you punish an infrequent overindulgence of the appetite, while you constantly distend your own belly with undigested food. You think theft a servile fault, but you too, O rich man, commit robbery when you encroach on things forbidden by God. Indeed every man who performs illicit actions is guilty of theft.

4. Why do I dwell on these petty details and speak in a sort of allegorical fashion, when absolutely unconcealed crimes make it clear that the wealthy commit not mere thefts but highway robbery

---

[17] Romans 2. 1.

on a grand scale? How often do you find a rich man's neighbor
who is not himself poor, who is really secure in his acts and position? Indeed by the encroachments of overpowerful men,[18] weak-
lings lose their property or even their freedom along with their
goods, so that it was not without reason that the Sacred Word
alluded to them both, saying: "Wild asses are the prey of lions in
the wilderness; so poor men are a pasture for the rich."[19] And
yet not only the poor but almost the whole human race is suffering
this tyranny. What else is the official career of eminent men but
the confiscation of all the property of their states? What else is
the prefecture of certain men, whose names I suppress, but plundering?[20] Nothing causes greater devastation in the poorer states than
the high officials. Honor is bought by a few to be paid for by the
oppression of the many; what could be more disgraceful or more
unjust than this? Wretched men pay the purchase price for honors
which they do not buy for themselves; they have nothing to do with

---

[18] Even the imperial estates suffered from such encroachments; cf. the
decree of Arcadius and Honorius, A.D. 399, providing for restitution of property unjustly seized on the imperial estates, and for a double penalty if
restitution was delayed beyond a period of three months, applying also to
those who had fled, unless they returned to restore the property stolen. The
penalty applied to judges also if they did not give evidence against the
exactores and *conpulsores* who were guilty. It is noteworthy that the decree
claimed that but for the imperial clemency a fourfold penalty should have
been exacted; one suspects impotence rather than clemency as the reason for
the lighter fine (Cod. Theod. X. 1. 16). On the general situation, cf. V. 8.
infra.

[19] Ecclesiasticus 13. 19.

[20] Compare the description of Arvandus, praetorian prefect of Gaul, given
by Sidonius Apollinaris *Ep.* I. 7. 3, "He governed his first prefecture with
great distinction, and his second with great destruction." Again, in *Ep.* V. 13
Sidonius described the "monster" Seronatus, "exhausting the individuals
scattered outside the towns by unheard of forms of indictions, and ensnaring
them by the sinuous deceits of his calumnies." The same Seronatus (*Ep.* II. 1)
"levies taxes as a master, exacts payments like a judge, slanders like a barbarian . . , fills the woods daily with fugitives, the villas with enemies, the
altars with accused men, the prisons with clergy." We learn, however, from
Ep. VII. 7. 2 that he was at last brought to justice and put to death, though
the government hesitated to act against him.

the bargain, but know only too well the payments made;[21] the world is turned upside down that a few men may be glorified; the honor of one man is the ruin of the human race.[22]

To conclude, the Spanish provinces know whereof I speak, for they have nothing left them but their name;[23] the provinces of Africa know it, whose very existence is at an end;[24] the lands of Gaul know it, for they are devastated, yet not by all their officials, and so they still draw the scanty breath of life in a few far corners, since the integrity of a few has supported for a time those whom the rapine of the many has impoverished.[25]

5. But my sorrow has led me to wander too far afield. To return to my former topic: is there any respect in which even the nobles are not contaminated by servile vices, or have they, forsooth, a right to commit sins they punish in their slaves? A slave may not even dream of such ravages as these nobles perform. This, however, is not quite true, for certain of the slaves, gaining noble rank, commit like sins, or even worse. Still the remaining slaves can hardly be held responsible for the fact that some few have so blessedly lost the condition of servitude.

Homicide is rare among slaves because of their dread and fear of

---

[21] So Sidonius, *Ep.* V. 13, said of Seronatus: "Some are freed by his venality, others by his vanity, none by his mercy."

[22] On this whole passage cf. Haemmerle, *Studia Salviana*, I. 4, pp. 29-33.

[23] Since Gaul was overrun by the barbarians earlier than Spain, the latter province suffered heavier taxation at the hands of the imperial prefects, who tried to make up the Gallic deficit in the imperial taxation from this source. Cf. Orosius VII. 41. 7: "There are certain Romans among them who prefer to sustain poverty in freedom among the barbarians than the constant oppression of taxation among the Romans."

[24] Africa, being under the praetorian prefect of Italy, as Spain was under that of Gaul, also suffered from the increase of taxation to make up for losses in Italy.

[25] See Sidonius *Ep.* III. 6. 3: "Certainly the provinces are much discussed; a good year depends less on the crops than the officials." Again, in *Ep.* IV. 24. 5, Sidonius illustrated the "integrity of a few" by persuading an official friend to grant a year's immunity from taxes, and cancellation of the interest due, to a more straitened taxpayer, to free him "from the barbarous demands of the collectors yapping around him."

capital punishment, whereas among the rich it is constantly committed because of their confident hope of immunity. Perhaps I am doing an injustice in reckoning the actions of the rich as sins, for when they kill their poor slaves they consider it an act of justice, not a crime.[26] Nor is this all; they also abuse their privilege in their vile breaches of chastity. What rich man keeps his marriage vows, who among them does not plunge headlong into passionate lust, who does not use his household slaves as harlots and pursue his madness against any one on whom the heat of his evil desires may light? They illustrate well the words of the Holy Scriptures about such men as they: "They are become as horses rushing madly on the mares."[27] Is it not a proof of what I just said, that the average man wishes to make his own by physical union whatever his eyes have beheld with desire? To use the term concubine may perhaps seem unfair, since in comparison with the vices mentioned above it seems almost a form of chastity to be content with a few mates and restrain one's lusts to a fixed number of wives.[28] I say "wives" advisedly because we have come to such a pass that many consider their maidservants as actual wives. Would that they were content to have only those whom they do so consider! But the truth is more foul and loathsome by far — for certain men who have contracted honorable marriages take additional wives of servile rank, deforming the sanctity of holy matrimony by low and mean

[26] This attitude, however, was in defiance of a decree of Constantine of A.D. 319 (Cod. Just. IX. 14. 1), which made a master who intentionally killed a slave guilty of homicide, whatever was the method used.

[27] Jeremiah 5. 8.

[28] The increase of concubinage in the fourth century led to progressive legalization of the institution. Constantine in A.D. 326 forbade it unconditionally (Cod. Just. V. 26); Arcadius and Honorius in 405 strictly limited the inheritance of concubines and their children (*Ibid.* 27. 2); Theodosius and Valentinian in 443 (*Ibid.* 27. 3) provided that natural sons might have full inheritance rights if they entered the curial class, and natural daughters if they married curials. The last decree illustrates also how fiscal necessities led to increasing leniency on the part of the government toward the frailties of the propertied class, especially when direct benefit to the treasury would result.

unions, not blushing to become the consorts of their slave women, toppling over the lofty structure of marriage for the vile beds of slaves, proving themselves fully worthy of the rank of those whom they judge worthy of their embrace.

6. Doubtless many of those who either are or wish to be nobles listened with lofty scorn to my statement that some slaves are less reprehensible than their masters. But since I made this remark not about all of them but only those whom it fits, no one has any cause for anger if he thinks himself a very different sort of man, for his anger would be enough to betray his membership in the group of which I spoke.[29] On the other hand, any nobles who abominate this wickedness should be angry at such men as these, who defame the very name of nobility by the extreme baseness of their misdeeds. For although men of that stripe are a heavy burden to all Christian people, still by their vileness they pollute especially the members of their own class. Therefore I have said that certain nobles are worse than slaves, and I have thus opened the way for contradiction, unless I can adduce proof for my words.

Take for example this crime, a very great one indeed, of which almost the whole mass of slaves is guiltless. Has any slave throngs of concubines, is any one of them defiled by the stain of polygamy or do they think they can live like dogs or swine with as many wives as they have been able to subject to their lust? The answer, I suppose, is obvious, that slaves have no such opportunities, for they surely would take them if they had. I believe this, but I cannot consider actions I do not see performed as having taken place. However dishonorable his intentions are, however evil his desires may be, no one is punishable for the crimes that he does not commit. It is generally agreed that slaves are wicked and worthy of our

---

[29] See Jerome *Adv. Rufinum* I. 11: ''When vice is attacked anonymously, the man who is angry at the attack accuses himself. It were the part of a prudent man, therefore, though annoyed, to hide his guilt and cover his clouded heart by a bright front.''

contempt. But, be that as it may, free-born men of noble rank are
the more to be reproached if in their more honorable condition they
are worse than slaves. Hence the inevitable conclusion is not that
bondmen ought to be absolved from responsibility for their wrongdoings, but that the majority of the rich are more to be condemned
in comparison with slaves.

Who can find words to describe the enormity of our present
situation? Now when the Roman commonwealth, already extinct
or at least drawing its last breath in that one corner where it still
seems to retain some life, is dying,[30] strangled by the cords of
taxation as if by the hands of brigands, still a great number of
wealthy men are found the burden of whose taxes is borne by the
poor; that is, very many rich men are found whose taxes are murdering the poor.[31] Very many, I said: I am afraid I might more
truly say all; for so few, if any, are free from this evil, that we
may find practically all the rich in the category to which I have
just assigned many of them.

Think a minute: the remedies recently given to some cities —
what have they done but make all the rich immune and heap up

---

[30] This mention of the notion, prevalent in the fifth century, of the old
age of the Roman power, is somewhat at variance with Salvian's usual point of
view. Sidonius used "the old age of the world" as a commonplace (cf. *Ep.*
VIII. 6. 3); Cyprian (*Ad Demetrianum* 4) made it the chief answer to the
usual charges against the Christians: "You blame the Christians because as
the world grows old its parts are weakened." Salvian, on the other hand,
saw the old régime as continuing with new vigor, gained from the barbarians,
to take the place of the old vices.

[31] The efforts of the central government to do away with such inequalities
are illustrated by the decree of Gratian, Theodosius and Valentinian, A.D. 383
(Cod. Theod. XI. 13. 1): "Let all the privileges granted to a few individuals
to the destruction of the many be annulled, and all who have received im-
munities of this sort by any means be reduced to an equal lot with the other
provincials . . . "; by the decree of the same emperors in 385 (*Ibid.* I. 20)
providing that all be bound "by the same equal form of levy"; and by that
of Arcadius and Honorius in 399 (*Ibid.* 1. 26) removing all privilege, making
all men equally subject to taxation, especially in "those provinces from
which the complaint arises." The repetition of such provisions illustrates
clearly enough the futility of enacting them, which increased in the fifth
century.

the taxes of the wretched?[32] To free the rich from their old dues they have added new burdens to those of the poor; they have enriched the wealthy by taking away their slightest obligations and afflicted the poor by multiplying their very heavy payments. The rich have thus become wealthier by the decrease of the burdens that they bore easily, while the poor are dying of the increase in taxes that they already found too great for endurance. So the vaunted remedy most unjustly exalted the one group and most unjustly killed the other; to one class it was a most accursed reward and to the other a most accursed poison. Hence I say that nothing can be more wicked than the rich who are murdering the poor by their so-called remedies, and nothing more unlucky than the poor, to whom even the general panacea brings death.

7. Then what a state of things it is, what a holy condition of affairs, that, if a noble begins to be converted to God, he at once loses his noble rank! What honor is paid to Christ among a Christian people in whose eyes religion makes a man ignoble? For as soon as a man has made an attempt to improve himself, he meets the abusive scorn of worse men, and thus all are compelled to some degree of evil living that they may not be considered contemptible. Not without cause did the apostle cry out: "The whole world lieth in wickedness."[33] He spoke truly, for it is right to say that the whole world is lying in wickedness when the good cannot hold their place in it. Indeed, everything is so full of iniquity that either all who live are evil, or the few who are good are tortured by the persecution of the many. Therefore, as I said, if any man of honorable rank devotes himself to religion, he at once ceases to be honored. For when a man has changed his garments,[34] forthwith

---

[32] See V. 8 *infra*. We are reminded, however, how much the rich also had to complain of the burdens of taxation, by the description (Sidonius *Ep.* V. 17. 5) of a church festival of which the crowning pleasure was the conversation of Sidonius and his wealthy friends with "no mention of the imperial officers or of the taxes, not a word to be betrayed, and no one to betray it."

[33] I John 5. 19.

[34] See V. 10, *infra*: "Thinking the service of God depends more on costume

he changes his rank; if he has been of high degree, he becomes contemptible; if he has been most glorious, he becomes the vilest of the vile; if he has been altogether full of honor, he becomes altogether wretched in aspect.

Yet certain worldly men and unbelievers wonder why they endure the wrath of God and his hatred, when they persecute him in the persons of all his saints; for all things are perverse and at variance with the ways of the past. If there is any good man, he is scorned as though he were evil: if a man is evil, he is honored as though he were good. Is it then strange that we who daily grow worse, endure worse tortures daily? [35] For men daily invent new evils and do not forsake the old; fresh crimes spring up, but the old are not abandoned.

8. Is there any room for further discussion? However hard and bitter our lot, we still suffer less than we deserve. Why should we complain that God deals harshly with us? We treat him much more rudely. We anger him by our impure acts and force him, unwilling though he is, to punish us. And although the spirit and majesty of God are such that he is not moved by any passion or anger, yet such is the aggravation of our sins that they drive him to wrath.

---

than on actions, they have changed their garments but not their hearts.'' Caesarius of Arles, who is said by Cyprian (*Vita* I. 1. 11) never to have given up in the slightest degree the customs of the brothers at Lérins, said in the first chapter of his *Regula ad monachos* (Migne, PL, LXVII, col. 1099): ''In the first place if any man come to conversion . . . let his lay garments not be changed, unless he have first made bills of sale for his possessions.'' Elsewhere he said (*Epistola ad germanos, ibid.* col. 1155): ''To lay aside secular garments and put on religious ones is the work of a moment. . . . Let him not be wont to wear a style of clothing either too mean, or displaying pride by frequent change, or of a ruinous elegance.'' Evidently, then, his idea of a religious habit was not a set uniform, but one distinguished from secular clothing chiefly by its simplicity. The emphasis laid by this prominent alumnus of the monastery at Lérins on the change in clothing as an indication of the adoption of a religious life seems adequate to settle the question much mooted among editors of Salvian, whether the change of garments in the present passage is to be taken literally or figuratively.

[35] See Cyprian *Ad Demetrianum* 10: ''And do you wonder that the wrath of God increasingly punishes the human race, when the sins to be punished increase daily?''

If I may say so, we subject his loving kindness to force, and seem
to lay violent hands on his mercy. For although he is so gentle that
he would like to spare us constantly, our perversity compels him
to punish our sins. As those who blockade well-fortified cities or
attempt to capture and undermine their mighty strongholds, cus-
tomarily lay siege to them with all sorts of machines and weapons,
so we attack the mercy of God with every kind of frightful sin as if
we, too, were using siege engines. Then we think God injures us,
though we are acting most injuriously toward him. Indeed every
fault of all Christians is an insult to his divinity. When we perform
those acts that are forbidden by God we trample underfoot the
orders of him who forbade us. It is impious to blame God's severity
for our misfortunes: we should instead accuse ourselves. For when
we commit the sins that cause our torture, we are ourselves the
authors of our torments. Why then do we complain of the bitterness
of our punishments? Each one of us punishes himself.

This is why the prophet said to us: "Behold, all ye that kindle
a fire, that have added fuel to the flame; walk in the light of
your fire and in the sparks that ye have kindled." [36] For the whole
human race is rushing headlong into eternal punishment by the
very course that the Scriptures describe. First we kindle the fire,
then add fuel to the flames, and lastly enter the flames that we have
prepared. When does man first kindle eternal fire for himself?
Surely when he first begins to sin. But when does he add fuel to the
flames? When he heaps up sins upon sins. When shall he enter the
everlasting fire? When he has already completed the irrevocable
account of wickedness by the increase of his sins, as our Savior
said to the leaders of the Jews: "Fill ye up then the measure of
your fathers, ye serpents, ye generation of vipers." [37] The men
whom the Lord himself told to fill up the measure were not far
from completing the full number of their sins. Because they were

---

[36] Isaiah 50. 11.
[37] Matthew 23. 32-33.

no longer worthy of salvation, they filled up the number of iniquities by which they were to perish. Whence also, when the ancient
Law recalled that the sins of the Amorreans [38] were fulfilled, it is
said that the angels spoke to the blessed Lot, saying: "Whomsoever
thou hast in the city, bring them out of this place, because the cry
of them is waxen great before the face of the Lord, and the Lord
hath sent us to destroy them." [39] For a long time, truly, that most
sinful people had been kindling the fires by which they perished,
and so when the tale of their iniquities was completed they burned
in the flames of their own crimes. For they deserved so ill of God
that they suffered in this world the Gehenna that is to come in the
later judgment.

9. But, you say, none now deserve the end of those men, for
none are to be compared with them in evil doing. Perhaps that is
true, still what do we make of the fact that the Savior himself said
that all who have spurned his Gospel are worse than they? And at
Capernaum he said: "If the mighty works which have been done
in thee had been done in Sodom, it would have remained until this
day. But I say unto you, that it shall be more tolerable for the
land of Sodom in the day of judgment than for thee." [40] If he said
the people of Sodom are less to be condemned than all who neglect
the Gospels, then we who in most of our actions show our neglect
of the Gospel teachings are in graver danger, especially since we
are not willing to be content with crimes long familiar, that seem
a part of our daily life. Many are not satisfied with the customary
vices, with litigation, slander and rapine, with drunkenness and
gorging at feasts, with forgeries and perjury, with adultery and
homicide. Finally, however inhuman the atrocities involved, all
the crimes involving injury to their fellow men are not enough for
them, but they must needs turn the blasphemous violence of their

---

[38] That is, the people of Sodom and Gomorrah; cf. I. 8, *supra*.
[39] Genesis 19. 12-13.
[40] Matthew 11. 23-24; cf. Luke 10. 12-15.

mad minds against the Lord also. For it is written of the wicked:
"They set their mouth against the heavens, and their tongue
walketh through the earth. . . . And they say, 'How doth God
know, and is there knowledge in the Most High?'" And again:
"The Lord shall not see, neither shall the God of Jacob regard
it." [41]

To such men this prophetic saying may well be applied: "The
fool hath said in his heart, 'There is no God.'" [42] For they who
declare that nothing is seen by God are very near to denying his
actual substance, as they deny his sight, and when they say that
he sees nothing they deny his very existence.

Although no evil deed has any rational foundation,[43] since there
is no bond between reason and wickedness, yet no blasphemy, in
my opinion at least, is more irrational than this or more insane.
What is so mad as for a man, who does not deny that God created
the whole world, to deny that he governs it? How can one admit
that God is its maker, and deny that he takes any care of what
he made? As if his intention in creating the universe was to neglect
it when completed! I say that he cares so much for his creatures
that I can prove that he cared for them even before their creation;
indeed, the very act of creation makes this clear. He would not have
created the world, if his care had not preceded the act, especially
since we know that in our human kind there is scarcely a man so
stupid that he would carry an undertaking through to completion
without the intention of taking care of it when finished. For a man
who tills a field does so in order to keep it for his own use after
it is cultivated; he who plants a vineyard means to take care of it
when he has planted it; he who gathers the nucleus of a herd means
to exercise his skill in increasing it. He who builds a house or lays
its foundations, even though he has as yet no finished dwelling-

---

[41] Psalms 73. 9, 11; 94. 7.

[42] *Ibid.* 53. 1.

[43] In the classical period this was already a popular proverb: *Scelera non
habent consilium*; cf. Quintilian *Institutio oratoria* VII. 2. 44.

place, still embodies in the building he is trying to erect the hopes of a future home.

Yet why should I speak of man alone, when even the smallest sorts of animals do all things with a view to future use? [44] Ants, hiding various sorts of grain from [the fields] [45] in underground storerooms, drag away and store their hoards because they cherish them in their desire to live. Why do the bees, when they lay foundations for the honeycomb or pluck their young from flowers, [46] search out thyme except from their eager desire for honey, or certain other flowerets but from love of the young they are to find there?

Has God then instilled this love of their own functions into even the least of living things, and deprived himself alone of the love of his works? Have you considered that all our love of good things has come down to us from his good love? He himself is the fount and source of all our benefits, and since, as it is written: "In him we live and move and have our being," [47] from him surely we have received all the affection we give our offspring; for the whole world and the whole human race are the offspring of their creator.

Therefore by that very love he has caused us to feel for our sons he wished us to know how greatly he loved his own. For we read, just as "the invisible things of him are clearly seen, being understood by the things that are made," [48] even so he wished his love for us to be known by the love that he gave us toward our own kindred. As it is written that he wished all fatherhood in heaven and in earth to be named after him, [49] so he wished us to recognize

---

[44] Cf. Lactantius *De ira Dei* 10. 44: "Nor is it probable that the smaller and humbler creatures should have a rule of life, while the larger and chief ones lack it."

[45] There appears to be a slight lacuna in the text, unless, as Hartel conjectures (cf. Pauly's note *ad loc.*), the preposition *ex*, for which an object is here supplied, has crept into the MS text from a marginal notation, *ex* standing for *exempla*.

[46] See Vergil *Georgics* IV. 200.

[47] Acts 17. 28.

[48] Romans 1. 20.

[49] Ephesians 3. 15.

his fatherly love. Yet why do I say fatherly? for his love is far
more than a father's. This is proved by the words of the Savior in
the Gospel, when he said: "For God so loved the world, that he
gave his only begotten Son for the life of the world." [50] But the
apostle also says: "God spared not his own Son, but delivered him
up for us all. How hath he not with him also freely given us all
things?" [51]

10. This confirms my former statement, that God loves us more
than a father loves his son. It is clear that his love surpasses a man's
love for his sons, since for our sake he did not spare his own child.
Nay, I add more, he did not spare his righteous Son, his only begotten Son, his Son who is himself God. What more can be said? And
this was done for us, that is for wicked, unjust and most irreverent
men. Who can justify this love of God toward us, save that his
justice is so great that no shadow of injustice can fall on him?
As far as human reason is concerned, any man would have acted
most unjustly if he had had his good son put to death for his worst
slaves. But for this very reason the love of God is the more surpassing and his goodness the more marvellous, that, as far as human
weakness is concerned, the greatness of his justice almost bears the
appearance of injustice. Therefore the apostle, to indicate as far
as he might the boundless mercy of God, said: "For when we were
yet without strength, in due time Christ died for the ungodly. For
scarcely for a righteous man will one die." [52] Certainly in this
one sentence he showed us the love of God. For if scarcely any one
undertakes to die for the greatest righteousness, Christ dying for
our iniquity proved what love he bore us. Why God should have
done this, the apostle tells us at once in the words that follow,
saying: "God commendeth his love toward us, in that, while we
were yet sinners, Christ died for us. Much more then, being now

---

[50] John 3. 16.

[51] Romans 8. 32. Note that the Vulgate reading is the future, *donabit*,
while Salvian had *donavit*.

[52] Romans 5. 6-7.

justified by his blood, we shall be saved from wrath through him.''[53]
He commends his love to us, in that he died for sinners; for a
benefit is of greater worth that is given to men unworthy of it.

So he says: "God commends his love toward us." How does he
commend it? Surely in that he bestows it on the undeserving. If
he had given it to holy men who deserved well of him, he would not
seem to have given what was not due, but what he owed them.

What then have we given in return for this great boon, or what
return ought we to make for it? First of all, what the most blessed
prophet testifies that he owes and will give, saying: "What shall
I render unto the Lord for all his benefits toward me? I will take
the cup of salvation, and call upon the name of the Lord." [54] This
is the first repayment, that we return death for death, and all die
for him who died for us, even though our death is of much less
account than his. Whence it comes that even if we take death upon
us, we cannot by this means repay our debt. But since we cannot
requite him more fully, we seem to be paying the whole, if we return him all that we can. This, therefore, as I said, is our first
payment.

The second is, if we do not pay our debt by death, to pay it by
love. The Savior himself, as the apostle says, by his death wished to
commend his love to us all, to lead us by the example of his loving
care to make a fitting return for such great affection. And just as
certain marvellous natural gems, when one brings them into contact with iron, though it be of the hardest kind, hold it in suspense
by an attraction that seems actually possessed of life, so also he,
the greatest and most glorious gem of the heavenly kingdom, wished
to come down from heaven to approach more closely to us, to draw
us, in spite of our hardness, to his care as if by the hands of
his love, that recognizing his gifts and benefits we might come to
know what it befitted us to do for so good a master when he had

---

53 *Ibid.* 5. 8-9.
54 Psalms 116. 12-13.

done so much for his wicked servants. Then should be fulfilled the
words of the apostle, that we should be killed all the day long for
his love, and neither tribulation nor distress nor persecution nor
famine nor nakedness nor the sword should be able to separate us
from the love of God, which is in Christ Jesus the Lord.[55]

11. Since our indebtedness to God is clearly established, let us
see what return we make him for all that we owe. What return,
indeed, but all the actions of which I have spoken before, namely,
whatever is indecent, whatever is unworthy, whatever leads to
injury of God, wicked deeds, disgraceful habits, drunken feasts,
bloodstained hands, vile lusts, mad passions and whatever else can
better be reckoned up by the conscience than in words! "For,"
said the apostle, "it is a shame even to speak of those things which
are done of them in secret." [56] Nor is this all, for it is an old charge,
and belongs no more to the present time than to the past. More
serious and lamentable is the fact that we are adding new sins to
the old, sins not only new but of a monstrous and heathen sort,
such as have not before been seen in the churches of God. We
blasphemously revile the Lord, saying that he is a God who does not
care for us, a God who pays us no attention, a God who neglects
us, who does not govern us, and hence he is pitiless and obdurate,
inhuman, harsh and cruel. For, since he is described as not regarding us, as careless and neglectful, what remains but to call him
harsh and cruel and inhuman? What blind impudence! what
sacrilegious boldness! It is not enough for us, that, bound in our
countless sins, we are in all things guilty before God, unless we
are also his accusers. Yet what hope, I ask, shall a man have, who,
while facing judgment himself, brings accusation against his judge?

12. If God does regard human affairs, some one may say, if he
cares for us, loves and guides us, why does he allow us to be weaker
and more miserable than all nations? Why does he suffer us to be

---

[55] Romans 8. 35-36, 39.
[56] Ephesians 5. 12.

conquered by the barbarians? Why does he permit us to be subject
to the rule of our enemies? [57] To answer very briefly, as I have already said, he suffers us to endure these trials because we deserve
to endure them. Let us consider the disgraceful habits, the vices
and crimes of the Roman people, as we have described them above,
and we shall then understand whether we can have any claim on his
protection when we live in such impurity. If we examine in this
light our customary argument that our misery and weakness show
God's neglect of human affairs, what do we really deserve? If he
permitted us, living in such vice and wickedness, to be exceedingly
strong, prosperous and completely happy, then perhaps there might
be some ground for suspicion that God did not see the evil-doing
of the Romans, if he allowed such wicked and abandoned men to
be happy. Since instead he bids such vicious and evil men to be
most abject and wretched, it is perfectly evident that we are seen
and judged by God, for our sufferings are fully deserved.

We, of course, do not think we deserve them, and consequently
are the more guilty and blameworthy for failing to recognize our
deserts. The chief accusation of wrongdoers is their proud asser-
tion of innocence. Among a number of men charged with the
selfsame crime none is more guilty than he who does not acknowledge his guilt even in his own thoughts. We have, therefore, this
single addition to make to our wrongdoings, that we consider ourselves guiltless.

But, you may object, grant that we are sinners and wicked men,
certainly you cannot deny that we are better than the barbarians,
and this alone makes it clear that God does not watch over human
affairs, because we, who are better, are subject to men worse than
ourselves. Whether we are better than the barbarians, we shall now
consider; certainly there can be no doubt that we ought to be
better. And for this very reason, we are worse than they, unless we

---

[57] This question is answered in a similar way in Augustine's homily, *De
tempore barbarico.*

are actually better, for the more honorable position makes any fault doubly blameworthy. The greater the personal dignity of the sinner, the greater is the odium of his sin.[58] Theft for example is a serious crime in any man, but a thieving senator is doubtless far more to be condemned than one of the lower classes. Fornication is forbidden to all, but it is a much more serious vice in one of the clergy than in one of the people. So also we, who are said to be Christians and catholic, if we are guilty of vices like those of the barbarians, sin more seriously than they, for sins committed by men who claim a holy name are the more abominable. The more lofty our claim to honor, the greater is our fault; the very religion we profess accuses our faults. A pledge of chastity increases the sin of lewdness; drunkenness is more loathsome in one who makes an outward show of sobriety. Nothing is more vile than a philosopher who pursues a vicious and obscene life, since in addition to the natural baseness of his vices, he is further branded by his reputation for wisdom. We therefore, who out of the whole human race have professed the Christian philosophy, for this reason must be believed and considered worse than all other nations, since, living under so great a profession of faith, in the very bosom of religion, we still sin.

13. I know it seems to most men intolerable that we should be called worse than barbarians. What possible good does it do us to have this seem intolerable? Our condition is made so much the more serious if we are worse than they and yet insist on believing ourselves better. "For if a man think himself to be something," the apostle said, "when he is nothing, he deceiveth himself. But let every man prove his own work."[59] We ought to put our trust in our works, not in our opinion; in reason, not lust; in truth, not in our will alone.

Since, then, some men think it unsupportable that we should

---

[58] See Juvenal *Sat.* 8. 141-142.

[59] Galatians 6. 3-4.

be adjudged to be worse, or even not much better than the barbarians, let us consider in what way we are better, and in relation to which of the barbarians. For there are two kinds of barbarians in the world, that is, heretics and pagans.[60] To all of these, as far as the divine law is concerned, I declare that we are incomparably superior; as far as our life and actions are concerned, I say with grief and lamentation that we are worse. However, as I said before, let us not make this statement of the whole body of Romans without exception. For I except first of all those men who have devoted themselves to a religious life, and then some laymen who are equal to them; or, if that is too much to say, at least very like them in their upright and honorable actions. As for the rest, all or practically all are more guilty than the barbarians. And to be more guilty is to be worse.

Therefore, since some men think it irrational and absurd that we should be judged as worse, or even not much better than the barbarians, let us see, as I said, how we are worse, and in relation to which barbarians. Now I say that except for those Romans alone, whom I mentioned just now, the others are all or almost all more guilty than the barbarians, and more criminal in their lives. You who read these words are perhaps vexed and condemn what you read. I do not shrink from your censure; condemn me if I do not succeed in proving my words; condemn me if I do not show that the Sacred Scriptures also have said what I now claim. I myself who say that we Romans, who judge ourselves far superior to all other nations on earth, are worse in many respects, do not deny that in certain ways we are superior. For while we are, as I have said, worse in our way of life and in our sins, yet in living under the catholic law we are incomparably superior. But we must consider this, that while it is not our merit that the law is good, it is our fault that we live badly. Surely it profits us nothing that

---

[60] The Goths and Vandals had been converted to Arianism; cf. Book IV. 14, 17 *infra*, for Salvian's account of the pagans among the barbarians.

our law is good, if our life and conversation are not; for the good law is the gift of Christ, whereas the faulty life is our own responsibility. On the contrary, we are more blameworthy if the law we worship is good and we who worship it are evil. Nay, we do not worship it, if we are evil, for an evil worshipper cannot be properly said to worship at all. He who does not worship sacredly that which is holy does not worship at all, and hereby the very law we hold accuses us.

14. Disregarding, therefore, the privilege of the law, which either does not help us or even brings just condemnation upon us, let us compare the lives, the aims, the customs and the vices of the barbarians with our own. The barbarians are unjust and we are also; they are avaricious and so are we; they are faithless and so are we; to sum up, the barbarians and ourselves are alike guilty of all evils and impurities.

Perhaps the answer may be made: if we are equal to them in viciousness, why are we not also equal to them in strength? Inasmuch as their wickedness is like ours and their guilt identical, either we should be as strong as they, or they as weak as we. That is true, and the natural conclusion is that we who are weaker are the more guilty. What proof have we? The proof is, of course, inherent in my demonstration that God does everything in accordance with judgment. For if, as it is written: "The eyes of the Lord are in every place, beholding the evil and the good:" [61] and in the words of the apostle: "The judgment of God is according to truth against all wicked men," [62] we, who do not cease to do evil, see that it is by the judgment of a just God that we endure the penalties for our evil-doing. But, you object, the barbarians commit the same sins, and yet are not as wretched as we. There is this difference between us, that even if the barbarians do the same things that we do, our sins are still more grievous than theirs. For our vices and

[61] Proverbs 15. 3.
[62] Romans 2. 2.

theirs can be equal without their guilt being as great as ours. All of them, as I said before, are either pagans or heretics. I shall discuss the pagans first, since theirs is the older delusion: among these, the nation of the Saxons is savage, the Franks treacherous, the Gepids ruthless, the Huns lewd — so we see that the life of all the barbarians is full of vice. Can you say that their vices imply the same guilt as ours, that the lewdness of the Huns is as sinful as ours, the treachery of the Franks as worthy of accusation, the drunkenness of the Alemanni as reprehensible as that of Christians, the greed of an Alan as much to be condemned as that of a believer?

If a Hun or Gepid is deceitful what wonder is it in one who is utterly ignorant of the guilt involved in falsehood? If a Frank swears falsely, what is strange in his action, since he thinks perjury a figure of speech, and not a crime? And why is it strange that the barbarians have this degree of vice, since they know not the law and God, when a majority of the Romans, who know that they are sinning, take the same attitude?

Not to speak of any other type of man, let us consider only the throngs of Syrian merchants who have seized the greater part of all our towns — is their life anything else than plotting, trickery and wearing falsehood threadbare?[63] They think words practically wasted that do not bring some profit to their speaker. Among these men God's prohibition of an oath is held in such high esteem that they consider every sort of perjury actually profitable to them. What wonder is it, then, that the barbarians, who do not know that falsehood is a sin, practice deception? None of their actions are due to contempt of the divine ordinances, for they do not know the precepts of God. A man ignorant of the law cannot act in defiance of it. This is our peculiar guilt, who read the divine law and constantly violate its terms, who say that we know God and yet

---

[63] Salvian's estimate of their numbers seems justified by the numerous inscriptions of Syrian and other orientals, found in Gaul; cf. *Corpus Inscriptionum Latinarum* XII, XIII.

walk roughshod over his commands and precepts; and therefore, since we despise him whom we believe and boast that we worship, the very appearance of worship is an injury to him.

15. Lastly, to say nothing of our other sins, who is there among laymen, except a very few, that does not constantly have the name of Christ on his lips to swear by it? Hence this is the oath most commonly used by nobles and baseborn men alike: "By Christ I do this . . . ; by Christ I act thus . . . ; by Christ I am not going to say anything else . . . ; by Christ I am not going to do anything else." And what results? The abuse has been carried so far that, as we said before about heathen barbarians, Christ's name seems now to be not a binding oath but a mere expletive. For among the great majority this name is held to be so trivial that men never have less intention of doing a thing than when they swear by Christ to do it. Although it is written: "Thou shalt not take the name of the Lord thy God in vain," [64] reverence for Christ has fallen so low that among all the vain words of this age scarcely any seems more vainly used than the name of Christ.

Then many swear by the name of Christ to do things not merely trivial and foolish but even criminal. For this is their usual manner of speaking: "By Christ I'll steal that . . . ; by Christ I'll wound that man . . . ; by Christ I'll murder him." It has come to such a pass that they feel themselves bound by religion to commit the crimes they have sworn in Christ's name.

Finally, let me tell an experience of my own. A short time ago, won over by the pleas of a certain poor man, I besought a man of considerable influence not to take from the poor wretch his property and substance, not to remove the sole prop and help that supported his poverty. Then he, who had swallowed the poor man's goods in ravenous haste, and had already devoured his prey with most ardent ambition and greed, glared at me with eyes blazing as if he thought I might take from him something he had not succeeded in

---

[64] Exodus 20. 7.

filching from the other, and said he could not possibly do as I asked, since he was acting in accordance with a sacred command or decree that he absolutely could not overlook. When I asked the reason, he said most emphatically, brooking no contradiction: "I have made a vow to seize that man's property. Consider then whether I could or should fail to accomplish what I have sworn by the name of Christ." Then I left him, having heard the reason for his most pious crime, for what else was I to do, when his action was shown to be so just and sacred!

16. At this point I ask all who are of sound mind: who would ever believe that human covetousness would reach such a pitch of audacity, would ever scorn God so openly that men should say it is for Christ's sake they intend to do a deed the very performance of which is an insult to Christ? What an unthinkable and monstrous crime! Of what daring are the wicked minds of men not capable? They arm themselves for robbery in God's name; they make him somehow responsible for their crimes, and although Christ forbids and punishes all sin they claim that they perform their wicked deeds for his sake.

Yet we, complaining of the injustice of the enemy, say that the heathen barbarians are guilty of perjury. How much less guilty are they who swear falsely by demons, than we who swear by Christ! How much less serious a crime it is to take the name of Jove in vain than that of Christ! In the one case it is a dead man by whom they swear,[65] in the other the living God by whose name they swear falsely. In the former instance there is no longer even a man; in the latter, the most high God; here, since the oath was taken in the most binding name, the greatest guilt and perjury must be involved; there, since that by which they swear scarcely exists, clearly there is no perjury, for since the God by whom they swear does not exist, there is no perjury when the oath is broken.

Finally, let him who wishes to know the truth of this matter

---

[65] A characteristic example of Christian euhemerism.

listen to the blessed apostle Paul uttering the very arguments I am giving. These are his words: "Now we know that what things soever the law saith, it saith to them who are under the law." And again: "Where no law is, there is no transgression." [66] In these two statements, did he not make clear that there are two divisions of the human race, those placed without the law, and those living under it? What men are there who now live under the law? Who indeed but the Christians? Such was the apostle himself, who said of himself: "I am not without law to God, but under the law to Christ." [67]

Who then are outside the law of Christ? Who but pagans ignorant of the Lord's law? Therefore it is of these that he says: "Where no law is, there is no transgression." By this one word he shows that only Christians transgress the law when they sin, but the pagans who do not know the law sin without transgression, since no one can transgress in a matter of which he is ignorant. We alone therefore are transgressors of the divine law, we who, as it is written, read the law and do not follow it. Hence our knowledge brings us nothing but guilt, since its result is only that we give the more offence by our sins, for what we know from our reading and in our hearts, we spurn in our wantonness and scorn.

So the words of the apostle to every Christian man were most justly spoken: "Thou that makest thy boast of the law, through breaking the law dishonorest thou God? For the name of God is blasphemed among the Gentiles through you." [68]

Of what crimes the Christians are guilty may be learned from this one fact, that they defame the name of God. And although we have been charged to "do all things for the glory of God" [69] we, on the contrary, do all things for his injury. Although the Savior daily calls to us: "Let your light so shine before men, that the

---

[66] Romans 3. 19; 4. 15.

[67] I Corinthians 9. 21.

[68] Romans 2. 23-24.

[69] I Corinthians 10. 31.

sons of men may see your good works and glorify your Father which is in heaven,'' [70] we, on the other hand, so live that the sons of men may see our evil deeds and blaspheme our Father which is in heaven.

17. This being the case, we may indeed beguile ourselves with the great prerogatives of the name of Christian, we who so act and live that by the very fact that we are said to be a Christian people we seem to be a reproach to Christ. On the other hand, what do we find of this sort among the pagans? Can it be said of the Huns: ''See what sort of men these are who are called Christians?'' Can it be said of the Saxons or the Franks: ''See what these men do who claim to worship Christ?'' Can the sacred law be blamed for the savage customs of the Moors? Do the most inhuman rites of Scythians or Gepids bring curses and blasphemy on the name of the Lord our Savior? Can it be said of any of these: ''Where is the catholic law that they believe? Where are the commandments of piety and chastity that they learn? They read the Gospel, and are unchaste; they listen to the apostles, and get drunk; they follow Christ, and plunder; they lead dishonorable lives, and say that they follow an honorable law.'' Can such things be said of any of these nations? Certainly not, but they are all truly said of us: in us Christ suffers reproach; in us the Christian law is accursed. Of us are said the words quoted above: ''See what sort of men these are who worship Christ. They are plainly lying when they say that they learn good things, and boast that they keep the commandments of the sacred law. For if they learned good things they would be good. Their religion must be like its followers: doubtless they are what they are taught to be. Thus it appears that the prophets they have teach impurity; and the apostles they read have sanctioned wickedness; and the Gospel which they have learned preaches the actions that they perform; in fine, the lives of the Christians would be holy, if Christ had taught holiness. So the object of their wor-

---

[70] Matthew 5. 16.

ship must be judged from his worshippers. How can the teacher be good whose pupils we see are so evil? In him they are Christians — they hear Christ himself and read his words. It is easy for us all to learn the teachings of Christ. See what the Christians do, and you will clearly discern the teachings of Christ.''

Finally, what distorted and wicked notions the pagans have always had about the sacraments of the Lord is shown by the bloody inquisitions of brutal persecutors, who believed that at Christian services only vile and abominable rites were performed. Even the origins of our religion were thought to spring from two great crimes, the first being murder and the second incest, which is worse than murder. Nor were these mere murder and incest, but a more wicked thing than the bare commission of either of these crimes, the incest of holy mothers, and the murder of innocent infants, whom, they thought, the Christians not only murdered, but — which is more abominable — devoured.

All this was supposed to be done to appease God, as if any evil would cause him greater offence! as an offering to atone for sin, as if any sin could be greater! to make him look with favor on sacrifices, as if any act could better arouse his aversion and horror! to win the right to eternal life, as if indeed, even supposing it could be won by such actions, it were worth while to attain it by such atrocious crimes!

18. We may understand from this what the pagans have come to believe about the character of Christians, who worship God in such sacrifices, and what sort of God they think could have taught such things as sacred rites. Yet how did this belief arise? How else but through those who are called Christians, but are not; who by their shameful and disgraceful lives sully the name of their religion; who, as it is written, ''profess that they know God, but in works deny him, being abominable and disobedient, and unto every good work reprobate'';[71] by whom, as we read, ''the way of

---

[71] Titus 1. 16.

truth is evil spoken of'' [72] and the sacred name of God violated by the profanity of sacrilegious men.

How very difficult it is to atone for subjecting the name of divinity to the evil-speaking of the heathen, we are taught by the example of the most blessed David. By the suffrage of his former acts of justice he deserved to win release by a single act of confession, from eternal punishment for his offences. Yet even the penitence that pleaded for him did not avail to win pardon for this grievous sin. For when Nathan the prophet had heard him confess his fault, and said to him: "The Lord hath put away thy sin, thou shalt not die," he added at once: "Howbeit, because by this deed thou hast given great occasion to the enemies of the Lord to blaspheme, the child also that is born of thee shall surely die." [73]

What followed? He laid aside his diadem, cast off his jewels, doffed the purple, gave up all the splendor of his royal state, and instead shut himself up alone in mourning, foully clad in sackcloth, drenched with his tears and besmirched with ashes. Yet though he sought the life of his little child with such lamentations and entreaties, and strove to move the tender heart of God with such fervent prayers, all his pleas and protests could not obtain his pardon, even though he had firmly believed that he should gain what he sought from God — which is the greatest aid to those who pray.

From this we learn that there is absolutely no sin for which it is harder to atone than that of giving the heathen occasion to blaspheme. For whoever has gravely sinned without causing others to blaspheme brings condemnation only on himself, but he who has made others blaspheme drags many men down to death with him, and must be held answerable for all whom he has implicated in his guilt. Nor is this all; whenever a man sins in such a way that his action does not give others occasion for blasphemy, his sin injures only him who has committed it, but does not insult the holy name of

---

[72] II Peter 2. 2.
[73] II Samuel 12. 13-14.

God by the sacrilegious curses of blasphemy. But if his wrong-doing has caused others to blaspheme, his sin must be immeasurably great, beyond the bounds of human guilt, for by the revilings of many he has caused incalculable insult to God.

19. Moreover, as I have said, this evil is peculiar to us Christians, because God is blasphemed only through the agency of those who know the good and do evil; who, as it is written: ''Profess that they know God, but in works deny him'';[74] who, as the same apostle says: ''Rest in the law and know his will, and approve the things that are more excellent; who have the form of knowledge and of truth in the law; who preach a man should not steal, and themselves steal; who say a man should not commit adultery and themselves commit it; who make their boast in the law and through breaking the law dishonor God.''[75]

The Christians are worse than other men for the very reason that they ought to be better. They do not justify their profession of faith, but fight against it by their evil lives. For evil doing is the more damnable in contrast with an honorable title; and a holy name becomes a crime in an impious man. Therefore our Savior also says in the Apocalypse to a lukewarm Christian: ''I would thou wert hot or cold; so then because thou art lukewarm, I will spue thee out of my mouth.''[76]

The Lord commanded every Christian to be fervent in faith and spirit. For it is written: ''That we may be fervent in spirit, serving the Lord.''[77] In this fervor of spirit the ardor of religious faith is made known; he who has the largest share of such ardor is recognized as fervent and faithful, while he who has none at all is known to be cold and an unbeliever. But he who is betwixt and between is a lukewarm Christian and hateful to the Lord, who therefore says to him: ''Would that thou wert hot or cold, now therefore

---

[74] Titus 1. 16.
[75] Romans 2. 17-23, selections.
[76] Revelations 3. 15-16.
[77] Romans 12. 11.

since thou art lukewarm I will spue thee out of my mouth.'' That
is to say: ''Would that you had either the heat and faith of good
Christians or the ignorance of pagans. For then either your warm
faith would make you pleasing to God, or at least for the time
being your ignorance of the law would give you some measure of
excuse. But as it is, since you know Christ, and neglect him whom
you know, you who have, so to speak, been received into the very
presence of God by the recognition of the faith, are cast out because
of lukewarmness.''

The blessed apostle Peter also made this plain when he said of
the lukewarm and vicious Christians, that is, those who live wicked
lives: ''For it had been better for them not to have known the
truth, than after they had known it, to turn from the holy commandment delivered unto them. But it is happened unto them
according to the true proverb, 'The dog is turned to his own vomit
again, and the sow that was washed to her wallowing in the
mire.' '' [78]

To make clear that this was said of those who live under the
name of Christian in the vileness and filth of the world, hear what
he says of such men in the same passage: ''For if, after they had
escaped the pollutions of the world through the knowledge of the
Lord and Savior Jesus Christ, they are again entangled therein,
and overcome, the latter end is worse with them than the beginning.'' [79] This, indeed, the blessed Paul repeats in like manner:
''For circumcision verily profiteth, if thou keep the law; but if
thou be a breaker of the law, thy circumcision is made uncircumcision.'' [80] He himself shows very clearly that by circumcision
Christianity is to be understood when he says: ''For we are the
circumcision, which worship God in the spirit and have no confidence in the flesh.'' [81] By this we see that he is comparing the

---

[78] II Peter 2. 21-22.
[79] *Ibid.* 2. 20.
[80] Romans 2. 25.
[81] Philippians 3. 3.

wicked Christians with pagans, and not merely comparing them but almost ranking them as of less account, when he says: "However, if the uncircumcision keep the righteousness of the law, shall not his uncircumcision be counted for circumcision? And shall not uncircumcision, which is by nature, if it fulfil the law, judge thee, who by the letter and circumcision dost transgress the law?"[82]

From this we learn, as I said before, that we are much more blameworthy, who have the law and reject it, than those who neither have it at all nor know it, for no one despises what he does not know. "I had not known lust," the apostle says, "except the law had said, Thou shalt not covet."[83] Nor do men transgress the law which they do not know, for, as it is written: "Where no law is, there is no transgression."[84] If men do not transgress the law which they have not, neither do they despise the terms of the law which they have not, for no one, as I said, can despise what he does not know.

We, therefore, are alike scorners and transgressors of the law, and thus we are worse than the pagans, because they do not know the ordinances of God, but we know them; they do not possess them, but we do; they do not perform precepts they have not heard, but we read and trample them under our feet. Hence what with them is ignorance is in us transgression, since there is less guilt in ignorance of the law than in contempt of it.

---

[82] Romans 2. 26-27.
[83] *Ibid.* 7. 7.
[84] *Ibid.* 4. 15.

THE FIFTH BOOK

1. I know that there are men, utterly lacking in faith and void of the divine truth, who think they have an easy answer to my arguments. They say that if the guilt of unfaithful Christians is so great that they sin more in disregarding the commands of the Lord which they know, than do the heathen tribes in their ignorance, then ignorance has proved of more benefit to the pagans than knowledge, and knowledge of the truth is only an obstacle to the Christians.

My answer must be this: it is not the truth that stands in our way, but our own vices; not the law that does us injury, but our evil ways. In brief, give us good ways of living and the decrees of the law are in our favor; take away our vices and the law helps us. "For we know," the apostle said, "that the law is good, if a man use it lawfully; knowing this, that the law is not made for a righteous man." Therefore, begin to be just, and you shall be free from the law, because the law cannot act against the holy life, in which it consists. "For we know," he said, "that the law is good, if a man use it lawfully; knowing this, that the law is not made for a righteous man, but for the lawless and disobedient, for the unholy, for the ungodly and for sinners, and if there be any other thing that is contrary to sound doctrine." [1] So the law is not so much fighting against you, my friend, as you against the law, nor does it by its good precepts take action against you, but you against it by your evil life. In fact, it is on your side, but you are against it. It gives you good counsel with holy words, while you fight against it with evil deeds, and yet not so much against it as against yourself. To oppose it is to oppose yourself, since in it lie your life and

---
[1] I Timothy 1. 8-10.

safety. When you desert the divine law, you abandon your own salvation. Thus our complaints of the Lord's law are like those of an impatient invalid against an excellent doctor. When his own fault has increased his illness, he accuses his physician of incompetence. As if, indeed, prescriptions could cure any illness if the patient did not obey them, or the regimen ordered by the physician work a cure if the patient did not follow it. What good can bitter draughts do the stomach if sweet ones are taken immediately after? What good can the silence of those about him do the delirious patient whose own ravings are killing him? Of what avail will the antidote be if the poison is poured over it?

Now in our case the law is the antidote, the poison our wickedness. The antidote of the law cannot cure us who are being killed by the poison of our own vice. But of these matters I have said enough before, and if occasion arises shall speak again later with God's help.

2. Meanwhile, since I mentioned above that there are two classes or sects of barbarians, namely, pagans and heretics, and I have already, I think, said enough of the pagans, let me now add what is necessary about the heretics. For my opponent may say: "Even if the divine law does not exact of the pagans that they keep commandments they do not know, it certainly does exact this of the heretics who know them; for they read the same books we do; they have the same prophets, the same apostles, the same evangelists, and therefore they are no less guilty than we are of neglect of the law. Really their neglect is much worse than ours, for although their Scriptures are the same, their actions are much worse."

Let us consider both points. You say that they read the same books we do. How can their books be the same, being badly interpolated and falsified by unscrupulous men? They are not the same at all, for they cannot be said to keep their identity unchanged if they are corrupted in any part. Having lost their full completeness they are not unharmed, and being robbed of the power of the sacraments they do not keep their true value. We alone, therefore, have the Sacred Scriptures in full, unviolated and complete, who either drink them at their fount, or at least drawn from the purest source by the agency of an incorrupt translation; we alone read them well. I wish we might fulfil them as well as we read them! But I fear that we who fail to keep them do not read them correctly either. For there is less guilt in not reading the holy words than in reading and violating them. The other nations either do not possess the law of God or have it in a changed and weakened form, and, as I said, to have it in such a condition is the same thing as not to have it at all.

If there are any among the barbarians who seem in their books to possess the Sacred Scriptures less interpolated and torn to pieces than the rest, still the corruptions in their texts are due to the tradition of their first teachers, whose disciples hold rather to their tradition than to the Scripture itself. For they do not abide by the instructions of the true law, but by the interpolations of an evil and distorted interpretation.

The barbarians, indeed, lacking the Roman training or any other sort of civilized education, knowing nothing whatever unless they have heard it from their teachers, follow blindly what they hear. Such men, completely ignorant of literature and wisdom, are sure to learn the mysteries of the divine law through instruction rather than reading, and to retain their masters' doctrines rather than the law itself. Thus the interpretation and doctrine of their teachers have usurped the authority of the law among them, since they know only what they are taught. So they are heretics, but unwittingly.[2] Indeed it is only among us that they are heretics,

---

[2] The rest of this chapter is quoted in an abridged translation by Voltaire in his *Dictionnaire philosophique*, *s.v.* ''Hérésie,'' with the prefatory remark that it is the most sensible attack on the spirit of intolerance that can be found. Voltaire had apparently forgotten or not read Augustine's treatise *Contra epistolam Manichaei* (Migne, PL, XLII, col. 173), in which (c. 1) he

and not among themselves, for they are so sure of their own ortho-
doxy that they libel us in turn by the accusation of heresy. As they
are to us, so are we to them. We are convinced that they injure the
holy incarnation in calling the Son inferior to the Father: they
think that we do injury to the Father in believing the two equal.
The truth is on our side, but they claim it for theirs. We truly honor
God but they think their belief honors his divinity the more. They
fall short in their Christian duty, but through what they think its
fullest performance; their lack of reverence seems to them true
piety. So they err, but with the best intentions, not through hatred,
but through love of God, believing that they honor and love him.
Although they have not the true faith, yet they think they possess
the perfect love of God. How they shall be punished for the error
of their false opinion on the day of judgment, none can know but
the Judge. In the meantime, God bears with them patiently, I
think, for he sees that though they have not the true faith, yet
their error is due to the love of what appears to be the truth,
especially since he knows that their wrongdoing is due to ignorance,
while among us men neglect what they believe. So their sin is the
fault of their teachers, while ours is our own; theirs is committed
in ignorance, ours in full knowledge; they do what they think right,
but we what we know to be perverse. Therefore with just judgment
the patience of God bears with them but punishes us, because
ignorance may be pardoned for a time, but contempt deserves no
lenience. For it is written: "The servant who knows not his lord's
will and does it not, shall be beaten with few stripes, but he who
knows it and does it not, shall be beaten with many." [3]

3. Let us not wonder that we are beaten with many stripes, since
we err not through ignorance but through rebellion. For knowing

---

prays for "a mind calm and tranquil, thinking rather of your correction than
your subversion. For although the Lord through his servants overturns the
realms of error, yet he bids the men themselves, in so far as they are men,
be amended rather than destroyed."

[3] See Luke 12. 47-48.

the good we do not perform it, and knowing the distinction between right and wrong we pursue the wrong. We read the law and trample underfoot what is lawful; we learn the decrees of the sacred ordinances only to increase the gravity of our sins after their prohibition; we say that we worship God, but give our service to the devil. After all this, we wish to receive good gifts from God, while we heap wrong upon wrong continually; we wish to have God do our will, though we are unwilling to do his. We treat with him as his superiors; we wish him to accede to our wishes constantly, though we constantly fight against his.

But he is just, however unjust we may be; for he punishes those he thinks deserve punishment, and bears with those he thinks deserve his patience. In each case his end is the same, that his chastisement of the orthodox may restrain their lust for sinning, and his forbearance at length bring the heretics to recognize the full truth of the faith, especially since he knows that those men are not apt to be unworthy of the catholic faith whom he sees superior to the orthodox in their way of living. All those of whom I speak are either Vandals or Goths,[4] for I say nothing of the multitude of Roman heretics, and shall not compare them with either Romans or barbarians, since their lack of faith makes them worse than the Romans, and their disgraceful lives than the barbarians. That the men of whom I speak are Romans, far from helping us,

---

[4] Orosius' account of the conversion of the Goths, while agreeing with Salvian's on the responsibility of the Romans for the heresy of the Goths, illuminates by contrast the comprehension and sympathy with which Salvian states the absence of moral responsibility on the part of the barbarians for a heresy that appeared to them orthodox. Salvian's attitude is the more remarkable in one whose devotion to Christ is so strong that at times he has Christ overshadow the other Persons of the Trinity. Orosius says (VII. 33. 19): "Before this the Goths sent ambassadors to ask that bishops be sent from whom they might learn the precepts of the Christian faith. Valens the emperor, with damnable perversity, sent teachers of the Arian creed. The Goths have held to the instructions of the first faith that they received. So by a just judgment of God they burned alive the man through whose fault they, when they die, are doomed to burn for their vicious error."

makes our case even worse. It is easy to estimate what the whole Roman state deserves, when part of the Romans offend God by their way of life, part by their lack of faith and their way of living also. Add that the very heresies of the barbarians spring originally from the false teaching they received from the Romans, and the inception of heresy among them becomes another heavy charge against us.[5]

4. But as for the way of life among the Goths and Vandals, in what single respect can we consider ourselves superior to them, or even worthy of comparison? Let me speak first of their affection and charity, which the Lord teaches us are the chief of virtues, and which he commends not only through the Sacred Scriptures but also in his own words, when he says: "By this shall all men know that ye are my disciples, if ye love one another."[6] Now almost all barbarians, at least those who belong to one tribe, under one king's rule, love one another, whereas almost all the Romans are at strife with one another. What citizen is there who does not envy his fellows? Who shows complete charity to his neighbors? All are indeed far from their neighbors in affection, however near in place; though living side by side, they are far apart in spirit. While this is a most grievous wrong, I wish it were true only of citizens and neighbors. But the situation is still more serious, for not even relations preserve the bonds of kinship. Who renders a brotherly service for his next of kin? Who pays to family affection the debt he knows is due to the name he bears? Who is as closely related by his affections as by blood? Who is not fired with a dark passion of ill will? Whose emotions are not the prey of envy? Who does not look on another's good fortune as his own punishment? Who does not reckon another's good as his own evil? Who finds his own good

---

5 See IV. 2 *supra*. As Zschimmer (*op. cit.*, 58 n.l.) points out, this is a very notable statement. Salvian clearly understands the historical connection of Roman Arianism with that of the Germans; either he actually knew that Ulfilas in his translation of the Bible made alterations to suit the Arian doctrines, or he is merely repeating some of the usual charges brought against Ulfilas and other Arian missionaries by contemporaries of the orthodox faith.

6 John 13. 35.

fortune so ample that he is willing that another should be fortunate also? Most men are now suffering a strange and incalculable
evil, in that it is not enough for any man to be happy himself unless
another is thereby made wretched. What a situation is this, how
savage, how rooted in the same impiety we deplore, how alien to
barbarians and familiar to Romans, that they proscribe one another
by mutual exactions. My last words, perhaps, give a wrong impres-
sion, for it would be much more tolerable if each man endured what
he himself had inflicted on others. The present situation is harder
to bear, for the many are proscribed by the few, who use the public
levies for their individual gain, and convert the bills of indebtedness to the public treasury to their private profit.[7] Nor is it only
the highest officials who do this, but the least too in almost equal
measure; not only the judges, but their obedient underlings as
well.[8]

For what cities are there, or even what municipalities and vil-
lages, in which there are not as many tyrants as curials?[9] Still
perhaps they preen themselves on their title, since it seems to be
one of power and honor. Brigands usually rejoice and exult at
being considered somewhat more ruthless than they really are.
What place is there, as I said before, where the very lifeblood of
widows and orphans is not drained by the leading men of their
states, and with them that of all godly men? For these last are
classed with widows and orphans, since they are either unwilling to

---

[7] For the efforts of the state to prevent such injustice, cf. especially Cod.
Theod. XI. 1. 20, 26.

[8] See Cod. Theod. XI. 7. 16, 20; 11. 1, for the penalties for undue aggression
by minor officials.

[9] See III. 5 *supra*. For the reverse of the picture, note the text of the
contemporary decree of Theodosius and Valentinian issued A.D. 443 (Cod. Just.
V. 27. 2) beginning: "If any man whether free or bound in the toils of the
curia . . ." In his own eyes the curial had become a slave rather than a
tyrant, and in those of the government as well, but the necessity of tyranny
toward the taxpayers was thereby increased. For the obligations of the office
and the difficulty of filling it at this time, see Cod. Theod. XII. 1, *De
decurionibus*.

protect themselves, out of devotion to their vows, or unable because of their simplicity and humility. Therefore not one of them is safe, indeed scarcely any are safe, except the very greatest, from the plunder and ruin of this universal brigandage, other than those who are a match for the brigands themselves. Matters have come to such an evil pass, to such a criminal condition, that only the wicked man may count himself secure.[10]

5. But certainly, you object, even though there are so many who persecute good men, there must be some who come to the rescue of those in distress, and, as it is written, "deliver the poor and needy out of the hand of the wicked." [11] "There is none that doeth good, no, not one:" [12] as the prophet showed by these words, good men are so rare that scarcely one seems to remain among us. Who offers help to those who are distressed and suffering, when even the priests of the Lord make no resistance to the violence of the unscrupulous? The majority of the clergy either say nothing, or, if they do speak, their words are no more effective than silence. With

---

[10] That similar conditions prevailed also in the eastern portion of the empire at this time is shown by the account of the Roman régime given by the Greek whom Priscus found at Attila's court (Priscus, "Historia Gothica," in De Boor, *Excerpta Constantiniana* I, 135-138; see also Bury, *History of the Later Roman Empire*, I, 213-223): "Their oppressions in time of peace are much more bitter than the calamities due to war, both on account of the harsh tributes and on account of the oppression of the wicked, since the laws are not enforced for all alike. If a rich or powerful man transgresses them, he does not pay the penalty for his misdeed; but if a needy man, who does not know how to conduct his affairs, transgresses, he must expect the penalty ordained by law; unless perhaps, before the sentence is decided, when much time has been spent in continual litigation and great amounts of money expended beside, his life ends. But the worst injustice of all is that law and justice are to be obtained only by bargaining and bribery. For no one will open the courts to any injured man before he turns over his money to the use of the judge and his assistants." Priscus countered with a description of the general justice of the Roman law and government, to which the exile replied that the laws of the Roman state were indeed good and the empire gloriously constituted, but the magistrates, less public-spirited than of old, were weakening and perverting it.

[11] Psalms 82. 4.

[12] *Ibid.* 14. 3.

many of them it is not lack of resolution, but what they consider a prudent discretion that commends this course.[13] They are not willing to declare the truth openly, for this the sensitive ears of the wicked cannot bear. Not content with shunning the truth, our oppressors hate and curse it; they fail to evince any reverence or respect when they do hear the truth, and show utter scorn for it, in their stubborn and rebellious conceit. Therefore, even those who have occasion to speak remain silent and refrain from immediate attacks on those whom they know to be guilty. They dare not publish the whole truth openly for fear of increasing oppression by a too emphatic insistence.

Meanwhile the poor are being robbed, widows groan, orphans are trodden down, so that many, even persons of good birth, who have enjoyed a liberal education, seek refuge with the enemy [14] to escape death under the trials of the general persecution. They seek among the barbarians the Roman mercy, since they cannot endure the barbarous mercilessness they find among the Romans.[15]

---

[13] Elsewhere Salvian speaks in the same vein (*Ad ecclesiam* IV. 8): ''In such a situation what do those men do whom Christ has appointed to speak? They displease God, if they are silent; men, if they speak. But, as the apostle said in answer to the Jews, it is more expedient to obey God than men.''

[14] An important bit of contemporary evidence for a fundamental step in the transition from the Roman régime in the country districts to feudalism.

[15] Orosius' similar statement in the case of Spain has already been cited; cf. IV. 4 *supra*. Sidonius (*Ep.* V. 7) speaks of the officials whose oppression of Gaul stands out in marked contrast to the clemency of the surrounding barbarians. The account given by Paulinus of Pella of Roman life among the Gothic invaders corroborates Salvian's statements, in a situation in which the victory of the Goths and the plundering before their departure made his favorable account the more remarkable. He lamented (*Eucharisticos* 285-290) the disadvantage of having had no Goths quartered in his house to protect him from the ravages when their tribe withdrew: ''for we know that certain of the Goths worked with the greatest humanity to benefit their hosts by their protection.'' Later his prayer (*Ibid.* 424-425) that ''some share of my ancestral fortune might remain from the barbarian plundering by right of war, and from the Roman crime, which has at various seasons fattened freely on my losses, against all justice'' was answered by a Goth's payment to him for a part of his old estate, which had fallen to the honest barbarian as part of his booty.

Although these men differ in customs and language from those with whom they have taken refuge, and are unaccustomed too, if I may say so, to the nauseous odor of the bodies and clothing of the barbarians,[16] yet they prefer the strange life they find there to the injustice rife among the Romans. So you find men passing over everywhere, now to the Goths, now to the Bagaudae, or whatever other barbarians have established their power anywhere,[17] and they do not repent of their expatriation, for they would rather live as free men, though in seeming captivity, than as captives in seeming liberty. Hence the name of Roman citizen, once not only much valued but dearly bought,[18] is now voluntarily repudiated and shunned, and is thought not merely valueless, but even almost abhorrent. What can be a greater proof of Roman injustice than that many worthy noblemen to whom their Roman status should have been the greatest source of fame and honor, have nevertheless been driven so far by the cruelty of Roman injustice that they no longer wish to be Romans?

The result is that even those who do not take refuge with the barbarians are yet compelled to be barbarians themselves; for this is the case with the greater part of the Spaniards, no small proportion of the Gauls, and, in fine, all those throughout the Roman world whose Roman citizenship has been brought to nothing by Roman extortion.

6. I must now speak of the Bagaudae,[19] who, despoiled, afflicted,

---

[16] A similar distaste is expressed by Sidonius (*Carmen* XII) in his description of the difficulties of composing six-foot verses when seven-foot barbarians breathe onions and garlic into your face at daybreak.

[17] Strictly speaking the Bagaudae were not barbarians, but revolted peasants from among the Roman citizenry, whose long-continued revolts had invested them in Roman eyes with a quasi-barbarian character; for the other barbarians note that in VII. 15 the Franks are described as especially hospitable.

[18] So the tribune of the soldiers at Jerusalem said to Paul: "With a great price obtained I this freedom," i.e., Roman citizenship. (Acts 22. 28.)

[19] The revolt of the Bagaudae, analogous in many respects to that of the Jacquerie in the 14th century, broke out in Gaul in A.D. 283-4 because of oppression in that province, due especially to overheavy taxation. The empire

and murdered by wicked and bloodthirsty magistrates, after they had lost the rights of Roman citizens, forfeited also the honor of the Roman name. We transform their misfortunes into crime, we brand them with a name that recalls their losses, with a name that we ourselves have contrived for their shame! We call those men rebels and utterly abandoned, whom we ourselves have forced into crime.[20] For by what other causes were they made Bagaudae [21] save by our unjust acts, the wicked decisions of the magistrates, the proscription and extortion of those who have turned the public exactions to the increase of their private fortunes and made the tax indictions their opportunity for plunder? [22]

Like wild beasts, instead of governing those put under their power, the officials have devoured them, feeding not only on their be-

---

was engaged in war against usurpers, and the revolt spread rapidly. Maximian won great praise for suppressing it, but the Bagaudae continued to plunder the country districts and towns, and spread through Gaul and Spain, adding seriously to the difficulty of guarding the frontiers. In the 5th century their revolt again assumed serious proportions; their troops were now regular armies and their local units closely equivalent to the individual German states in menace to the unity of the empire, breeding increasing discontent with the official oppression. The last mention of the Bagaudae in the Chronicle of Idatius is in the year A.D. 449, and the movement seems to have come to an end not long after this. For the contemporary references, of which Salvian's account is the most detailed, cf. Seeck, s.v. "Bagaudae," in Pauly-Wissowa, Real-Encyclopädie.

20 That a man should not be held responsible for a crime committed under compulsion is recognized by a decree of Honorius and Theodosius in A.D. 416 (Cod. Theod. XV. 14. 14) prohibiting suits for crimes committed during the barbarian raids, "either through flight or through the herding together of refugees . . . for an act done to escape death is not considered a crime."

21 Salvian uses the term Bagaudae, apparently a word of Celtic origin, for which Seeck suggests the meaning "warlike," as equivalent to "outlawed rebels."

22 The ten chief men of each town were responsible for handing over to the agents of the central government all that was due from their district in payment of the indiction, the term used from the time of Diocletian for the general provincial taxation on the basis of the amount of arable land, cattle and laborers in each locality. The periodical revisions of the taxable property also depended largely on the town officers, and usually caused much oppression of the poorer taxpayers, as Salvian here says. In this case, also, as in so many others, the rich could more easily gain substantial relief by bribery than the poor could do.

longings as ordinary brigands would do, but even on their torn
flesh and their blood. Thus it has come to pass that men who were
strangled and half killed by brutal exactions began to be really
barbarians, since they were not permitted to be Romans. They
were satisfied to become what they were not, since they were no
longer allowed to be what they had been; and they were compelled
to defend their lives as best they could, since they saw that they
had already completely lost their liberty.

How does our present situation differ from theirs? Those who
have not before joined the Bagaudae are now being compelled to
join them. The overwhelming injuries poor men suffer compel them
to wish to become Bagaudae, but their weakness prevents them.
So they are like captives oppressed by the yoke of an enemy, enduring their torture of necessity, not of their own choice; in their
hearts they long for freedom, while they suffer the extremes of
slavery.

7. Such is the case among almost all the lower classes, for the
same circumstances force them to two very different alternatives.
They are most strongly compelled to wish for freedom, but the compulsion they suffer deprives them of power to carry out their wish.
Perhaps it may be asserted that the very men who have these desires would wish for nothing better than to be free of any occasion
to feel them, for what they wish is the greatest misfortune. They
would be much better off if they had no need for such ambitions.
But what other wish can these poor wretches have? They must
endure the frequent, even continuous, ruin of state requisitions,
always menaced by severe and unremitting proscription; they desert their homes to avoid being tortured in them, and go into volun-
tary exile to escape heavy punishment. To such men the enemy
are kinder than the tax collectors. This is proved by their actions,
for they flee to the enemy to avoid the oppression of the levies.[23]

---

[23] See Cod. Theod. XI. 1. 7 for the decree of Constantius and Constans in
A.D. 361 relieving of payments *pro his qui aufugerint* any senators who could
prove that they possessed none of the property of fugitive holders; and

Such taxation in itself, however harsh and brutal, would still be less severe and painful if all shared equally in the common lot. But the situation is made more shameful and disastrous by the fact that all do not bear the burden together; the tributes due from the rich are extorted from the poor, and the weaker bear the burdens of the stronger. The only reason why they do not bear the whole burden is that the exactions are greater than their resources. They are suffering the most diverse and dissimilar misfortunes, envy and need. For envy is involved in the payment, and need in the means by which it is made. If you consider the amount they pay, you will think them wealthy; but if you consider what they have, you will find them in dire need. Who can square the accounts of such injustice? They make the payments due from the rich while they suffer the poverty of beggars.

My next point is still more serious. The rich themselves from time to time make additions to the amount of taxation demanded from the poor. You may ask how it is, when their assessment has already reached a maximum figure, and the payments due from them are very large, that the rich can possibly wish to increase the total. But I did not say that they increase their own payments, for they permit the increase simply because it does not cost them anything additional.

Let me explain. Frequently there come from the highest imperial officials new envoys, new bearers of dispatches, sent under recommendation to a few men of note, for the ruin of the many. In their honor new contributions and tax levies are decreed. The mighty determine what sums the poor shall pay; the favor of the rich decrees what the masses of the lowly shall lose; for they themselves are not at all involved in these exactions.[24] Do you say that

---

XI. 1. 31 for the similar decree of Honorius and Theodosius in A.D. 412. Salvian's description is closely paralleled by the passage from Priscus quoted in note 10.

[24] The contrast between these practices and the imperial theory is shown by the five decrees in Cod. Theod. VIII. 11: "That the heralds of public good fortune are to receive no gifts from public levies or from forced payments."

it is impossible not to give due honor and entertainment to the envoys sent by our superiors? Then be the first to contribute, you men of wealth, who are first to pass such decrees; be first to lavish your property who are first in largess of mere words. You who give, give of mine and thine alike; though absolute justice would require that any one who wishes sole claim on the resulting favor should also bear the expense alone. However, we poor men accede to the wish of the rich. What you few order let us all pay. What is so just and humane as this? Your decree burdens us with new debts; at least let this indebtedness be shared between us. What can be more unjust or unworthy than that you alone should be free from debt, who are making us all debtors?

The poor, indeed, in the extremes of their misery, pay all the exactions of which I have spoken, in utter ignorance of the object or reason of the payments. For who is allowed to discuss the payments, or inquire into the reasons for the amounts due? The sum is openly published only when the rich fall out with one another, and some of them feel slighted because they learn that assessments have been passed without their advice and management. Then you will hear some among them say: "What an unconscionable crime! Two or three decide the ruin of the many; a few powerful men determine what is to be paid for by many poor wretches!" For each individual rich man thinks it due to his honor to object to any decree passed in his absence, but he does not consider it due to justice to object to any wrong being enacted in his presence.

Finally, what they have criticized in others they themselves afterward establish in law, either in requital for the earlier contempt, or as proof of their power. As a result the most unhappy poor are like men far out at sea, buffeted by conflicting winds; they are overwhelmed by the billows that break over them now from one side, now from the other.

8. But surely, you say, those who are unjust in this respect are known to be moderate and just in another, and atone for their

wickedness in the one matter by their generosity in the other. For in proportion as they burden the poor with the weight of new indictions they sustain them by proffering new alleviations; in proportion as the lesser men are weighed down by new tributes, they are relieved by new remedies.

But this is not the case, for the injustice is alike in both the exactions and the remedies. As the poor are the first to receive the burden, they are the last to obtain relief. For whenever, as happened lately,[25] the ruling powers have thought best to take measures to help the bankrupt cities to lessen their taxes in some measure, at once we see the rich alone dividing with one another the remedy granted to all alike. Who then remembers the poor? Who summons the needy and humble to share in the common benefit? Who allows the man who is always first in bearing the burden to have even the last place in receiving relief? What more can I say? Only that the poor are not reckoned as taxpayers at all, except when the weight of taxation is being imposed on them; they are outside the number when remedies are being distributed.

Under such circumstances can we think ourselves undeserving of God's severe punishment when we ourselves continually so punish the poor? Can we believe that God ought not to exercise his judgment against us all, when we are constantly unjust? For where, or among what people, do these evils exist save only among the Romans? Who commit such grave acts of injustice as ours? Take the Franks, they are ignorant of this wrong; the Huns are immune to it; there is nothing of the sort among the Vandals, nothing among the Goths. For in the Gothic country the barbarians are so far from tolerating this sort of oppression that not even

---

25 See IV. 6 *supra*. No writer gives further details on these measures, and they are not mentioned in the Codex. Salvian's description of the profit made by the rich out of attempts at relief is confirmed by phrases in Cod. Theod. XII. 1. 173, of A.D. 410: "For relieving the fortunes of the poorer curials and restraining the oppression of the powerful. . . . Let them fear the knowledge of your power and dare make no attempt at relieving the rich and destroying the needy."

Romans who live among them have to bear it. Hence all the Romans in that region have but one desire, that they may never have to return to the Roman jurisdiction. It is the unanimous prayer of the Roman people in that district that they may be permitted to continue to lead their present life among the barbarians.

Yet we are surprised that the Goths are not conquered by our resistance, when the Romans would rather live among them than at home. Not only have our kinsmen no desire at all to escape from them to us, but they even leave us to take refuge with them. I could find occasion to wonder why all the poor and needy taxpayers [26] do not follow their example, except for the one factor that hinders them, namely, that they cannot transfer their poor possessions and homes and their households. For, since many of them leave their tiny fields and shops to escape the enforced payment of taxes, how could they help wishing to take off with them, if it were at all possible, the property they are compelled to abandon? They are not capable of doing what they would probably prefer, hence they do the one thing they can. They put themselves under the care and protection of the powerful, make themselves the surrendered captives of the rich and so pass under their jurisdiction.[27] Still I should not consider this a serious or unfitting procedure; on the contrary, I should laud the public spirit of the powerful to whom the poor entrust themselves, if they did not sell their patronage, if the defence they claim to give the poor were

---

[26] That is, free farmers, not *coloni*, for the latter would not be liable to direct taxation. The constant use of diminutives in reference to their property — *agelli, resculae, habitatiunculae* — shows the type of small farmer meant. The passage is an important one as an indication of the existence of independent small landholders in Gaul in Salvian's time.

[27] See Cod. Theod. XII. 1. 146 of A.D. 395: "We have noted that many hide under the shadow of the powerful to defraud their country of the payments due"; and, in general, Cod. Theod. XI. 24; *De patrociniis vicorum*. A decree of A.D. 319 (*ibid*. XI. 3. 1) recognized as the cause of many arrears in the taxes that "some men, taking advantage of the temporary needs of others, get possession of the best farms on condition of holding them tax free without making up their arrears to the fiscus."

due to their humanity and not to their greed. It is a serious and grievous situation, that the rich make a show of protecting the poor only in order to rob them, that they defend the wretched only on condition of making them more wretched still by this defence. For all those who seem to be enjoying protection assign to their patrons the bulk of their property before they receive any help, and thus the sons' inheritance is destroyed that the fathers may be secure.[28] Protection for the parents is assured by the beggary of the children. See then the aid and patronage afforded by the great: they do nothing for the benefit of those who come under their care, but only for their own. Some aid is granted the parents for the time being, but only on condition that in the future the children shall lose everything. It is a mere process of sale, and certain of the great are sure to demand a very dear price for everything they offer. I said it was a process of sale — I wish they would sell in the ordinary sense of the term, for in that case perhaps they would leave something to the purchaser! But this is a new sort of buying and selling; the seller gives nothing and receives everything, while the buyer receives nothing and loses all that he had. Now practically every sales agreement has this characteristic, that the element of desire is on the side of the buyer, and that of need on that of the seller, inasmuch as the buyer wishes to increase his substance and the seller to diminish his. This, however, is an unheard-of sort of trading, in which the property of the sellers increases while nothing remains to the buyers but sheer beggary.

What an intolerable and monstrous thing it is, one that human hearts can hardly endure, that one can hardly bear to hear spoken of, that many of the wretched poor, despoiled of their tiny holdings, after they have completely lost their property, must still pay taxes for what they have lost! Though possession has been forfeited, the

---

28 In Cod. Just. XI. 54. 1, A.D. 468, an attempt is made to prevent patronage by making testaments in such cases invalid; in Cod. Theod. XI. 24. 4 such patronage is made subject to very heavy fines.

assessment is not cancelled:[29] they are without property but are overwhelmed with taxes. Who can fairly estimate this evil? The poor wretches pay taxes for the invaders who have swooped down on their estates. After the father's death, the sons have no claim on the little farms that should rightly be theirs, but are forced to pay ruinous taxes for them. As a result, what else is accomplished by this great wrongdoing except that men stripped naked by private robbery, die under the public exactions, and taxation ends the lives of those whose property has been carried off by plunderers?[30]

Therefore some of those of whom I speak, who are either shrewder than the rest or have been sharpened by necessity, have lost their homes and farms by such encroachments, or have fled before the taxgatherers, because they cannot hold their property, and seek out the farms of the rich and great, to become their *coloni*.[31]

Those who are driven by the terror of the enemy flee to the forts,[32] and those who have lost their immunity as free men take refuge in some asylum[33] out of sheer desperation. So also these men, who are no longer able to guard the home and condition of their birth, subject themselves to the lowly yoke of serfdom. They have been reduced to such a necessitous state that they are cut off not only from their former possessions, but also from their rank. They are exiled not alone from their property but from their very selves; losing all that was theirs along with their freedom, they

---

[29] Salvian uses the word *capitatio*, which, as Haemmerle (*op. cit.* II. 11) points out, must be here equivalent to *iugatio*, not to the poll tax.

[30] For attempts to remedy this wrong, cf. Cod. Theod. XI. 3. 1-5, providing for proper registration and payment of arrears on land acquired ''in any way whatsoever.''

[31] That is, they give up their full citizen status, and become bound to the soil, being no longer subject to direct taxation. This would seem a harsher alternative than the preceding, yet actual conditions lead Salvian to reckon it as the wiser course.

[32] *Castella* had already become frequent sanctuaries in exposed territories.

[33] Churches had taken the right of sanctuary formerly held by pagan temples; cf. Cod. Theod. IX. 45.

lack any title to their holdings and forfeit the very rights of liberty.[34]

9. Even this might through sheer necessity seem somehow tolerable, if there were not further misfortune to follow. Their lot is made more bitter by a worse injustice still. For they are received as strangers; they become natives only on the terms of their present condition. Recalling the example of that evil sorceress of old who is said to have changed men into beasts, we might say that all who are received on the farms of the rich are transformed as if by Circe's potions. For the owners begin to count those whom they have received as outsiders and aliens, as their own property; they turn into slaves men known to be free-born. Do we wonder that the barbarians are able to capture us, when we take our brothers captive? It is not at all strange that our states are being devastated and destroyed. We have long been providing by the oppression of the multitude for our own eventual capture, falling into captivity by our enslavement of others. Much later than we deserve, do we now at length suffer the treatment that we have meted out to others, and in the words of the Holy Scripture, eat the labor of our own hands.[35] Under the judgment of a just God we are paying what we owe. We showed no mercy to exiles; behold, we ourselves are in exile: we deceived wanderers; behold, we ourselves, now wanderers, are deceived in turn: we took advantage of circumstances to ruin free-born men; behold, we ourselves are beginning to live on alien soil, and fear the same ruin.

How great is the deceptive blindness of sinful minds! We are suffering from the condemnation of God's judgment and still do not acknowledge that we are being judged. Some of the saints wonder that the others who have thus far not endured any such

---

[34] Compare the commentary on their status in Haemmerle, *op. cit.* II. 19-25, where Salvian's use of the terms *coloni* and *inquilini* as interchangeable is discussed.

[35] Psalms 128. 2.

fate are not reformed by our example! Not even those of us who are already smitten by God are being corrected by the torments justly due to our wickedness. What intolerable pride is ours! However many are enduring the punishment that their sins require, no one deigns to acknowledge the cause of his trouble. The reasons for our pride are perfectly obvious: even though we are at last suffering a little, we do not yet suffer as we deserve. So great is the mercy of God that he does not wish us to endure the full penalties for our misdeeds, but only a part of what is due; he chastens the wicked, but not to the full measure of their sin. He wishes us to acknowledge our misdoings rather than to endure their penalties, to the end that by his loving and salutary correction he may show us what we deserve to suffer, but not inflict on us the stripes we deserve. In this he follows the words of the blessed apostle, who said: "Dost thou not know that the goodness of God leadeth thee to repentance? But after thy hardness and impenitent heart thou treasurest up unto thyself wrath against the day of wrath." [36]

In truth our actions suit the words of the apostle, for God calls us to repentance, but we treasure up wrath; he invites us to receive pardon, but we daily heap up our offences. We bring force to bear on him by our iniquities; we ourselves arm the divine wrath against us. We compel God against his will to take vengeance on our monstrous crimes; we give him scarcely any opportunity to spare us. For although no token of injustice can ever light on him or appear in him, our actions are such that if he did not take vengeance on our sins he would seem to be unjust.

10. Surely, you say, a man who has once been a sinner may have ceased to do wrong. Is there any end to wrongdoing? Do not men give up life sooner than iniquity? What man does not die in his evil pursuits, to be buried with his sins and crimes? Truly, one might apply to such men the words of the prophet: "Their

---

[36] Romans 2. 4-5.

graves are their homes forever, and they are compared to foolish
cattle, and are become like them.''[37] If only they were like cattle!
It would at least have been something gained, to have gone astray
through mere brute folly. To have sinned, not through ignorance,
but in despite of God, is worse and deserves a heavier penalty. Do
you claim that this is the case with the laity only, and not with even
a few among the clergy? With worldly men only, and not with
many of the religious also, or rather men given over to worldly
vices under the empty show of religion? These, to be sure, after
the shameful guilt of their past misdeeds, have gained themselves
the honorary name of sanctity. They have altered in their profession but not in their actual way of life, and, thinking that the
service of God depends on costume more than on action, have
changed their garments but not their hearts. Why should men
think their guilt less hateful, who, though they are said to have
performed a sort of penance, do not put off their old habits when
they lay aside their former style of dress? Their actions as a whole
are such that there is less reason to suppose that they have already
done penance for their misdeeds than that they afterwards repented
of their penitence. There is less ground to think that they have
repented their evil life than that they have since regretted their
promise of a good one.

Many men know that I am speaking the truth, and can even bear
witness to my words in their own conscience. Chief among these
are the religious who have gained some reputation by a general
repentance and now seek after new honors, and buy powers they
formerly lacked. They are so anxious to be not merely men of the
world, but more than worldly, that what they were before their
repentance does not now suffice them unless they may become
greater than they were in the past. Do they not repent of their
conversion?

So also do those men repent of their conversion and their brief

---

[37] Psalms 49. 11-12.

thought of God, who, abstaining from intercourse with their wives, do not refrain from invasion of other men's property; who, professing physical continence, run riot in incontinence of spirit. A strange sort of conversion, truly! They do not do what is permissible, but commit forbidden sins. They refrain from lawful wedded life but not from rapine.

What vain delusion is this? Sins were forbidden us by God, not marriage. Your deeds do not suit your convictions; you who call yourselves adherents of virtue should not consort with crime. What you are doing is utterly absurd; this is not conversion to God but aversion from him. If, as is rumored, you have left off long since the functions even of lawful wedlock, now at last give up your sin. It is indeed just that you should refrain from crime of all sorts, but if you think this impossibly difficult, at least give up your greatest and most monstrous sins. Grant, whoever you are, that the neighbors whose land adjoins yours cannot remain prosperous; grant that the poor cannot support life near you; grant that you persecute the indigent and plunder the wretched; grant that you cause affliction to all men, provided that they are outside your own circle: still, I beg, at least spare your own family. And if you think it too hard and burdensome to spare all who are yours, then spare those who have preferred you not only to their other relatives and kinsmen, but even to those most closely bound to them and their dearly loved children. Yet why should I speak of their loved ones and their children, when they have preferred you almost to their very life and hope? There is nothing praiseworthy in this, as everyone who has committed the error now recognizes. But what has that to do with you, whom even their mistakes have advantaged? Your debt to such men is the greater because they have erred from too great trust in you. They were indeed blinded by devotion, and consequently are branded and censured by all; but even so you are under greater obligations to them because they have incurred the blame of all for love of you.

11. What is there to compare with this among the barbarous Goths? Who among them injures those who love him, attacks his friends, and cuts the throats of his dear ones with his own dagger? You attack those who love you, you cut off the hands of those who offer gifts, you kill your closest friends, and do you not fear and tremble? What would you do if you had not felt the present judgment of God in the scourging you have just received? You increase the count and constantly add new crimes to your former misdeeds. Think what punishment awaits your worse deeds, when even lesser faults are regularly punished by demons. Be content now, I pray, with robbing your friends and companions. Let it be enough that the poor have been harried and beggars despoiled by you, that hardly any one can keep from trembling in your presence, no one can feel secure. Torrents rushing down from Alpine crags, or flames driven by the wind, are more easily borne. No such death as this — to use a well known figure — do sailors die, devoured by the engulfing whirlpool or by Scylla's proverbial dogs. You evict your neighbors from their little farms, those nearest you from their houses and property. Would you "be placed alone in the midst of the earth,"[38] as it is written? This is the one end you cannot gain. Seize all that you can, occupy by force all that you can, still you shall always find a neighbor. Consider, please, other men, whom even you, willingly or not, regard with honor; consider others, whom even you, willingly or not, admire. They are above others in honor, but on a level with them in their own estimation; they are greater in their power and less in their humility. You yourself, to whom I am now speaking, surely know whom I mean, and you of whom I now complain ought to recognize whom I honor by this praise. I only wish that there were many who deserve such praise; the nobility of a great number might work healing for all.

But suppose that you do not wish to win praise; tell me, why do you wish to be worthy of condemnation? Why is nothing dearer

---

[38] Isaiah 5. 8.

to you than injustice, nothing more delightful than avarice, nothing more cherished than the seizure of other men's goods? Why do you judge nothing more precious than wickedness, nothing more excellent than rapine? Learn the true good from a pagan, who says: "One should be fenced about by charity and goodwill, not by arms." [39]

So your delusions lead you astray; the wickedness of your blind and evil heart deceives you. If you wish to be upright, to be powerful, to be great, you ought to surpass other men not in ill will but in honor. I once read somewhere: "No one is wicked but a fool; for if he were wise, he would prefer to be good." Do you, therefore, if you can at last return to sanity, put off your wickedness, if you wish wisdom. For if you hope to be at all wise or sane, you must discard all that you have been and change completely. Deny yourself that you may not be denied by Christ; cast yourself off that you may be received by him; lose yourself, that you may not perish. For the Savior says: "Whosoever will lose his life for my sake shall find it." [40] Wherefore love this profitable loss, that you may gain true safety. For God will never set you free, unless you have first condemned yourself.

---

[39] Pliny *Panegyric* 49: "In vain has he girded himself with terror, who was not fenced about with charity; for arms are stirred up by arms."

[40] Luke 9. 24.

THE SIXTH BOOK

1. I have been dealing with personalities for a long time now, and seem to have exceeded the rules of argument. For undoubtedly the reader (if anyone for Christ's sake does read these words written from love of Christ) is thinking or saying of me: "Since the subject he is pursuing is a general one, of what use is it to heap up so many accusations against a single person? Suppose — for it is credible — that the man of whom he speaks is as he describes him; still how can one man's goodness be blocked by another's guilt, or — a point of much greater importance — how is the general cause injured by one individual's crime?"

The injury indeed I can prove by clear examples. For instance, Achar[1] once stole a part of an accursed thing, and the trespass of one man was the ruin of all. David ordered the children of Israel to be numbered, and the Lord punished his fault by the destruction of the whole people.[2] Rapsaces spoke scornfully of God, and God smote a hundred and eighty-five thousand men because the froward tongue of one profane man spoke evil of him.[3] Hence it was not without justice that the blessed apostle Paul ordered a noxious sinner cast out of the church and showed why he gave this order, saying: "A little leaven leaveneth the whole lump."[4] From this we clearly see that even one evil man very often works the destruction of many. Nor is this without justice. The reader should recognize that what I said above concerning one wicked man is not beside the point, since we read in the Scriptures that the wrath of the Divine Majesty has very frequently been kindled on account of

---

[1] See Joshua 7, where the name is given as *Achan.*
[2] II Samuel 24.
[3] Isaiah 36-37.
[4] I Corinthians 5. 6.

one man's guilt. But my argument is not limited by this consideration, for we do not need to assume that one man blocks the way of
all, since all are blocking each other; it is not fitting to consider that
all are imperilled by one, since they are all imperilled by their own
actions. For all men are rushing headlong into destruction, or at
least, to put it somewhat more mildly, almost all. Where can the
Christian people find such good fortune that the number of evil-
doers may be less than the number of the good, or failing that, be
merely equivalent to it? How lamentable and grievous is our
present wretchedness! How changed is the Christian people now
from its former character! Of old, Peter, the chief of the apostles,
punished with death the falsehood of Ananias and Sapphira.[5] The
most blessed Paul also expelled one wicked man from the church,
that he might not infect a great number by his presence.[6] But we
are content to have an equal number of good and evil men. Why
should I say we are content? We ought rather to exult and dance
for joy, if we could achieve such an equal balance. See to what
depths we have fallen, to what state we have been reduced after
that glorious purity of the Christian people which kept them all
unspotted, for now we think that the church would be happy if it
contained even as much good as evil. How could we fail to consider
it blessed if half its members were guiltless, since now we lament
that they are almost all guilty?

Since this is the case, it was useless, useless indeed, to speak so
long of one evil man, useless to weep for one man's crimes, since
all or almost all require our tears and lamentations. There are
many who are of this sort or who wish to be so, which is no less
incriminating, and who strive by their zeal for evil to seem guilty
of the charge. On this account, even if their lesser capacity accomplishes less evil, they are themselves as wicked as the rest, for it is

---

[5] Acts 5.
[6] I Corinthians 5.

their lack of ability and not their will that prevents them. Their
hopes alone are within their own control, and in these they are
criminals; they yield to none in their desire for wrongdoing, and
in this, as far as their means permit, they strive to excel. Different
though the two cases are, their rivalry is like that of good men, for
as the good desire to outdo all others in honorable aims, so the evil
yearn to surpass in depravity. As the glory of good men is to grow
daily better, even so the glory of the wicked is to become worse;
and as the best wish to reach the height of all virtues, so the worst
hope to claim the palm in all vices. To our misfortune this is particularly characteristic of us, the Christians, since, as I have already
said, we think wickedness is wisdom. Of these God spoke particularly: "I will destroy the wisdom of the wise and will bring to
nothing the understanding of the prudent."[7] When the apostle
cried, "if any man seemeth to be wise, let him become a fool, that
he may be wise,"[8] he meant that if a man wishes to be wise, he
should be good, for no one is truly wise unless he is truly good.
We, on the contrary, through the viciousness of our perverse spirits
and our "reprobate minds"—to use the scriptural phrase[9]—
reject goodness in favor of folly. Loving corruption more than
wisdom, we think we become daily wiser in proportion as our
depravity increases.

2. Yet what hope of betterment is there in us, I ask, who are not
led into evil by mistaken opinion, but strive with all the eagerness
of our perverted natures to appear constantly worse and worse?
This is the reason why I have long lamented that we are much
worse than the barbarians, for ignorance of the law excuses them,
whereas our knowledge of it accuses us. They prefer the evil to the
good through inexperience of the truth, because they do not know
what things are good; we, by our knowledge of the truth, know very

---

[7] *Ibid.* 1. 19.

[8] *Ibid.* 3. 18.

[9] Romans 1. 28.

well what things are good, [but consider them inferior to the evil in many] [10] ways.

In the first place, there is almost no crime or vice that does not accompany the games.[11] In these the greatest pleasure is to have men die, or, what is worse and more cruel than death, to have them torn in pieces, to have the bellies of wild beasts gorged with human flesh; to have men eaten, to the great joy of the bystanders and the delight of onlookers, so that the victims seem devoured almost as much by the eyes of the audience as by the teeth of beasts.[12] That such things may take place the whole world is ransacked; great is the care with which the search is carried on and perfected. Hidden retreats are entered, pathless ravines are searched, impenetrable forests traversed, the cloud-bearing Alps are climbed, the depths of valleys plumbed, and in order that the flesh of men may be devoured by wild beasts, the last secrets of the world of nature are revealed.

My opponents object that this is not done all the time. True,

---

[10] Here there is a lacuna in the MSS. I have followed Pauly's conjecture to fill out the sense, but am inclined to agree with Zschimmer, *op. cit.*, p. 35, that the abrupt introduction of the subject of the games indicates a more substantial loss in the text.

[11] Salvian's diatribe against the games has been one of the most quoted portions of his work as Grégoire and Collombet note (*Oeuvres de Salvien*, II, 476), it was much used by the French clergy in the 18th century, especially as a source for Lenten sermons. The Italian translation by S. Carlo Borromeo (Milan, 1579) is actually entitled *Libro di Salviano Vescovo di Marsiglia contra gli spettacoli ed altre vanità del mondo.* The subject was one on which the majority of the Fathers wrote with vehemence, and there is naturally a considerable degree of similarity in their attacks. Salvian's chapters on the spectacles are perhaps closest to Tertullian, *De spectaculis*, and to what Lactantius has to say on the subject in various sections of his *Institutiones divinae*.

[12] This sentence shows that in spite of all attempts to check the custom, men were still being "thrown to the lions" in the middle of the 5th century. Constantine in A.D. 325 decreed (Cod. Just. XI. 44): "Bloody spectacles in a time of civil peace and domestic quiet do not meet with our favor, wherefore we absolutely prohibit the existence of gladiators." Rittershausen aptly queries whether the spectacle of men torn and devoured by wild beasts was more suited to civil peace and quiet than were gladiatorial combats.

and a glorious excuse it is for wrongdoing, that it is not constantly carried on — as if any time were appropriate for actions that injure God! Are evil deeds well done because they are not done incessantly? Even murderers are not always employed in murder, but they are still murderers when they are not actually killing, for their hands are at all times stained with bloodshed. Robbers do not steal all the time, but they do not cease to be robbers, for when they are not engaged in theft, their minds are occupied with it. Certainly men who take pleasure in the animal fights of the arena are by no means free from the guilt involved in such spectacles, even when they are not actually looking at them. Would they not enjoy watching them always if they could?

Nor is this the only possible example of our sins, but there are still greater ones. For instance, do not the consuls even now have hens fed after the custom of the sacrilegious pagans? Are not auguries still sought from the flight of birds, and almost all those superstitions kept up which even pagan writers of old thought laughable?[13] Now when the very men who give their names to the years and with whose office the years themselves begin do such things, are we to believe that years begun under these auspices can continue their course propitiously?[14] I wish that these actions might pollute only the consuls who are responsible for them. But the situation is the more desperate because while such things are done with the public consent, the honor of a very limited number becomes the guilt of all, and so, although only two men are inaugurated in any given year, scarcely any one in the whole world escapes infection.

---

[13] See Minucius Felix *Octavius* 26.

[14] Already in the fourth century the chief functions of the consuls at Rome had come to be the giving of their names to the official year, and giving games to the people; this example therefore has an added pertinence in the discussion of the games. See Seneca *De ira* III. 31, in the importance of the *consul ordinarius* as compared with the consuls later in the year, who were deprived of that immortality for their names, which until the general adoption of the Christian era was really considerable.

3. Let this much suffice about the games, seeing that they are, as you say, not performed all the time. We shall speak, instead, of everyday obscenities. These the hosts of demons have contrived of such a sort and so innumerable that even honest and upright hearts, though they can scorn and tread down some among them, yet can scarcely find a way to overcome them all completely. Armies about to engage in battle are said either to intersect with pitfalls the places through which they expect the troops of the enemy to march, or plant them with stakes, or fill them with caltrops, so that even if some of their snares fail to entrap a victim, none of the enemy can fail to be caught. In like manner the demons have prepared so many treacherous lures in this life for the human race that even though one escapes many of them, he is finally caught by one or another.

And since indeed it would take too long to tell of all these snares, that is, the amphitheaters, the concert halls, games, parades, athletes, rope dancers, pantomimes and other monstrosities of which one is ashamed to speak, since it is shameful even to know of such wickedness, I shall describe only the vices of the circuses and theaters. For the evils that are performed in these are such that no one can mention them, or even think of them without being polluted.[15] Other vices as a rule claim only some one portion of our being; for instance, base thoughts affect the mind only, immodest glances the eyes, shameful sounds the ears, so that when any one of these has gone astray, the rest can still be free from wrongdoing. But in the theaters no part of our bodies is free from guilt, for our minds are polluted by evil desires, our ears by hearing and our eyes by what they see, and all these are so disgraceful that a man cannot even describe them without loss of decency.

Who without injuring his modesty can tell of those representations of base acts, those obscenities of words and voice, those dis-

---

[15] See Seneca *Ep.* VII. 2: "Nothing is so ruinous to good character as to spend time at any spectacle."

graceful motions and foul gestures? The very fact that they forbid description shows what great sin there is in all these. Some of the very greatest crimes can be named and discussed without injury to the character of the speaker, as homicide, robbery, adultery, sacrilege and so forth; it is only the vice of the theaters that cannot even be attacked without loss of modesty. So in arraigning these vile and disgraceful abuses the prosecutor has a strange experience, in that, although the honesty of the would-be accuser is unquestioned, he cannot without prejudice to his honor relate or attack them. All other evils pollute those who perform them, not those who merely see or hear them. You may, for instance, hear a man blaspheme, but since your mind disapproves of his sacrilege you are not polluted by it. Or if you happen to be present during a robbery, you are not defiled by the act, inasmuch as it is abhorrent to your principles. The indecencies of the spectacles alone involve actors and audience in substantially the same guilt. For all those who approve such performances and take pleasure in seeing them perform them through the medium of their sight and approval. To such men the words of the apostle apply with a peculiar force, since not only "they which commit such things are worthy of death" but also "those who have pleasure in them that do them." [16]

Therefore in these pictures of vice the whole people commits fornication mentally, and any who happen to come to the spectacle chaste go home from it adulterers. They are guilty of this fornication not only when they go home, but also when they come to the theater, for the very desire of the obscene makes a man unchaste who is hurrying toward an impure spectacle.

4. You see then in what actions all or the majority of Romans participate. None the less, we who do such things say we are forsaken by God, though we ourselves are forsaking him. Let us suppose that our Lord would like to watch us even though we do not deserve it: can he do so? See countless thousands of Christians daily

---

[16] Romans 1. 32.

spending their time at shows representing shameful acts. Can God look at them at such a time? Can God watch over men who are revelling in the circuses and wantoning in the theaters? Or do we perhaps think it fitting and desirable that when God sees us in the circuses and theaters, he should see with us what we ourselves see there, and look with us at the disgraceful sights at which we gaze? One of two things must happen; either, if he deigns to look on us, he must also see our surroundings, or if he averts his eyes from them, which he surely does, then he must avert them equally from us, who are among them.

In spite of this, without interruption we continue to do those things of which I speak. Do we perhaps suppose that, like the ancient pagans, we have a god of theaters and circuses? For they built the theaters and circuses long ago because they believed that such vanities were a delight to their idols.[17] How can we imitate them in this, who surely know that our God hates such things? Of course, if we know that these vile shows please God, there can be no objection to our performing them incessantly. But if in our hearts we know that God abhors and abominates them, that as they are the devil's food so are they also a cause of offence to God, then how can we say that we worship God in the church, we who always serve the devil in the obscene games with full knowledge and understanding and with deliberate intention? What hope, I ask, shall we have before God, who injure him not by chance or by ignorance, but after the manner of those old giants of whom we read that they attempted to scale the heavens in their mad ambition and climbed, as it were, into the clouds? So we, by the injuries that we constantly inflict on God throughout the world, as if by common consent, are making war on heaven.

Therefore we offer up to Christ — O monstrous folly! — to Christ we offer up circuses and mimes, and we do this chiefly when we receive some benefit from him, when some mark of prosperity is

---

[17] See Lactantius *Inst. div.* VI. 20.

granted us by him, or a victory over the enemy is bestowed on us by his divine favor! How do we seem in this to differ from a man who injures a generous benefactor, or responds to endearments with cutting abuse, or pierces with his dagger the lips that seek to kiss him? I ask all the rich and powerful men of this world, what punishment they think fitting for a slave who plots evil against a good and loving master, who quarrels with a master who deserves only good of him, and returns only foul words for the liberty that he has received. Undoubtedly he is guilty of the greatest wrong-doing who returns evil for good, when he should not even feel free to return evil for evil. But this is what we do who are called Christians: we arouse a merciful God against us by our licentious acts, we insult him by our filthy deeds when he is propitious, we lash him with abusive words when he speaks gently to us.

5. To Christ then — O monstrous folly! — we offer circuses and mimes, to Christ in return for his benefits we offer the obscenities of the theaters, to Christ we dedicate the vilest shows as sacrificial offerings. Was this the teaching given us by the Savior, incarnate for our sake? Was this his preaching, or that of his apostles? For this did he endure the humiliation of human nativity and take upon himself a shameful origin in his mortal birth? For this he lay in a manger, whom angels served as he lay there. For this he willed to be wrapped in swaddling clothes, and wearing them ruled heaven; for this he hung upon the cross, whom the world feared as he hung there. "Who though he was rich," the apostle said, "yet for your sakes became poor, that ye through his poverty might become rich." [18] "And being in the form of God," I quote further, "he humbled himself unto death, even the death of the cross." [19]

These then are the precepts that Christ gave us at the time of his passion. A glorious return we are making for his suffering, who, having received redemption by his death, offer him in return

[18] II Corinthians 8. 9.
[19] Philippians 2. 6, 8.

most disgraceful lives! The blessed Paul said: "For the grace of our Lord Jesus Christ hath appeared, teaching us that, denying ungodliness and worldly lusts, we should live soberly, righteously, and godly in this present world; looking for that blessed hope and glorious appearing of the great God and our Savior Jesus Christ; who gave himself for us, that he might redeem us from all iniquity and purify unto himself a people worthy of acceptance, zealous of good works.[20]

Where are men who do those things for which the apostle says Christ came? Where are those who flee from worldly lusts? Where are those who live righteous and godly lives, who show in their good works that they hold the blessed hope, and by living immaculate lives prove that they await the kingdom of God, since they deserve to receive it? "The Lord Jesus Christ," Paul said, "came to purify unto himself a people worthy of acceptance, zealous of good works." Where is that pure people, that acceptable people, that people of good works, that people of righteousness? "Christ," the Scripture says, "suffered for us, leaving us an example, that we should follow his steps."[21] So we follow the Savior's steps in the circuses; we follow the Savior's steps in the theaters. Is this the example Christ left for us? We read that he wept, not that he laughed. In both he gave us an example, for weeping is the remorse of the heart, laughter the corruption of uprightness. For this reason he said: "Woe unto you that laugh now; for ye shall weep;" and again: "Blessed are ye that weep now, for ye shall laugh." [22] But we do not think it enough to laugh and rejoice, unless we rejoice in sin and madness, unless our laughter is mixed with impure and disgraceful actions.

6. Who can describe this delusion of ours, this folly? Are we really unable to enjoy ourselves day by day, and to laugh, without turning our laughter and joy into crime? or do we perhaps con-

---

[20] Titus 2. 11-14.
[21] I Peter 2. 21.
[22] Luke 6. 25, 21.

sider wholesome enjoyment profitless and find no pleasure in innocent laughter? What wickedness is this, I ask, and what insanity? Let us laugh indeed, let us rejoice unstintedly, and as constantly as you please, if only we do so innocently. What folly and madness it is for us to think laughter and joy worthless unless they involve injury to God! Injury indeed, and a very great one. The spectacles involve a sort of apostasy from the faith, a fatal violation of the creed itself and of the divine sacraments. For what is the first confession of faith made by Christians in baptism for their salvation? What else than their vow to renounce the devil and his pomps and spectacles and his works? So in the very words of our profession of faith spectacles and pomps are the works of the devil.[23] How then, O Christian, shall you after baptism seek the spectacles, which you confess are the work of the devil? You have once renounced the devil and his spectacles, and therefore as a rational and intelligent being must recognize that in resorting again to them, you are returning to the devil. For you have renounced them both at the same time and declared them to be one and the same. If you return to one, you return to them both. For your words were: "I renounce the devil, his pomps and spectacles and his works."[24] What follows in your baptismal vows? "I believe in

---

[23] Tertullian makes a similar connection between *spectacula* and *pompa diaboli* in *De spectaculis* 4. On his other uses of the phrase, and its generally symbolic meaning at this time, cf. P. de Labriolle's article, "Pompa Diaboli," *Bulletin du Cange*, II (1926), 170-181. The actual word *spectacula* was not included in the baptismal vow, but in Salvian's interpretation was inherent in the pomp and works of the devil. So Tertullian, in the passage cited above, says: "If then the whole apparatus of the spectacles is proven to consist of idolatry, there is no doubt that our vow of renunciation at the font refers also to the spectacles, which are by their idolatry in the service of the devil and his pomp and angels."

[24] See Isidore, *Etymologiae* XVIII. 59: "These spectacles of cruelty and vanity were instituted not only by the vices of men but by the orders of demons also. Therefore a Christian should have nothing to do with the insanity of the circus, with the indecency of the theater, with the cruelty of the amphitheater, with the atrocities of the arena, with the voluptuousness of the games. For he who prefers such sights denies God, being made a traitor to

God the Father Almighty and in Jesus Christ his Son." First then, you renounced the devil that you might believe in God, for he who does not renounce the devil does not believe in God and therefore he who returns to the devil forsakes God.

Furthermore, the devil is present in his spectacles and pomps, and therefore when we return to the devil's spectacles, we abandon our Christian faith. Thus all the sacraments of our belief are broken, and all that follows in the creed is shaken and totters; for nothing that follows remains intact if the chief clause has fallen. Tell me then, you who are a Christian, how you think you are keeping the latter portions of the creed, whose first clauses you have abandoned? The limbs without the head are worth nothing, and everything depends on its own first principles; these surely, if they perish, will drag all the rest down with them to destruction. If the main stock is removed, the other parts either cease to exist or if they continue are useless, for without its head nothing can subsist.

If any one thinks the wickedness of the spectacles a trivial matter, let him consider well all that I have said, and he will see that in them is not pleasure but death. For what else is it but death, to have lost the source of life? When the foundations of our creed are overthrown, life itself is strangled.

7. I must return again to my oft-repeated contention, what have the barbarians like this? Where in their lands are circuses, where are theaters, where those other wicked vices that are the ruin of our hope and salvation? Even if they had such things, being pagans, their error would involve less offence to what is sacred, and less guilt, for though such sights as these are impure, still they would not involve violation of a sacrament.

But as for us, how can we answer in our own behalf? We hold the creed and overthrow it. We are equally ready to confess the

---

the Christian faith, who seeks again what he once renounced at the font; that is, the devil, his pomps and works."

gift of salvation and to deny it. Where then is our Christianity, when we only receive the sacrament of salvation [25] to the end that falling from grace we may thereafter sin more grievously than before? We prefer vain shows to God's churches, we scorn his altars and honor the theaters. To conclude, we love and honor everything else; only God, in contrast with worldly pleasures, is vile in our sight.

One case in itself proves the truth of my contention, disregarding all the rest. Whenever it happens, as it does only too often, that on the same day we are celebrating a feast of the church and the public games,[26] I ask it of everyone's conscience, which is it that collects greater crowds of Christians, the rows of seats at the public games or the court of God? Do all men throng to the temple in preference to the theater, love the words of the Gospel more than those of the stage — the words of life or of death, the words of Christ or of a mime? Without doubt, we love more that which we place first. For on every day when the fatal games are given, whatever festival of the church it may be, not only do men who claim to be Christians fail to come to the services, but any who do happen to have come unwittingly, if they chance to hear, while in the church, that games are being given, leave the building at once. The temple of God is scorned for a rush to the theater; the church is emptied and the circus filled; we leave Christ alone on the altar and feast our adulterous eyes on the foulest sights of the vile games. So it is with the greatest justice that the Lord God says to us:

---

[25] That is, baptism.

[26] Another instance of popular disregard for imperial edicts. Cod. Theod. II. 8. 20, in A.D. 392, forbade circuses on Sunday except when the emperor's birthday fell on that day. Another decree, *ibid.* II. 8. 23, of A.D. 399, forbade theaters and races and all sorts of public shows, with the same exception. In A.D. 409 (*ibid.* II. 8. 25), the prohibition held even for the emperor's birthday and the anniversaries of his rule. A few years after Salvian's book was published, the emperors Leo and Anthemius in the East (Cod. Just. III. 12. 9, A.D. 469) inflicted heavy penalties for presence at the spectacles on Sunday, and on any officials who should authorize such performances "on the pretext of public business."

"For your filthiness you have been driven out in banishment."
And again he says: "The altars of this laughter shall be brought
to nothing."[27]

8. At least, you say, this answer can be made, that such things
are not done in all the cities of the Romans. True, and I shall even
go so far as to say that they are not now being done in all places
where they have been hitherto. For instance, no shows are given
now in Mayence, but this is because the city has been destroyed and
blotted out;[28] nor at Cologne, for it is overrun by the enemy. They
are not being performed in the most noble city of Trèves, which
has been laid low by a destruction four times repeated,[29] nor finally
in many other cities of Gaul and Spain. Then woe to us and our
iniquities, woe to us and our impurities! What hope have Christian
congregations in the sight of God when these evils cease to exist in
the Roman cities only from the time when the cities themselves

---

[27] Sources? Compare Isaiah 16.4 and 10.

[28] Haemmerle, *op. cit.*, I. 27-28, puts the destruction of Mayence in A.D. 405-
406 (see Jerome, *Ep.* 123; Migne, PL, XXII, col. 1057), and that of Cologne
between 438 and 440, as it is here connected with the fourth sack of Trèves.
Salvian, *Ep.* I, agrees with this in his account of the effect on his relatives of
the recent sack of the city.

[29] The dates of the four destructions of Trèves here mentioned have been
much discussed with widely differing conclusions. The 12th century *Gesta
Treverorum* described four captures of the city, but, ranging as they do from
that of the "Greeks" under the Arian Constans in A.D. 380 to that of the
Franks in 463, they do not suit the conditions required by Salvian's text.
The recent tendency has been to ascribe all four captures of the city to the
Franks, and to set them fairly close together, emphasizing the phrase *ter
continuatis vicibus* in VI. 15 *infra*. Rudolph and Kenterich (*Quellen zur
Rechts- und Wirtschaftsgebiete der rheinischen Städte: kurtrierische Städte:
I. Trier*, Bonn 1915, 5-6) incline to date the first capture in A.D. 411-412, the
second and third in the period from 412 to 416, and the fourth in 427-428,
dates that connect well with Salvian's account and with local conditions. The
earlier and later dates assigned by some commentators, while suitable as far
as the history of Trèves is concerned, are less consistent with the conditions
required by Salvian's account. For summaries of various opinions on this point,
see Haemmerle, *Studia Salviana* I, 19-26. Haemmerle himself suggests the
date 406 as that of a sack by the Vandals, and 411-413, 418, 438-439 or
earlier, as Frankish destructions of the city. This conjecture is not far from
that of Rudolph and Kenterich.

have come into subjection to barbarian jurisdiction? This mark of vice and impurity seems to be a native characteristic of the Romans, an inborn trait, for wherever there are Romans, these evils prevail. Do you think that this is a serious and unjust accusation? Serious indeed, if it is without foundation. But how can it fail to be false, since the activities of which I spoke are now carried on in only a few Roman cities? Most of our cities, you claim, are not now polluted by the taint of these vices; even though they are the same places which were the homes of our old wickedness, still their former indulgences have ceased.

So we must now consider the question, why those cities still seem to be the haunts of the games, whereas the games have ceased. They are still the homes and abiding places of disgraceful vice because all sorts of vile deeds have hitherto been enacted in them. Moreover, the only reason for the cessation of the games themselves is that they cannot be given at the present time because of the misery and poverty in which we live. That they were presented before was due to our depravity; that they are not given now, to our necessity. For the collapse of the imperial fiscus and the beggary of the Roman treasury do not permit money to be lavished on trifling matters that make no return. Let men squander as much as they please, casting their money into the mire; they cannot lose as much as they could formerly, for they have not as much to lose. In respect of our lustful desires and our base pleasures we should certainly like to have more abundance, if only that we might be able to transmute our wealth into disgraceful filth. The amounts squandered in our beggary are an indication of what we should like to spend if we were rich and magnificent. The bane and ruin of our present depraved condition is that though our poverty has nothing left to lose, our sinful souls yearn for more wealth to cast away.

We cannot therefore console ourselves at all on these grounds, that is, by saying that the former extravagances are not now being committed in all our cities. For the only reason for their abandonment is that cities where they were carried on in the past are no longer in existence, or that in the places where such things used to be done, [means are lacking][30] to perform them. Thus the spectacles are no longer possible in the cities where they were formerly performed; as God himself said to sinners through his prophet: "The Lord remembered these things and it came into his mind, and the Lord could no longer bear, because of the evil of your doings and because of the abominations which ye have committed; therefore is your land a desolation, and an astonishment and a curse."[31] So it has come to pass that the greater part of the Roman world is become a desolation and an astonishment and a curse.

9. Would that these abominations had only been committed of old and that Roman depravity would at length cease such performances! Then perhaps, as it is written, God would be merciful to our sins. But we do not so act as to propitiate him. We constantly add evils to evils and pile sins upon sins, and though many of us have already perished we seek to complete our own destruction. Who, tell me, seeing another man killed beside him is not in terror for himself? Who can see his neighbor's house burn and not try by every means in his power to keep his own from being set on fire? But we not only see our neighbors burning[32] but know that the flames have already spread over the greater part of our own bodies. What unspeakable evil is this that we are suffering? We are on fire, on fire, I say, and yet we do not fear the flames that burn us. That the evils committed formerly are at last diminishing is the result of our miseries, not the fruit of a true repentance.

This is easily proved; only give back our former prosperity and

---

[30] The text is badly corrupted, and no satisfactory emendation has been proposed. The bracketed words are supplied on the basis of the preceding sentence.

[31] Jeremiah 44. 21-22.

[32] Baluze, referring this phrase to the burning of Trèves, somewhat gratuitously concluded that Salvian could not have been a native of that city.

you shall see at once the old interests everywhere restored. Note
this also: as far as men's wishes are concerned, even if the games
are no longer actually being given in many places, yet they still
exist as of old, for the Roman people everywhere wish them given.
When nothing but sheer necessity hinders a man from an evil deed,
the mere desire for a base act is as much to be condemned as the
action. For if, as I said, according to the words of our Lord:
"Whosoever looketh on a woman to lust after her is guilty of the
adultery conceived in his heart," [33] we can understand that while
of necessity we do not commit disgraceful acts worthy of condemnation, we are nevertheless guilty if we only desire forbidden
things.

Why should I mention desire? Most men actually do these
things whenever they can. When the inhabitants of other cities
come to Ravenna or Rome they join the Roman plebs in the circus,
and the people of Ravenna in the theater. Therefore let no one
consider himself acquitted on the ground of his distance from the
spectacles. All are united in the turpitude of their actions who join
one another in their desire for disgraceful deeds.

Yet we flatter ourselves on the uprightness of our ways, the
rarity of our vices. So I shall carry my charges farther: not only
do men still yield as of old to the pollution of those infamous games
but their guilt in this is much greater than before. For in the past
the various members of the Roman world flourished unimpaired;
the public wealth had made the storehouses inadequate; the citizens
of all the towns had abundance of riches and delights, and amid
such overflowing prosperity the authority of religion could hardly
exercise due censorship of conduct. Then indeed those who ex-
ploited base desires found rich grazing on all sides, but there was
no lack of wealth to satisfy their greed; no one worried about the
public disbursements and expenses, for the cost was not felt. The
state indeed seemed in a way to seek an opportunity to squander

---

[33] Matthew 5. 28.

what it could scarcely continue to hold. Thus the heaped-up wealth
that had already begun to exceed just bounds furnished abundance
for lavishness even in trivial matters.

But of the present situation what can we say? Our old abundance
has deserted us; the resources of former times are gone, and we
are in a wretched state, but do not cease our frivolities. Although
even orphan wastrels are usually benefited by poverty, leaving off
the error of their ways as soon as they have squandered their
wealth, we seem to be a new class of profligates, in whom opulence
has ceased to dwell, but dissipation persists. The causes of our corruption lie not as with other men in outside enticements, but in
our hearts, and our minds are the source of our depravity, so that
[we] are not [moved] to amend our ways by the loss of our
wealth, but [go on] [34] sinning through love of wickedness.

10. Although I may have shown sufficiently what serious vices
the Romans have, from which the barbarian tribes are free, still
I shall add many points that I have omitted. But before I continue,
let me remind you that a fault of any sort which dishonors God
should in no sense seem a trivial matter to anyone. It is never
permissible to dishonor an illustrious and powerful man, and anyone who dishonors such a one is held guilty in the eyes of the law
and is condemned in due course as responsible for the injurious
action. How much more difficult of atonement is the accusation
of injury to God! The fault of the wrongdoer always increases in
proportion to the position of the person injured, since necesssarily
the greater the person of the man who suffers abusive action, the
greater is the guilt of the man who commits such action. Wherefore
we read in the law that even those who seem to have committed
only slight offence against the sacred ordinances have nevertheless
been most severely punished; to the end that we might know that
nothing pertaining to God should be considered unimportant. Even

---

[34] The corrupt text is here emended according to Pauly's conjectures.

what seemed to be a petty fault became a grave one, inasmuch as it was an injury to the divine power.

What did Oza, the Levite of God, do against the divine commandment, when he tried to steady the ark of the Lord? There was no law laid down regarding this. Yet immediately he took hold of it, he was struck down, apparently not because he did anything in an impudent fashion or with an undutiful intention, but his very service was undutiful because he exceeded his orders.[35]

When a man of the Israelites had gathered wood on the Sabbath, he was struck down and killed by the judgment and command of God, who is truly a most gentle and merciful judge, who would doubtless have preferred to spare rather than to kill, if the consideration of severity had not outweighed consideration of mercy. For one incautious man perished to save many from perishing thereafter through lack of caution.[36]

But why do I speak of single individuals? The children of Israel in their journey through the desert, because they longed for their accustomed meat, lost a part of their number. The desire for meat had not yet been forbidden them, but God, I think, wished to further the observance of the law by the suppression of rebellious desires. He intended the whole people to learn the more easily how earnestly one should avoid what God forbade in his divine writings, since even those acts injured him which he had not yet forbidden by law.[37]

The same people also murmured at the hardships they underwent, and for this reason were punished by the Lord's rods, not because it is forbidden a man to groan at hardships, but because their murmurs were displeasing to God, inasmuch as they seemed to accuse him of causing them too much labor. From this we should learn how much a man enjoying the blessings of good fortune ought

---

[35] II Samuel 6. 6-7.
[36] Numbers 15. 32-36.
[37] *Ibid.* 11.

to seek to please God, since it is not even permitted to complain of those ills that seem painful.

11. What is the purpose of these examples? What else than that nothing should seem trivial that causes injury to God? For we were talking of the public games, which are truly mockeries of our hopes, mockeries of our life. While we sport in the theaters and circuses, we perish, according to the Sacred Word which says: "It is as sport to a fool to do mischief." [38] So we too, when we laugh amidst disgraceful and shameful sights, are committing crimes, and crimes of no slight extent. Our wrongdoing is the more worthy of punishment for this very reason, that though it seems to be of a most trivial nature, it is really pestilential and deadly in its outcome. There are two chief evils, for a man to destroy himself and for him to injure God; both of these are committed in the public games, where through criminal and shameful sights the eternal salvation of the Christian people is utterly destroyed, and through a sacrilegious superstition the divine majesty is violated. There can be no doubt that the games injure God, consecrated as they are to idols. For Minerva is worshipped and honored in the gymnasia, Venus in the theaters, Neptune in the circuses, Mars in the arena, Mercury in the palaestra, and thus the superstitious worship varies according to the character of its sponsors.[39] Impure actions of all sorts are performed in the theaters; there is wanton luxury in the palaestras, immoderate vice in the circuses, madness in the arenas. In one of these is wantonness, in another lasciviousness, in another intemperance, in another insanity, in them all the devil; nay, in each individual place where shows are held, not merely one devil, but devils of all varieties, for they preside over the places dedicated to their worship. Therefore in spectacles of this sort neither allurements nor vices are found alone. It is sacrilege for a Christian to mingle with this superstition, sharing in the worship of those in

---

[38] Proverbs 10. 23.
[39] See Tertullian *De spectaculis* 10-11.

whose festivals he takes delight. While such a thing is always serious enough, it becomes more intolerable when either our adversity or our prosperity, exceeding the ordinary measure of our life, makes our acts more blameworthy. In adversity there is double need to appease God, and in prosperity to avoid grieving him. Surely he must be appeased when he is angry, and must not be alienated when he is propitious; for our adversities come to us through his wrath, our prosperity through his favor. But we do everything by contraries.

How, do you ask? Listen. First, if won over by his own mercy — for we never so live that we deserve his favor — if, as I say, at any time won over by his own mercy God gives us peaceful seasons, plentiful crops, tranquillity rich in all good things and abundance increasing beyond our hopes, we let ourselves be so corrupted by great prosperity and fortune, we let ourselves be so depraved by insolent manners that we altogether forget God and ourselves. Although the apostle says that every benefit of the peace given by God depends on this: "That we lead a quiet and peaceable life in all godliness and honesty," [40] the only use we make of the quiet he gives is to live in drunkenness and luxury, in wantonness and rapine, in all manner of crime and wickedness. We look on his goodly gift of peace as an opportunity for licentiousness, and take the quiet given by his truce as a chance to sin more freely and safely.

Therefore we are unworthy of heavenly gifts, who make no good use of God's kindness, and see in the means of good works only material for vice. Hence it comes that the peace which we so abuse itself works against us, and is actually harmful to us, since we use it to our detriment. Is this worthy of belief? We change nature itself by our wickedness, and the good things that God has made as his loving gift to us are turned to evil by our wanton lives.

12. We who are corrupted by prosperity, you say, are corrected

---

[40] I Timothy 2. 2.

through adversity. Long peace had made us unruly, but we are brought back by strife to moderation. In what cases have the dwellers in our cities, who were licentious in prosperity, begun to be chaste in adversity? When has drunkenness, which increased in the time of our peace and prosperity, ceased under the ravages of the enemy?

Italy has already been devastated by many disasters: have the vices of the Italians therefore ended? The city of Rome has been besieged and taken by storm:[41] have the Romans therefore ceased their mad blasphemy? Barbarous nations have overrun the states of Gaul: have the crimes of the Gauls therefore changed in character, as far as their evil habits are concerned? Tribes of Vandals have crossed over into the Spanish countryside: the fortune of the Spaniards has indeed changed, but not their corruption. Lastly, that no part of the world might be immune from fatal destruction, wars have begun to cross the seas, they have devastated and overthrown cities shut off by the waves, in Sardinia and Sicily, the imperial granaries. Having, as it were, cut off the vital channels of the empire, they captured Africa, which may be called its heart. What then? As barbarians entered that land, did its vices cease, even through fear? Or, as even the most worthless slaves are usually reformed for the time being, did terror drive them to modesty and self-restraint? Who can rightly estimate this evil? The barbarians' arms clashed about the walls of Cirta and Carthage [42] while the Christian congregation of the city raved in the circuses and wantoned in the theaters. Some had their throats cut

---

[41] That the reference here is to the sack of Rome by Alaric in A.D. 410 is clearly shown by the order of events cited; if it had been intended, as those who use this passage to prove that Salvian's book was written after A.D. 455 assume, to refer to the Vandal sack, it would hardly have been made the first of a series of events ending with the Vandal destruction of Carthage some years before their sack of Rome.

[42] Gaiseric captured Carthage in A.D. 439, after ten years of general Vandal control in Africa. The orthodox clergy were given their choice of slavery or exile, as were the nobles. Church property was given over to the Arians.

without the walls, while others still committed fornication within; part of the people were captive to the enemy without, while part within the city were captive to their own vices. It is hard to decide which suffered the worse misfortune. The former indeed were captive externally in the flesh, the latter inwardly in the soul. Of the two deadly evils, it is less, I think, for a Christian to endure captivity of the body than of the soul, according to the teachings of the Savior himself in the Gospel, that the death of the soul is much more fatal than that of the body.[43]

Or do we perhaps believe that those men were not captive in soul, who then rejoiced in the time of their people's captivity? Was he not captive in mind and heart, who laughed amid the punishments of his people, who did not know that his throat was being cut along with theirs, that in their deaths he also died? Outside the walls, as I have said, and inside them too, was heard the din of battle and of the games; the voices of dying men mingled with the voices of revellers; the outcry of the people slain in the war could scarcely be distinguished from the clamor of those who shouted in the circus. What was accomplished by this but the hastening of the destruction of the people who chose such a course, though God perhaps did not yet wish to destroy them?

13. These places, however, are far away, almost removed to another world, and seem irrelevant to the discussion when I consider that even in my own country,[44] in the Gallic states, almost all men of high degree have been made worse by their misfortunes. I myself have seen men of lofty birth and honor, though already despoiled and plundered,[45] still less ruined in fortunes than in morality; for, ravaged and stripped though they were, something still remained to them of their property, but nothing of their character. They were so much more hostile to themselves than to alien

---

[43] Luke 9. 24-25.

[44] This phrase was overlooked by those commentators who held that Salvian was born in the province of Africa.

[45] That is, in the first sack of the city of Trèves.

enemies that, though they had already been ruined by the barbarians, they now completed their own destruction. It is sad to tell
what we saw there; honored old men, feeble Christians, when the
ruin of their state was already imminent, making themselve slaves
to appetite and lust. What are the first grounds of accusation? That
they were honored, old, Christians, or in danger? Who would deem
it possible that such things should be done by old men even in
utter security, or by boys in a crisis, or at any time whatever by
Christians? They reclined at feasts, forgetful of their honor, forgetting justice, forgetting their faith and the name they bore.
There were the leaders of the state, gorged with food, dissolute
from winebibbing, wild with shouting, giddy with revelry, completely out of their senses, or rather, since this was their usual condition, precisely in their senses. In spite of all this, what I have
next to say is still worse: not even the destruction of their towns
put an end to their excesses. The wealthiest city of Gaul was taken
by storm no less than four times.[46] It is easy to recognize the city
of which I speak. The first captivity should surely have sufficed to
mend the ways of the citizens, so that the renewal of their sins
would not have renewed the destruction. But what followed? The
tale is incredible. The constant repetition of misfortunes in that city
increased its crimes. Like that fabulous monster whose heads multiplied as they were cut off,[47] so also in the most excellent city of

---

[46] The reference to Trèves is obvious. This estimate of the city is supported
by the general testimony of the writers of the early empire. Ausonius puts
Trèves in the fourth place in his *Ordo urbium clarissimarum*, the first being
assigned to Rome, the second to Constantinople and Carthage, and third to
Antioch, so that Trèves is second only to Rome in western Europe. The choice
of the city as the seat of the praetorian prefect of Gaul is a significant indication of its preëminence. See also Cod. Theod. XIII. 3. 11, *De medicis et profes-
soribus* (A.D. 376): ''For the most glorious city of Trèves we have thought
best to make a somewhat more ample allowance, that thirty *annonae* be paid
to a teacher of rhetoric, twenty to a teacher of Latin grammar, and twelve
to one of Greek, if a worthy one can be found.''

[47] That is, the Lernaean hydra. The labors of Heracles were a popular subject for light verse; cf. Ausonius *Monosticha de XII aerumnis Herculis*.

Gaul, wickedness gathered strength from the very blows that punished it. You would have thought that the punishment intended to end the crimes of its people acted instead as the begetter of vice. What then? By the daily multiplication of swarming evils it has come to such a pass that the city could more easily exist without inhabitants than any of its citizens could do without crime.

So much then for this city. What of another not far distant but of almost equal magnificence?[48] Has it not suffered the same ruin of fortunes and of morals? For aside from all else, when it was utterly demoralized by the two chief evils common to all, avarice and drunkenness, it finally reached such a state of rabid greed for wine that the very rulers of the city did not rise from their feasts when the enemy were actually entering the gates. God wished to make clear to them why they perished, since at the moment of their final disaster they were leading the very life through which they had come to ruin. I myself saw lamentable sights there, with no distinction between boys and old men. The scurrility and levity of all were alike; all vices reigned at once — extravagance, drinking bouts, wantonness — all the people revelled together. They drank, gamed, committed adultery. Old and honored men waxed wanton at their feasts; men already almost too feeble to live proved mighty in their cups; men too weak to walk were strong in drinking; those whose steps tottered were nimble dancers. What more can be said? Through all that I have recounted they became so degraded that the words of the Sacred Scripture were fulfilled in them: ''Wine and women make men of understanding to fall away from God.''[49] For while they drink, dice, rape and play the mad-

---

[48] Brouwer, *Antiquitatum et Annalium Treverensium libri XXV* (1671), V. 14, p. 275, identified this city as Mayence, which seems to fit better than Metz or Cologne, the description of utter ruin. In VI. 8 *supra*, Salvian mentioned Mayence especially as having been destroyed, while Cologne was only spoken of as being full of the enemy. Haemmerle, *op. cit.*, I. 18, follows Baluze in identifying the city here mentioned with Cologne instead.

[49] Ecclesiasticus 19. 2.

man, men begin to deny Christ. After all this do we wonder that men who have long since undergone moral ruin suffer the ruin of their fortunes? Let no one think that such a city perished only at the time of its physical destruction, for the deeds of its people had brought its ruin long before their death.

14. I have told the fate of the most famous cities. What of the many others in various parts of Gaul? Have they not fallen, too, because of like vices on the part of their citizens? All were so completely possessed by their crimes that they did not fear any danger; they had foreknowledge of captivity and did not dread it. Fear indeed was taken away from these sinful men to prevent them from the exercise of caution. Therefore, though the barbarians were settled almost within their sight, men felt no fear, the cities remained unguarded. Such was the blindness of their hearts, or rather of their sins, that although doubtless no one wished to die, no one did anything to ward off death. Everything was in the grip of carelessness and sloth, negligence and gluttony, drunkenness and sleep, as has been written of such men: "Because a deep sleep from the Lord was fallen upon them." [50] A deep sleep indeed fell upon them that destruction might follow closely. For when, as it is written, a sinner's iniquity is full [51] and he is due to perish, foreknowledge is taken from him, that he may not escape his doom. But enough of this. I have made my point sufficiently clear, I think, that not even in the time of the greatest danger did the vices of the people come to an end before the actual overthrow of their cities.

15. Perhaps such things have occurred in the past, but have now come to an end, or will do so at some future time. Yes, forsooth, if today any city or province that has been smitten by God's scourge or devastated by the enemy appears humbled, converted and amended, if practically all who bear the Roman name do not

---

[50] I Samuel 26. 12.
[51] Genesis 15. 16.

prefer death to reformation, the end of their life to the end of their vices! This can be quickly tested by the example of the greatest city of Gaul, three times destroyed by successive captures,[52] yet when the whole city had been burned to the ground, its wickedness increased even after its destruction. Those whom the enemy had not killed when they pillaged the city were overwhelmed by disaster after the sack; those who had escaped death in the capture did not survive the ruin that followed. Some died lingering deaths from deep wounds, others were burned by the enemy's fires and suffered tortures even after the flames were extinguished. Some perished of hunger, others of nakedness, some wasting away, others paralyzed with cold, and so all alike by diverse deaths hastened to the common goal.

Worse than all this, other cities suffered from the destruction of this single town. There lay all about the torn and naked bodies of both sexes, a sight that I myself endured. These were a pollution to the eyes of the city, as they lay there lacerated by birds and dogs. The stench of the dead brought pestilence on the living: death breathed out death. Thus even those who had escaped the destruction of the city suffered the evils that sprang from the fate of the rest.

What followed these calamities? Who can assay such utter folly? The few men of rank who had survived destruction demanded of the emperors [53] circuses as the sovereign remedy for a ruined city. O that I might here and now be gifted with eloquence adequate to cope with this shocking event, that there might be at least as much

---

[52] This phrase offers some support for the adoption of dates for the first three captures of the city close to each other in point of time: cf. note 29 *supra*.

[53] Haemmerle, *op. cit.*, I. 22-23, pointed out the importance of this plural for dating the third sack of Trèves, since the joint rule of Honorius and Constantius, A.D. 420-421, was the only possible date before Salvian's withdrawal to Lérins, when there could have been two *imperatores* in the West to whom such an appeal could have been made. Hence the third sack of the city must have taken place at about 420. He suggests further that the people of Trèves hoped by the circuses to attract more residents for the rebuilding of the city.

virtue in my complaint as there is sorrow at its cause! Who can even decide what chiefly merits accusation in the tale, irreverence or stupidity, extravagance or insanity? In these terms the whole is comprised. What is more irreverent than a petition that works injury to God? What is more stupid than not to consider your petition carefully? What so clear a proof of hopeless extravagance as to desire luxuries in a time of general mourning? Or more insane than to be in the midst of evils without any understanding of them?

Among these, however, insanity is the least culpable, for the will is not at fault when sin is committed through sheer madness. Therefore those of whom I speak deserved the greater blame, because, though sane, they acted senselessly. Do you, O citizens of Trèves, long for circuses when you have been plundered and captured, after slaughter and bloodshed, after stripes and captivity, and the repeated destruction of your ruined city? What is more lamentable than this stupidity, more grievous than this folly? I confess I thought you most miserable when you were suffering destruction, but I see that you are now more miserable when you demand public shows. At first I thought you had lost only your material property in the capture of your city; I did not know that you had lost also your intelligence and control of your senses. Do you then ask for theaters, and demand a circus from our emperors? For what condition, I ask, what people and what city? A city burned and destroyed, a people captive and killed, who have perished, or mourn their dead; a city of which nothing survives but sheer calamity, whose people are altogether anxious in their grief, worn out by tears, prostrate in bereavement, so that it is hard to say whether the lot of the living or the dead is worse to bear. So great are the miseries of the survivors that they surpass the ill fortune of the dead.

Do you then seek public shows, O citizen of Trèves? Where, pray, are they to be given? Over the pyres and ashes, the bodies and blood of the dead? For what part of your city is free from these? Where has blood not been shed, where are bodies and mangled limbs not strewn? Everywhere the city's appearance betrays its capture, everywhere are the horror of captivity and the image of death.[54] The remains of a most unhappy people lie on the graves of their dead, yet you ask for circuses; the city is blackened by fire, yet you put on a festive countenance; all things mourn, but you rejoice! Yea more, by your infamous pleasure you provoke God, and by your vile superstitions arouse his divine wrath. Can there be any wonder that such a fate has befallen you, when threefold destruction has not corrected you, so that you richly deserved to perish by the fourth?

16. I have given the above account in somewhat full detail to prove that we have borne all our sufferings not through the failure of God's providence or through his neglect, but because of his justice and judgment — a most just dispensation and worthy retribution — and that no portion whatever of the Roman world and Roman name, however greatly chastised by afflictions sent from heaven, has ever been corrected. Thus we prove that we do not deserve to enjoy prosperity, since we are not corrected by adversity.

Good gifts are given us from time to time, however, unworthy though we are. The good God, like a most indulgent father, sometimes lets us be humbled for our sins, but does not suffer us to be afflicted long. So at one time he chastises his children by adversity, in accordance with his discipline, and again favors them with peace, according to his mercy. As the best and most skilful doctors give different cures for various diseases and succor some by sweet, others by bitter drugs; cure certain ills by cautery, others by soothing poultices; employ ruthless surgery for some, but pour healing oil on others; seeking the same good health by utterly different cures: so also our God, when he restrains us by harsher blows, is seeking to cure us by cautery and surgery; when he favors us with good fortune he is offering us soothing oil and poultices — for by means

---

[54] The Vergilian phrase, *imago mortis* (*Aeneid* II. 360).

of different treatments he wishes to restore us all to the same good health.

Gentle treatment usually corrects even the most incorrigible slaves whom punishment has failed to reform, and kindness subdues those whom the lash failed to make submissive to their masters. Babies, too, and almost all stubborn children, whom threats and blows do not make amenable, are often led to obedience by goodies and endearments. Hence we should realize that we are more worthless than the worst slaves, and more stupid than foolish children, since torments do not correct us as they do bad slaves, nor coaxings win us over as they do naughty children.

17. I think I have now proved adequately that punishment has not corrected any part of the Roman people; it remains to prove that neither the gifts nor the gentle words of God correct us. What then are the gifts and gentle words of God? What indeed but our peace and quiet, the calmness of prosperity that attends on our hopes and wishes? Let me give you a particular instance, since the case demands it.

Whenever we are in fear, distress and danger, when cities are besieged by the enemy or provinces devastated, or the members of the state wounded by any other adversities, and we offer prayers and vows to the heavenly hosts for help, then if by the aid of the divine mercy our cities are saved, the devastation ended, the hostile armies routed and all fear removed by God's grace, what do we immediately do? Do we endeavor to recompense our Lord God by our worship, honor and reverence for the benefits we have received at his hands? For this is the fitting action and in accordance with human custom, that those who give us gifts may receive due return for them. This then perhaps we do, giving God recompense in human fashion, and making a good return for the good we have received of him.

So we run at once to the Lord's house, and prostrate ourselves on the ground, we supplicate him, our joy mixed with tears, and bedeck his doorway with votive garlands, we adorn his altars with gifts, and since we ourselves are making a festival of gifts to him, transfer the joy of our countenance to his temples also. Or at least, an act no less pleasing to him, we renounce the vices of our former lives, we give good works as a sacrifice to him, and offer up a new conversion in return for our new joys. Lastly we declare a holy war on all uncleanliness, shun the madness of the circus, curse the vileness of the shows in the theater, vow a new life to the Lord and, to obtain his protection forever, dedicate ourselves to God.

18. Although all that I have described should be given to God for his recent benefits, let us consider what we actually do. Men run at once to the games, fly off to their old insanity, the folk pour into the theaters, the whole people riot madly at the circuses. God gives us good gifts to assure our merit, but we, as often as we receive his benefits, multiply our crimes. He by his mercies calls us to righteousness, but we rush headlong into wickedness; he by his mercies calls us to repentance, but we rush to destruction; he calls us to chastity, but we rush into impurity. A noble response we make to his holy favors, nobly do we recognize and honor his gifts, who repay the kindness we have received from him by an equal measure of injustice! Is this not injury to our God, or can any injury be less deserved, [when] great and frequent [gratitude] is needed instead? [55]

But since by the taint of wickedness ingrained in our nature we cannot fail to be prey to vice except by ceasing to live at all, what hope of good is there in us? Those who sin through ignorance correct themselves when they learn their error; those who do not know the true religion begin to change their way of life when they change their faith. Lastly, those who are spoiled by excessive abundance and security, as I said, cease their depravity when they are no longer secure. We do not err through ignorance, nor are we

---

[55] The lacuna indicated by Halm is supplied according to Pauly's conjecture.

outside the true religion, nor corrupted by prosperity and security:
quite the reverse. We know the true religion, so ignorance cannot
serve as our excuse; we lack the peace and wealth of our former
days; all that we had has been taken from us or changed — only
our vices have been increased. Nothing remains of our former peace
and plenty but our crimes, which have made our prosperity cease.

Where are now the old resources and honors of Rome? The Romans were of old the mightiest of men, now they are without
strength; of old they were feared, but now they live in fear; barbarous nations paid tribute to them, but to these same nations they
are now tributary.[56] The enemy sell us the very daylight; almost
our whole safety is purchased for a price. Alas for our misfortunes! to what a pass have we come! For this we give thanks to the
barbarians, that we are allowed to ransom ourselves from them at
a price. What could be more abjectly wretched than to live on such
terms? Yet after all this we think that we are living, we whose lives
depend on tribute! We even make ourselves additionally ridiculous by pretending that the gold we pay is merely a gift. We call
it a gift, yet it is really a ransom — but a ransom paid on unusually
hard and wretched terms. When captives have been redeemed, they
gain their liberty, whereas we pay ransom constantly and are
never free. The barbarians deal with us like those masters who hire
out for wages slaves not needed for their own service. In like
fashion, we are never free of the payments due: we pay ransom
constantly in order to have the privilege of continuing endlessly to
pay.

---

[56] Tribute had been paid to barbarians in return for guarantees of the
integrity of the frontier since the early empire: beginning with the fourth
century such tributes came to be due more and more to weakness, rather than
to policy, till the condition was reached which Salvian here describes.

THE SEVENTH BOOK

1. My description, at the end of the previous book, of the weakness and misery of the Romans, may seem to be at variance with my general proposition. I admitted that the very people who, as pagans, conquered and ruled the world, are being conquered and enslaved, now that they have become Christians. Is not this clear evidence of God's neglect of human affairs? The charge is easily refuted by what I said long ago about the pagan nations. Those who know the law of God and neglect it are more guilty than those who fail to observe it through lack of knowledge.

However, if God is willing, since we have reached the point in our undertaking at which something should be said of the old Romans, we shall, with God's help, prove that his favor to them in the past was as just as is his present severity toward us, and that his help to them in former times was as fully deserved as is our punishment now.[1]

Would that this same punishment were of benefit to us! Much harder and more grievous than punishment is the fact that no amendment follows. The Lord wishes to cure us by his chastisement, but improvement does not result. How can we explain this evil? Cattle and flocks are cured by surgery; when the diseased organs of mules, asses and swine have been cauterized they acknowledge the healing effect of the fire, and at once when the corruption of the infected parts has been burned away or cut out, living flesh grows in place of the dead tissue. But we are burned and cut, yet are not healed by the surgeon's tools or the burning of the cautery.

---

[1] Since this promise is not carried out, we have here a clear indication that Salvian's book either was not finished, or has since been mutilated. The manner of his projected proof of the point raised may be surmised from his description in Book I. 10 of the virtues of the early Romans.

189

What is more serious, such care makes us even worse. It is not mere chance that we undergo the same treatment as flocks and cattle afflicted by incurable diseases. For in all parts of the world, since the healing care that is given us has no effect, our lives are being brought to an end by death and destruction. Indeed, not to repeat what I said some time ago, how can we define these disorders except by saying that we are at the same time living in misery and in luxury? Grant that luxury is the vice of the fortunate (though no one can be both infamous and happy at the same time, since there is no true happiness without honor), grant that these are the vices of a long peace and plentiful security, why then are they found where there is no longer peace or security? Almost throughout the Roman world peace and security have ceased. Why do only the vices they engender survive? Who can tolerate licentiousness in a needy man? Wantonness in poverty earns the more reproach, and a worthless fellow is more heavily censured if his condition is wretched.

The whole Roman world is at once wretched and voluptuous. What poor man is also wanton? What man awaiting captivity thinks of the circus? Who laughs in the shadow of death? Yet we, in the fear of captivity, continue to frequent the games, and shadowed by the fear of death, we laugh. You would think the whole Roman people had been steeped in Sardonic herbs:[2] they are dying, yet they laugh. So in almost every part of the world tears follow close upon our laughter; and the saying of our Lord comes home to us at the present time: "Woe unto you that laugh, for ye shall weep."[3]

2. The great length at which I have spoken of the disgraceful character of the public spectacles may have led you to assume that the abstinence of the barbarians from this particular vice of

---

[2] One of the best known of ancient proverbial expressions; cf. Isidore, *Etymologiae* XIV. 6. 40: "the herb recalled by many writers and poets, which contracts men's jaws and kills them while they seem to laugh."

[3] Luke 6. 25.

ours is their only point of moral superiority to us, inasmuch as we are not polluted as they are by the crime of carnal lust and the filth of mortal fornication. Let us then, if you please, compare the Romans in this respect also with other nations. I cannot indeed think of any with whom we may be more justly compared than those whom God has put into the very bosom of the state and made owners and lords of the Roman land. Although there was absolutely no ground to dispute his judgment in this, still, since he has taken away from us the best part of our territory, and given it to the barbarians, let us see whether he seems to have exercised justice in this transfer.

No one questions that the Aquitanians and the Nine Peoples [4] had the very marrow of the Gallic provinces, rich in every sort of fertility, and not in fertility alone, but in qualities sometimes ranked above this, charm, beauty and luxury. Almost all that district is still covered with close-planted vines, flowering meadows, plowed fields, fruit orchards, charming groves, springing fountains, flowing streams or waving grain, so that the owners and masters of the land truly seem to have taken for their own not so much a section of ground as a likeness of paradise. What conclusion can be drawn from this? Unquestionably those men ought to have been more fervent in service to God whom he had especially enriched by the most abundant evidence of his favor. What is more right and fitting than that those whom their Lord seemed especially to have favored by his gifts should themselves make an earnest effort to please him by their religious worship, particularly since God lays no heavy or burdensome demands on us? For he does not call on us to plow or hoe, to spade up the earth or prepare the ground for vines, nor, to sum up, does he exact from his slaves what we require of ours. What does he himself say? "Come unto me, all ye that labor and are heavy laden, and I will give you rest; take my yoke

---

[4] The inhabitants of Novem Populana, the southwestern province of Gaul, between Aquitania and Spain.

upon you and learn of me, for I am meek and lowly of heart, and ye shall find rest unto your souls; for my yoke is easy, and my burden is light.'' [5]

So we see that the Lord calls us not to labor but to rest. What does he exact of us, what does he order us to offer him, save only faith, chastity, humility, sobriety, mercy and sanctity? All these assuredly do not burden but adorn us. Nor is this all; they adorn our present life to the end that they may adorn even more the life to come. O good and loving master, of inestimable mercy! He has given us the gifts of religion at the present time that he may later reward us for the gifts he now gives! These virtues, then, all the Aquitanians should have cultivated, and indeed, as I said before, they should have made more especial efforts in this direction, since they had received the especial gifts of God. What resulted from their prosperity? What was bound to result? Was it not the exact reverse of what should have happened? In all the provinces of Gaul these men who are first in wealth, are first also in vice: nowhere is pleasure more shameless, life more vicious, or moral standards more corrupt. This is the return they have given God for his sacred gifts, that as far as by his generosity he had drawn them to his favor, so far they by their abuse have labored to arouse his anger.

3. Or is this perhaps false, and are all my statements due to envy rather than truth? I shall not use the method of proof some men employ in the courts, bringing in as witnesses outsiders or persons unsuitable to testify for some other reason. I shall cross-question the very men by whom these things have been done. I have spoken falsely if they deny me. They confess, and indeed, which is much more serious, they confess without any apparent grief. For now in their confession they have the same attitude as in their commission of the fault. Just as then they were not ashamed to perform disgraceful acts, so now they do not in the least repent having per-

---

[5] Matthew 11. 28-30.

formed them. We must indeed make exception for a very small number of men distinguished for their holiness, who, as one of their number has said, "have given their wealth to redeem their crime." [6] Of these we must make an exception, men who, we believe, were actually guilty only of lesser crimes even in the midst of the almost universal entanglements of vice, and who merited conversion by God's divine power. Now one for whom favor is reserved has not been altogether injurious to his master in his actions. What more can I say? I think that a man whom God has persuaded at last to cease from his wrongdoing has always had God in mind, even in the midst of his error.

The rest, however, at least the great majority and the most noble, are all very nearly of a kind: the intemperance of all is a devouring whirlpool, their life a brothel. Why should I speak of brothels? Even those I think are less wicked than the men of whom I spoke. For the prostitutes in them have not experienced the marriage bond, and so do not defile what they do not know; their shameless lives require atonement, it is true, but they are not liable to the charge of adultery. Add to this that such haunts are few, and few the prostitutes who have condemned themselves to a most unhappy life in them. Among the Aquitanians, on the other hand, what city in its richest and most elegant quarters was not practically a brothel? What rich and powerful man did not live in lustful vice? Who among them did not plunge into the pit of the most sordid associations? Who honored his wife by a faithful observance of his marriage vows? Nay, as far as passive endurance of their lust is concerned, who among them did not reduce his wife to the status of his maidservants and degrade the sacrament of holy matrimony so far that no woman in the house was made to seem more contemp-

---

[6] See Paulinus of Nola *Ep.* 33. 3. The passage was identified by C. Weyman, "Salvianus und Paulinus von Nola," *Historisches Jahrbuch* XV (1894), 372-373. This is the only case in which Salvian gives a clue to the personal identity of the rare exceptions he makes to the general vice of prominent men; he could scarcely have chosen a more appropriate one.

tible by her husband's conduct than she who was made chief in it by the dignity of marriage?

4. Perhaps some one is thinking that what I say is not strictly accurate; for the matrons of southern Gaul did continue to exercise their rights and to hold honor and power as mistresses of their households. That is true. Many of them indeed did keep unimpaired their right of government, but scarcely one kept her marriage rights unpolluted. Our present object of investigation is not the power of women, but the infamous conduct of their husbands. However, I should not even say that the matrons kept their power uninjured, since a wife who has not kept her connubial rights safe and inviolate has not kept her full rights of domination. When the master of the house acts as husband of the maidservants, the mistress is not far removed from the mean position of the slave. Who among the rich men of Aquitania did not so act? Who among them has not been considered by his shameless maids, and with good reason, as either adulterer or husband? For, as the prophet said: "They were as fed horses in the morning; everyone neighed after his neighbor's wife."[7] Those of whom he spoke sinned perhaps less grievously, and, I think, with less intention of wrong than did our men. The Aquitanians more truly resembled the post horses: they whinnied not after a few women merely, but after all their household maids — that is, after their own herds — and, like those beasts called the stallions of the herd, they waxed wanton with the heat of their intoxicating passion, and attacked whatever woman was first exposed to the onslaught of their shameless lust. Since this is the case, I ask the wise what sort of families they think were found where such men were heads of the households? What corruption do they think there would be among the slaves, where there was such great vice among the masters? For if the head is diseased no part of the body is sound, and no member performs its functions when the dominating part is not functioning. Moreover,

---

[7] Jeremiah 5. 8.

the master's relation to his house is that of the head to the body, its very life, setting up standards of living for all its members. The most unfortunate aspect of the matter is that all follow the worse example more readily, and evil associations corrupt good manners more easily than good ones will correct the evil. Furthermore, since even good and honorable heads of families cannot make their slaves good, what do you think becomes of the household morality when the master himself sets an example of lewdness? And yet in such a case we have not only an example of immorality but a sort of enforced necessity, since the slave women are compelled to obey their wanton masters against their will, and the lust of those in power is the compulsion of their subjects. From this we may see how great was the filth of shameless vice when women subject to the most depraved of masters were not allowed to be chaste even when they wished.

5. It may be difficult, you think, to prove this, and no traces are likely to be found remaining of the past debauchery and lust. See, then, how many of these men, even though they no longer have any country, and are living as paupers in comparison with their past wealth, are really worse than before. They are worse not only in that they continue to live as they did formerly, but in the very fact that their crimes never cease. Indeed their evil deeds, though not worse than before in character, are more numerous; thus, even though no new devices lend novelty to their sins, the number of their misdoings is increased.

Add to this that, as I have said, it is old men, and poor ones, who live in such a fashion; for each of these points increases the evil. Surely it is less shocking for young men and rich to sin. But what hope of cure is there for men who are not recalled from their wonted vice either by miserable poverty or by extreme age? Some of them, I suppose, are relying on a foolish assurance of long life or the intention of eventual penitence; is it not a strange prodigy that men should be given over to vice even at the very time of

death? This being the case, what more can be said? I add one
more point, however, that many are living in this fashion today,
even among the enemy, and subject as captives to daily fear and
danger, and although it was on account of the excessive wickedness
of their lives that God surrendered them into the hands of the
enemy, they do not forsake their vice even among the barbarians.

6. Perhaps those among whom they now live are of such a character that these vices please them, and they would be most grievously offended if they were to see the Romans living chastely in
the midst of their vices. If this were the case, still the wickedness
of others ought not to make us wicked. It should be of more importance in every man's eyes to be good on his own account than
to be wicked for another. We should strive to please God by our
uprightness rather than men by our vices. Consequently, even if a
man lives among unchaste barbarians, he ought to seek chastity,
which is of service to him, rather than lewdness, which pleases his
lustful enemies. But note a point that serves to increase our guilt:
among chaste barbarians we ourselves are unchaste.[8] I shall say
even more; the barbarians themselves are offended by our vices.
Among the Goths no one is permitted to indulge in fornication;
only the Romans in their land, by national and titular prerogative,
are allowed this vice. What hope, I ask, have we then in the sight
of God? We love vice, while the Goths execrate it; we flee from
purity, while they love it; fornication with them is a perilous vice,
but with us a mark of honor. Do we think that we can stand before God, do we think that we can attain salvation, when every
crime of impurity, every disgraceful vice, is committed by the Romans and censured by the barbarians? At this point I ask those
who consider us better than the barbarians to tell me which of these
evils are committed by even a very few of the Goths, and which of
them are not committed by all or nearly all of the Romans? Yet

---

[8] The chastity of the Germans had long been a Roman tradition; cf. Tacitus
Germania 19.

we wonder that the lands of the Aquitanians and of us all have
been given by God to the barbarians, though those same barbarians
are now purifying by their chastity the places polluted by the fornication of the Romans.

7. Is this the case in Aquitania alone? Let us pass under review other parts of the world also, and not speak exclusively of the
Gauls. Have not the same crimes or greater ones destroyed the
provinces of Spain? Even if the divine wrath had handed these
lands over to any other barbarians you might name, the enemies of
chastity in them would have suffered tortures worthy of their vices.
But as an added evidence of the condemnation of their shameless-
ness they were delivered into the hands of the Vandals, the most
shamefast of barbarians. In the captivity of Spain God wished
to give a twofold evidence of his hatred of carnal lust and love of
chastity, when he put the Vandals in command solely on account
of their preëminent chastity and subjected the Spaniards to them
solely on account of their surpassing lewdness. What do I mean by
this? Were there not anywhere in the world stronger barbarians
to whom the Spanish lands might be surrendered? Many, without
doubt, nay, all of them were stronger, if I am not mistaken.[9] But
he handed the people of Spain over to the weakest of the enemy
expressly to show that it was not the strength but the merit of the
Vandals that conquered, and that we were not being overwhelmed
by the power of our foes, who then seemed most unheroic, but only
by the wickedness of our vices, that the saying of the Lord to the
Jews might be fulfilled in us: "According to their uncleanness
and according to their transgressions have I done unto them, and
hid my face from them." [10] Elsewhere speaking to the same people,
he said: "The Lord shall bring a nation against them from far . . .

---

[9] It was not until Gaiseric's capture and sack of Carthage and later of
Rome that the Vandals took on in the eyes of the Romans the character that
has since made their name proverbial.

[10] Ezekiel 39. 24.

with the hoofs of his horses shall they tread down all thy streets; they shall slay thy people by the sword.'' [11]

So all that the Lord said has been fulfilled in us, and our punishment has vindicated the force of his divine words.

8. Since the majority of barbarian nations have drunk Roman blood and torn our flesh, we may ask why it is especially into the power of those once considered the most cowardly of the enemy that the Lord has delivered the greatest resources of the state and the wealthiest people who bear the Roman name. Why else indeed, except to make us recognize, as I said before, that the outcome depended on merit, not on strength, and that this should serve to confound and punish us, that we were given into the power of the weakest, and must recognize the correction of God's hand in the fact that not the bravest but the most despised of our enemies overcame us. For we read that whenever God has willed that men should clearly see his great works, the action has been performed through the medium of a few men, of men of the lowest sort, so that his divine handiwork might not be ascribed to human power.

Thus indeed Sisera, the captain before whom the Hebrew army trembled, was laid low by a woman; [12] a woman's hand struck down Abimelech, the stormer of cities, [13] and the ironclad hosts of the Assyrians were routed by the help of a widow. Not to speak of women only, did not the Lord wish Benedad, king of Syria, whom thirty-two kings and armies of like proportions served, as well as countless thousands of his own people, to be conquered by a few serving-men, so that God himself might be recognized as the author of so great a victory? [14] Against the Midianites also, who, as the Book of Judges relates, had filled all the land like locusts, Gideon was ordered to fight with a few men, not because he had not more in his army, but he was forbidden to lead many men to battle for

---

[11] Deuteronomy 28. 49; Ezekiel 26. 11.
[12] Judges 4.
[13] *Ibid.* 9. 53.
[14] I Kings 20.

fear that a multitude might claim some share in the victory as their own. When Gideon had gathered together thirty thousand armed men, the Lord spoke thus to him: "The people that are with thee are too many for me to give Midian into their hands." [15] What followed? He left Gideon, to fight against countless thousands of barbarians, only three hundred men. Indeed, he commanded the force of soldiers to be reduced to such a scanty number in order that their lack of men might prevent any claim of credit for a victory divinely won. Why he did this, the Lord himself declared most plainly: "Lest Israel vaunt themselves against me, saying: 'Mine own hand hath saved me.' "

Let all the wicked hearken, I say, let all the presumptuous hearken, and all who excel in power; let all men hear what the Lord says: "Lest Israel vaunt themselves against me, saying, 'Mine own hand hath saved me.' "

9. Let all men hear, I repeat, who utter blasphemies against the Lord, let all hear who put their trust in man. God declares that all men speak against him who presume to think that they can be freed by their own might. Who is there among the Romans who does not hold this opinion? Who is there in our number who does not blaspheme in this respect almost constantly? It is common knowledge that the state has no longer any strength, yet not even now do we acknowledge to whose favor we owe it that we still live. Whenever God gives us a degree of prosperity beyond our hopes and deserts, one man ascribes it to fate, another to chance, another to the strategy of our leaders, another to their foresight, another to the administration, another to his patron, but none to God.

Yet we wonder that his divine hand fails to give us some things for which we wish, though we deny him credit for what he has given in the past. What else are we doing, when we ascribe the good things he gives us to the blind workings of chance, the ability of our leaders, or any other minor agencies? Following such argu-

---

[15] Judges 7. 2.

ments we ought to thank the earth for our yearly harvests, the vineyards for the vintage, the sea for hauls of fish, the forests for the wood we cut, the sheep for our clothing, and other beasts for the meat with which we are filled. What sense is there in our willingness to be grateful to God for his other gifts when we deny him gratitude for his greatest benefits? What man of our condition would be satisfied to have another thank him for some minor favor if he had denied him credit for his greatest gifts? So though we cannot thank God worthily, we shall fall far short of what is due him if we are grateful to him only for the means of daily life, and withhold from him our gratitude for helping us in time of trouble, freeing us in the midst of dangers and preserving us by his constant protection when we are placed in the midst of barbarous nations.

Not so do the Goths or the Vandals regard him, being better in this respect than ourselves, though trained by heretical teachers. However, I have grounds to suspect that certain men are offended by what I say. Since the truth must outweigh the fear of giving offence I shall say it nevertheless, and say it repeatedly: not so do the Goths or the Vandals act, for when they are in danger they beg help of God and they call their prosperity the gift of his divine love. In fact our misfortune in the last war furnished proof of this difference between us. For the Goths through fear put their hope in God, and we through presumption put ours in the Huns. The Goths sought peace and we denied it; they sent bishops to make terms and we rejected them; they honored God even in the person of alien priests and we despised him in our own. Was not the outcome of these events consonant with the actions of each side? To them in the depths of fear was given the palm of victory; to us in the height of confidence was given confusion, so that the words of our Lord were clearly exemplified in us and in them: ''For whosoever exalteth himself shall be abased, and he that

humbleth himself shall be exalted.''[16] To them was given exalta-
tion for their humility and to us humiliation for our pride.

10. This the general of our forces learned when he entered as a
captive the same city of the enemy that he had boasted he would
enter that same day as victor.[17] He proved indeed the words of the
prophet: ''For a man's way is not his own, nor is it in his own
power to walk and direct his steps.''[18] Since he thought his actions were under his own control, he could neither direct his steps
nor find the way of safety. So we read: ''He poureth contempt
upon the prince and causeth him to wander in the wilderness where
there is no way. . . . He has been brought to nothing, even as the
waters which run continually.''[19] In him, indeed, in addition to his
actual misfortune, the present judgment of God was clearly shown.
He has endured all the sufferings that he had boasted he would
inflict on others. Because he trusted that the enemy could be
taken without God's aid and consent, he has himself been captured; he claimed foreknowledge and wisdom and has met with
disgrace for his presumption; he himself has worn the chains he
prepared for others.

What clearer proof, I ask, could there have been of the judgment of God, than that the general who boasted of plundering
should be counted as booty; that he who counted his triumph already won should be led in another's triumph — be surrounded,
seized, and bound, his arms twisted behind his back; that he should
see those hands tied whose prowess he vaunted; that he should become a spectacle for women and children, see barbarians making
sport of him, endure the derision of both sexes, and though he had

---

[16] Luke 14. 11.

[17] Litorius had been put in command in Gaul by Aëtius. Made overconfident
by his success at Narbonne, he undertook in A.D. 439 to besiege Toulouse, then
the Gothic capital, with the aid of Hunnish auxiliaries, but was defeated and
captured.

[18] See Proverbs 16. 9; 20. 24.

[19] Psalms 107. 40; 58. 7.

the greatest pride in his bravery, meet a coward's death? Would that this might have been a speedy cure for his wrongdoing, without longer suffering! But, as befits the greatness of his punishment, wasted by the days of his captivity and by the prolonged anguish of a barbarian prison,[20] he was reduced to such misery that he roused the pity of the enemy, and this most men think harder and more bitter to bear than the imprisonment itself. Why did these things happen? Surely because, as I have already indicated, the enemy were humble before God, whereas we were rebellious; they believed the victory lay in his hand, we that it lay in our own — a sacrilegious and wicked conception that makes our sin so much the worse and more injurious to us. Lastly, we learn from an authentic report that the king of the enemy [21] himself lay on haircloth and prayed up to the very day of the conflict; when battle was imminent he lay in prayer, and rose only to fight. Before he assumed command in the battle he fought in prayer, and so went forth to the fight with confidence in a victory already earned by his prayers.

11. Moreover, the experience of the Vandals was not dissimilar: when our people went against them in Spain and had as much confidence in a complete victory as they had recently against the Goths, the same overweening pride engulfed them in the same disastrous ruin.[22] Then the words of the prophet were fulfilled for our army: "The Lord shall reject thy confidence and thou shalt not prosper in it." [23]

For we trusted in our own wisdom and strength against the

---

[20] Idatius (*Chronicon* A.D. 439) gives a different version: "He himself was wounded and captured, and after a few days was put to death." His notorious paganism and dependence on soothsayers made Litorius a particularly apt contrast to the piety of the barbarian king.

[21] Theodoric I, king of the Visigoths.

[22] In A.D. 432 when Boniface and Castinus were conducting the war in Spain against the Vandals with an army largely Gothic, the jealousy of the two leaders led to a disastrous defeat of the Romans in battle, when the Vandals had been almost at the point of surrender due to famine. The defeat ended the Roman rule in Spain.

[23] Jeremiah 2. 37.

command of the Lord, who said: "Let not the wise man glory in his wisdom, neither the mighty man in his might, but let him that glorieth glory in this, that he understandeth and knoweth me, that I am the Lord." [24]

So we have not been conquered undeservedly, for the enemy sought better aid than we did. While we prided ourselves on arms and auxiliaries, on the side of the enemy the Book of the Divine Law opposed us. To its help most of all the fear and terror of the Vandals then resorted, to oppose to us the Divine Word and to open up to those who came against them in rivalry the writings of the Sacred Book which may be called the very voice of God. At this point I ask: who of our number ever did this, or who would not have been derided if he had thought it should be done? He would have been scorned indeed, as almost all religious acts are derided among us. Then what value can our claim to a religious title have for us, what use is it to say we are catholic, to boast that we possess the true faith, to despise the Goths and Vandals, reviling them as heretics, when we are living in a truly heretical depravity? The words of the Divine Scripture addressed to the Jews who trusted in the law are most fittingly applied to us: "How do you say, 'We are wise and the law of the Lord is with us?' . . . Trust ye not in lying words, saying, 'The temple of the Lord, the temple of the Lord, the temple of the Lord, are these.' For if ye thoroughly amend your ways and your doings; if ye oppress not the stranger and the fatherless and the widow and shed not innocent blood in this place, then will I cause you to dwell in this place, in the land that I gave to your fathers for ever and ever." [25] By this surely it is shown that if we do not amend our ways, it is useless for us to vaunt our claims to catholicism.

Enough of this has been said already, and more must perhaps be said later, though there seems little need to discuss the point fur-

---

[24] Jeremiah 9. 23-24.
[25] *Ibid.* 8. 8; 7. 4-7.

ther, since the judgment of God is constantly manifested. Recent history shows his verdict both upon us and upon the Goths and Vandals; they increase daily while we diminish; they gain in power while we are humbled; they flourish and we wither away. So the words of the Holy Scriptures concerning Saul and David may be truly spoken of us also: "David waxed stronger and stronger, and the house of Saul waxed weaker and weaker." [26] For the Lord is righteous, as the prophet says: "He is righteous and his judgments are upright." [27]

12. We are judged by the ever-present judgment of God, and thus a most slothful race has been aroused to accomplish our destruction and shame. They go from place to place, from city to city, and destroy everything. First they poured out from their native land into Germany, which lay nearest them, a country called barbarous, but under Roman control. After its destruction, the country of the Belgae burst into flames, then the rich estates of the luxurious Aquitanians, and after these the whole body of the Gallic provinces. This ruin spread gradually, however, in order that while one part was being visited with destruction, another might be reformed by its example.[28] But when has there been any amendment among us, or what part of the Roman world, whatever its affliction, is corrected by it? As we read: "They are all gone out of the way, they are altogether become useless." [29] And in like manner the prophet cried out to the Lord, saying: "Thou hast stricken them but they have not grieved; thou hast consumed them, but they have refused to receive correction; they have made their faces harder than a rock; they have refused to return." [30]

---

[26] II Samuel 3. 1.

[27] Psalms 119. 137.

[28] The *Germany* of this account was, of course, the Roman military district along the Rhine. The pauses in the course of the invasion are naturally explained by the custom of the Germanic tribes of "following up with the plow their conquests by the sword."

[29] Psalms 14. 3; 53. 3.

[30] Jeremiah 5. 3.

How truly this applies to us the present situation shows. Gaul long endured devastation; did Spain, her near neighbor, mend her ways? Not undeservedly, since they showed no fear whatever, and no reform, the people of Spain began to catch fire from the flames by which the Gauls were consumed.[31] The worst and most evil aspect of all this is, as I have said before, that the fires which, to speak figuratively, consumed the bodies of these sinful men, did not burn away their vices.

Thus God has been compelled by our crimes to scatter the enemy's forces as a scourge for our sins, from place to place, from city to city, and to send nations aroused almost from the very ends of the earth even across the sea, to punish the crimes of our people in Africa. Why was this? Having been led forth from their own country, could the Vandals not have remained within the Gallic states? Could fear have prevented these tribes from abiding there, who had already devastated all the land without injury from us? But suppose they had cause for alarm in Gaul, why should they have feared to settle and stay in Spain, where they had completely crushed our armies in battle, where they were already triumphantly victorious, having reached such a height of valor as to learn that after trial in a war long anticipated, the strength of the Roman state, even with barbarian reënforcements, could not equal theirs?

13. They could have stayed there, then, and were not afraid, but surely the heavenly hand that had dragged them thither to punish the vices of the Spanish compelled them also to cross the straits to devastate Africa. In fact, they themselves confessed that they did not act of their own volition, for they were driven and urged on by a divine command. From this we may learn how great are our misdoings, since to destroy and punish us the barbarians are compelled

---

[31] Orosius' account of the Vandal conquest of Spain furnishes a parallel for Salvian's estimate of the barbarians (*Historia adv. paganos* VII. 40. 10): "After grave destruction of property and men, of which they themselves now repent, they drew lots and distributed the land and still live in possession of it."

to move against their will, following the words of the devastator of
the land of Israel, the king of the Assyrians, when he said: "And
now without the will of the Lord am I come up against this land?
The Lord said unto me, 'Go up against this land, to destroy it.' " [32]
And elsewhere the Sacred Word says: "Therefore thus saith the
Lord of Hosts, the God of Israel: 'Behold, I will send and take
Nabuchodonosor [33] the king of Babylon, my servant, and when he
cometh, he shall smite the land of Egypt.' " [34]

From this we may know that all things which are afflicted are
indeed smitten by the judgment of God; their overthrow, however,
as I have often remarked, is due to sin. So whatever is done on
account of sin is not to be ascribed to God, since a deed is rightly
ascribed to that cause which has made it unavoidable. For example,
a murderer sentenced to death by the judge is actually punished by
his own crime; a thief or a man who has committed sacrilege is
consumed not by the flames that burn his body, but by his own
sin. Whence we see that the Vandals did not cross to Africa because of God's severity but because of the sins of the Romans in
that country. By their grave and long continued iniquity these
people were forcing the Vandals to come before they actually left
their native land. Therefore we must understand that only God's
mercy postponed the punishment so long due, and their misdeeds
and crimes at length brought upon these sinful people the chastisement they deserved. Or are we to believe that they did not deserve
their fate? Have any people better deserved ruin than these, in
whom all sorts of shameful and indecent lust have flourished at
once? For the rest of the world, though bound by some disgraceful
vices, has some virtue still remaining: men who are subject to
drunkenness are free from malevolence; those who live in a fever
of lust do not suffer from raging greed; finally, many who are

---

[32] Isaiah 36. 10.
[33] That is, Nebuchadnezzar.
[34] Jeremiah 25. 8-9; 43. 11.

accused of physical incontinence are commended by the simplicity of their minds. But among the people of Africa, with few exceptions, you will find none with an equal measure of good and evil, for almost the whole population is evil. So the purity of their original nature has been shut out and their vices have, as it were, created a new character among them.

14. Indeed, aside from a very few servants of God, what was the whole territory of Africa but one house of vice, like that bronze vessel of which the prophet said: "Woe to the bloody city! to the bronze vessel whose scum is therein, and whose scum hath not gone out from it, because the blood shall not go out from it!"[35] He compared the city, as we see, to a bronze vessel and its iniquity to blood, that we might know that the iniquity of the people in a city is like blood seething in a brazen pot. And again, not unlike this is another saying of the Sacred Word: "The houses of Israel have all been made a mixture before me of brass and iron and tin and lead, in the midst is silver mixed with the mass. Therefore say this; thus saith the Lord God: 'Inasmuch as ye are all made one mass I shall blow upon you and melt you in the fires of my wrath.'"[36]

How are the very dissimilar metals that the Scriptures have named melted together in one furnace? Surely in the diversity of metals the unlike qualities of men are figured. Thus even silver, that is, metal of the nobler sort, is cast in the same fires as the rest because men have debased the gifts of their nobler natures by their degenerate lives. Even so we read that the Lord spoke also of the king of Tyre through his prophet: "Son of man, take up a lamentation upon the king of Tyrus, and say unto him, 'Thus saith the Lord God: thou hast been the seal of likeness, and a crown of beauty in the delights of paradise; every precious stone was thy covering, the sardius and topaz and emerald.'"[37] Again he says:

---

[35] Ezekiel 24. 6.
[36] Ibid. 22. 18-20.
[37] Ibid. 28. 12-13.

"With silver and with gold hast thou filled thy treasuries, from the multitude of commerce hast thou filled thy storehouses." [38] Do not all these things seem to have been said expressly of the people of Africa? Where are greater treasuries, where is greater commerce, where are fuller storehouses? "With gold," he says, "hast thou filled thy treasuries from the multitude of thy commerce." I add more: Africa was once so rich that the abundance of her commerce seems to have filled not only her own treasuries but those of the whole world as well.

What did the prophet say next? "Thine heart was lifted up because of thy beauty, because of the multitude of thine iniquities have I cast thee to the ground." [39] How does this apply to the power of Africa, and how does that land seem to have been laid prostrate on the ground? How except that when she lost the height of her former power, she also lost her almost celestial honor? "And I shall bring forth," said the prophet, "a fire from the midst of thee, it shall devour thee." [40] What could be truer than this? The fire of sin went forth from the midst of their iniquity, and devoured the happiness of former times. "And all they that know thee among the people shall be sore afflicted over thee." [41] We might think that this phrase did not apply to them, were it not that the destruction of Africa is the sorrow of the human race. "Thou art become destruction," said the prophet, "and never shalt thou be any more." [42] It is only too well known that everything in that province has been completely destroyed; all that we can do is to prevent those evils which are now being punished from being continued forever.

15. May God in his merciful kindness not permit this! Indeed, as far as the deserts of our crimes are concerned, there is no reason

[38] *Ibid.* 28. 4-5.
[39] *Ibid.* 28. 17.
[40] *Ibid.* 28. 18.
[41] *Ibid.* 28. 19.
[42] *Ibid.* 28. 19.

why he should not. What misdeeds are not constantly committed there? I shall not speak of them all, for their enormity is such that they cannot be known or discussed. I shall talk chiefly of the obscene nature of their indecencies, and, which is more serious still, of their acts of sacrilege. I pass over their insane greed, a vice shared by the whole human race; I pass over their inhuman avarice, an evil characteristic of most of the Romans; let their drunkenness be left unmentioned, since it is common to noble and base alike; let swelling pride be omitted, for this is so particularly the province of the rich, that they would perhaps think they were losing something of their just due if anyone else wished to claim any share in it. Finally, let almost all the wickedness involving frauds, forgeries and perjuries be passed over, for no Roman city was ever free from these evils. Yet this crime was the especial prerogative of all the people of Africa. For just as the filth of a boat is washed down into the bilge water in its depths, so vices seem to have flowed into their habits from the whole world. I know of no wickedness that did not abound there, whereas even pagan and barbarous nations, though they have evil ways especially characteristic of their own races, still do not merit reproach in all things. The race of the Goths is treacherous but chaste, the Alans unchaste but not treacherous; the Franks are deceitful but hospitable, the Saxons savage in their cruelty but admirable for their chastity; to conclude, all races have their own peculiar vices accompanied by their own good qualities. But among the people of Africa practically without exception there is nothing but evil. If inhumanity is the subject of our accusation they are inhuman; if drunkenness, they are drunken; if falsehood, they are most false; if deceit, they are unexcelled in deceitfulness; if greed, they are surpassingly greedy; if perfidy, theirs is unequalled. Their impurity and blasphemy must not be confused with these other sins, since in the evils of which I have spoken above they have surpassed the vices of other nations, but in these they have outdone their own.

16. To speak first of their impurity — who does not know that all Africa has always flamed with the torches of obscenity, so that you would think it not a land and abiding place of men, but an Aetna of unclean fires? As Aetna has always seethed with certain inner flames of heat implanted in it by nature, so also has Africa with the abominable fires of fornication. I do not wish you to believe my words alone in this matter, but to seek the corroboration of the whole human race. Who can fail to recognize that all the people of Africa are unchaste unless they happen to have been converted to God, and changed by their religious faith? This however is as rare and strange as to see a Gaius who is not a Gaius or a Seius who is not a Seius.[43] It is as unusual and rare for an African not to be unchaste as for him not to be an African.

So general is the vice of impurity among them that whoever ceases to be indecent seems to be no longer an African. I shall not discuss the individual cities nor mention all the different localities, for fear of seeming to search out examples too curiously. I shall content myself with one city instead, the chief of all the cities of that land, and in a way the mother of them all, the eternal rival of Rome's citadel, of old in arms and courage, afterwards in splendor and dignity. It is Carthage of which I speak, the greatest rival of the city of Rome, and a sort of Rome in the African world; she alone suffices as an example and witness of my words, since she has contained within herself all the resources and governance of statecraft in the world.

There you would find all the appurtenances of the public offices, schools of the liberal arts, the studies of the philosophers, training schools in languages and ethics; there also were military forces and the powers that control the army, there was the office of the pro-

---

[43] Gaius and Seius appear frequently as the John Doe and Richard Roe of Latin authors. Gaius is most commonly used, perhaps because of the *Ubi tu Gaius, ego Gaia,* of the marriage ceremony. In Cod. Just. Titius is used instead of Seius. Tertullian uses Gaius Seius and Lucius Titius; cf. *Ad nationes* I. 4.

consul, there the daily judge and ruler of the province — in name, indeed, proconsul, but in power a very consul; there lastly were the administrators of the state properties, their honors differing from one another in rank and name — procurators, as I may call them, of the public streets and crossroads — governing all the wards of the city and all sections of the people. With this one city we may well be content as an example of the others, and as evidence of their condition, so that having seen the character of the city where the officials have always been of the highest grade, we may infer what those towns were like that had the supervision of less honored men.

At this point I almost repent of my promise made above, to omit almost all the vices of the people of this province and to speak chiefly of their obscenities and blasphemies. For I see the city overflowing with vice, boiling over with every sort of iniquity — full indeed of people, but even fuller of dishonor, full of riches but fuller still of vice; men striving to outdo one another in depravity and lust, some vying with their mates in rapacity, others in indecency. Some are languid with wine, others distended with feasting, some garlanded with flowers, others smeared with unguents, all wasted by various forms of dissipation, but sunk in the same mortal error. Not all, indeed, were intoxicated with winebibbing, but all were drunk with their sins.

You would judge such a people lacking in sanity, not in full possession of their senses, steady neither in mind nor in gait, attacking each other in a mob like drunken men. Now we must consider also another charge of a serious kind, unlike this in its nature but not unlike it in gravity, unless its greatness sets it in a different class. I mean the proscriptions of orphans, the afflictions of widows and the crucifixion of the poor. All these made their moan daily to God, and prayed for an end of their sufferings. Nay, what is worse, they were sometimes driven by their bitter woes even to pray for the arrival of the enemy. These have now at last obtained from

God the privilege of enduring with the rest such ruin from the barbarians as they formerly suffered alone from the Romans!

17. But let us pass over these matters, for they may be paralleled in practically every part of the Roman world, and I promised to mention them only briefly. As to the unchastity and impurity which I have been discussing, would these not have been sufficient of themselves to destroy Africa? What part of the state was not full of indecency, what street or bypath was not a place of shame? Lust had so cut off most of the crossroads and streets with its snares, and entangled them with its nets, that even those who utterly abhorred such vices could scarcely avoid them. You might compare them to brigands lurking in ambush and snatching their spoils from passers-by; they so hedged in the paths, the winding roads and byways with their close-set traps, that scarcely anyone could be cautious enough not to fall into some of their treacherous snares, however many he escaped. All the citizens reeked, if I may use the expression, with the stench of lust, all inhaled the fetid odors of their mutual impurity. Yet this horrid condition inspired no loathing in them, for the same plague had infected them all. You would think the city a sinkpot of lust and fornication, like the muck collected from the offscourings of all the streets and sewers. What hope could there be in such a place, where, except for the temple of the Lord, there was nothing to be seen but filth?

Yet why should I except the temple of God? The church was, to be sure, completely under the care of the priests and clergy, whom I prefer not to discuss. I am bound by reverence for my Lord's ministry, and think that those men who served at the altars alone preserved their purity, as we read that Lot stood alone on the mountain when the people of Sodom perished. As for the people, however, who among such countless numbers was chaste? Chaste, did I say? Who was not guilty of fornication, or adultery, and that too without ceasing? Therefore must I cry out again — what hope could there be in that people? One adulterer sometimes pollutes a whole church congregation, but there you could scarcely find one chaste man among thousands, if you searched most diligently, even in the church.

I have much more than this to say. Would that what I have said included the whole accusation, and that these men in their indecency had been content to satisfy their lust with fornication of fallen women only! Their fault was still more serious and wicked than this, for nearly all the vices of which the blessed apostle Paul complained so bitterly existed in Africa. "The men leaving the natural use of women burned in their lust toward one another; men with men working that which is unseemly, and receiving in themselves that recompense of their error which was meet. And even as they did not like to retain God in their knowledge, God gave them over to a reprobate mind, to do those things which are not convenient."[44] Was it not of barbarous and savage races that the blessed apostle spoke? Nay verily, but of us, that is, expressly of the Romans, whom indeed the people of Africa, since they were not able of old to overcome them in power and might, have now outdone in the only way left to them, to wit, in lust. Whoever thinks he has a right to be angry at my words should rather be incensed at the apostle, for what I have said of the character of the inhabitants of Africa, he once said of their masters, the Romans.

18. Perhaps the vices of which I spoke were hidden, or the men in charge of the public morals in different places took care that the diffusion of such crimes should not sully the eyes of the people. If this had been done, however many had been defiled by the actions themselves, all would not have been injured by the sight and thought of them. However disgraceful a vice is, it does not as a rule deserve full credence when it is committed secretly. But to commit the greatest sins and feel no shame for what one has done, demands censure passing that of the sins themselves. What more prodigious wrong could have been performed there? In a Chris-

---

[44] Romans 1. 27-28.

tian city, in a church which the apostles founded by their teachings,[45] which martyrs had crowned by their passion, men took upon
themselves the functions of women, without any shame to cloak
their action, without the shield of modesty; as if their sin would be
too slight if only the authors of these evils were stained by them,
through the public knowledge of their vice it became the wrongdoing of the whole city. The entire city saw this and suffered it,
the judges saw and condoned it, the people saw and applauded,
and thus when fellowship in disgraceful lust was spread through
the city, the general consent made it common to all. But, you say,
perhaps there was at length an end to the evil and some emendation of the wrong. Who could believe or even hear calmly that men
converted to a feminine passivity not only their natural functions
but even their looks, their step, their clothing and everything characteristic of the male sex and appearance? So completely was nature reversed in them that although nothing should be more shameful to men than to seem to have any feminine characteristics,[46]
nothing seemed to certain of these men more disgraceful than to
seem in any respect masculine.

19. You may argue that this disgrace was that of a few men
only, and what was not perpetrated by the majority could not injure all. Indeed, I have said before that very often among the
people of God the crime even of one man has been the ruin of
many, as the people were betrayed by the theft of Achar, a pestilence arose from the jealousy of Saul, and a plague came from the
numbering of the people by the blessed David. For the church of
God is like an eye. If even a little mote fall into the eye, it blinds
the whole sight; so, if even a few men in the body of the church

---

[45] Tertullian, himself a native of Africa, does not include Carthage in the
list of apostolic churches (*Liber de praescriptionibus* 32), but in Salvian's
time the orthodox church of Africa claimed an apostolic origin in their con-
troversy with the Donatists, and it was natural that Salvian should accept their
claim.

[46] See Tertullian *De idololatria* 16: "Finally I find no type of clothing
censured by God, save the feminine when worn by a man."

act indecently, it darkens the whole light of the church. Therefore the Savior called the chief part of the church its eye, saying: "The light of the body is the eye: if therefore thine eye be single, thy whole body shall be full of light. But if thine eye be evil, thy whole body shall be full of darkness." [47] Whence the apostle asked: "Know ye not that a little leaven leaveneth the whole lump?" [48] I should not say, however, that there was in Africa a little of this evil, but overmuch, not that most of the people there were effeminate, but that the effeminacy of the few was the corruption of the many. Even if there are few who live disgracefully there are many who are stained by the filth of the few. As one harlot makes many commit fornication, so the abominable unions of the effeminate few infect the vast majority of the people.

Nor do I know which of them are worse in the sight of God, since in the Sacred Scriptures they are condemned by one and the same decree. "Neither effeminate, nor abusers of themselves with mankind, shall inherit the kingdom of God," [49] said the apostle. This makes it the more lamentable and deplorable that such a sin should appear to be the wrongdoing of the whole city, and that the honor of the Roman name should be branded with the infamy of prodigious wickedness. Men took the garb of women and made their steps more mincing than women do; they wrought for themselves the tokens of a monstrous impurity and swathed their heads with the wrappings of feminine veils. And this they did publicly in a Roman city, the greatest and most famous city in that region! Was this not a disgrace to the Roman power, which permitted a most execrable wrong to be openly committed in the very bosom of the commonwealth? A great and strong power, capable of preventing the greatest crime, must approve the actions which with full knowledge it suffers to be committed, for he who has prohibitory power sanctions any action that he does not prevent.

---

47 Matthew 6. 22-23.
48 I Corinthians 5. 6.
49 *Ibid.* 6. 9-10.

20. Once again, impelled by my grief, I ask those who are angry at my words in what barbarian nations such things have at any time been done or permitted with general impunity? Finally, to save the necessity of longer discussion or investigation of this point, let us compare the actual devastators of Africa with the people whom they conquered. What actions of this sort have been performed by the Vandals? Surely barbarians, swollen with pride, puffed up with victory, rendered lax by the abundance of riches and luxuries, would have been changed by their unusual good fortune and prosperity, however chaste and continent they had always been before. They had, as it is written in the Scriptures, entered "a land flowing with milk and honey," [50] a fertile land, so rich in all delicacies as to be almost intoxicating in its plenty. Under these conditions it would be no cause for surprise that a barbarous tribe should wax wanton where nature herself seems unrestrained. Who would doubt that the Vandals, upon entering such a country, would plunge into all manner of filthy and unclean vice? Or, to speak more moderately, that they would at least copy the constant behavior of the people of Africa, into whose province they had come? Indeed, if that were all they did, they would deserve to be judged most continent and moderate, whom good fortune had not rendered more corrupt. For how often do you find a wise man whom prosperity does not change, whose faults do not increase with his fortunes? It is certain that the Vandals were most temperate, if they, the victors, merely resembled their captive subjects.

In such great abundance of wealth and luxury, however, not one of them was rendered effeminate. Does that seem a small matter? Certainly the Romans of noble birth made effeminacy a regular practice. What more have I to add? Not one of the Vandals was polluted by the incest of the effeminate Romans about him. Certainly, effeminacy had long been considered by the Romans as a virtue rather than a vice, and those men thought themselves models

---

[50] Exodus 13. 5.

of manly strength who had put others to the basest uses. For this reason the attendant boys, who once followed the soldiers, were given as a reward for services well performed on campaign, the privilege of being shamefully used as women, since they had proved themselves brave men. What a crime was this! Such were the actions of Romans, and Romans not of the present time; nevertheless — not to accuse the men of old — they were not the ancient Romans, but those who had already become corrupt and dissolute, no longer living up to their former reputation, but resembling Greeks more than Romans. Hence, as I have often said before, it should cause no surprise that the Roman state is at length suffering what it has long deserved.

21. This vice began among the Romans before Christ's Gospel, but that it did not cease after the Gospel was preached among them is still more grievous. After recalling this fact, who can help admiring the Vandals? They entered the wealthiest cities, where such vices were common, and took over the riches of dissolute men in such a way that they rejected their corrupting customs and now possess and use those things that are good, and avoid the degrading influence of those that are evil.[51] This ought to be enough in their praise even if I add nothing more; for they have abominated the illicit acts of men. Still more noteworthy is it that they have also abstained from the corruption of women; they have shrunk from evil haunts and brothels, they have avoided illicit unions and the company of harlots. Can it be credible that the Romans permitted these things and barbarians abhorred them? Is there anything more to be said after this? There is indeed, and much more. That they have avoided foul actions is the lesser part; for a man can abhor disgraceful deeds without abolishing them. Their great and singular merit is that not only do they themselves avoid pollution by this

---

[51] That Salvian spoke too soon is suggested by Procopius *De Bello Vandalico* II. 6. His description of the habits of the Vandals "since the time when they gained possession of Libya" includes all the luxuries and vices that Salvian thinks they rejected.

stain, but they take care that others shall not be polluted. Indeed, a man is in some sort a guardian of human welfare who not only endeavors to be good himself, but also strives to bring it about that others may cease to be evil.

What I have said is a great point, surely, great and of pre-eminent importance. Who could believe that the Vandals in the Roman cities committed such sins? Sexual vice has been completely abolished by them. How was it removed? Not as some crimes are wont to be prohibited by the Romans, who decree that there shall be no theft, and go on thieving; who decree that there shall be no adultery, and are first to commit it. Yet I should scarcely say that they commit theft, for theirs is no mere theft but highway robbery. A judge punishes a petty theft in another though he is himself a robber: he punishes rapine, though he is himself guilty of the same crime; he punishes the cutthroat, though he himself wields a sword; he punishes those who break down bars and doors, though he him-self destroys cities; he punishes those who burglarize houses, though he himself robs the provinces. Would that this were true only of those who are set in positions of power and to whom the very honor conferred on them gives some right to carry on their robberies; it is worse and more intolerable that even private citizens do the same, that is, men who have previously held high office. The honor once given them affords them this much advantage, that they may keep forever the legal right to plunder. So even when they have ceased to wield public administrative power, they do not cease to enjoy the private right of plundering. Thus the power they had as judges is slighter than that they have as private citizens, for in the former case successors were sure to be appointed for them, but now they have no successors.

See then how much legal decrees are worth, what profit we gain from the passage of ordinances which those men most scorn who administer them! The humble and lowly are forced to obey, the poor are compelled to accede to the orders of their superiors, and if they fail in their obedience, they are punished. The same rule is observed in this case as in that of the taxes: the poor are the only ones to obey the public decrees, as they alone pay the taxes. Thus in the laws themselves and in the execution of justice, injustice is most criminally wrought, since the lesser men are compelled to observe as sacred the laws that their betters continually trample under foot as of no importance.

22. Indignation has led me to exceed somewhat the appointed order of my discourse; let me now return to the original topic. I said that the cities of Africa were full of monstrous vices, and especially the queen and mistress of them all, but that the Vandals were not polluted. How unlike the Romans did these barbarians prove themselves, in cleansing the stains of our disgrace! For they have removed from every part of Africa the vice of effeminacy, they have even abhorred intercourse with harlots, and have not only shunned or done away with it for the time being, but have made it absolutely cease to exist. O kindly Master, O good Savior! How much the desire of discipline accomplishes with your help, through which the vices of nature can be changed, as they have been by the Vandals! Let us see how they have been changed, since it is important to show not only the results of this action, but also the method by which it was made effective. It is difficult to have lewdness removed by a word or order, unless it has been done away in fact, and to have decency required by a command unless it has been enjoined before. Knowing this to be true, they removed unchastity while preserving the unchaste; they did not kill the unfortunate women, lest they should stain their prevention of vice with cruelty, and sin themselves in the very act of destroying the sins they desired to abolish. But they corrected the erring in such a way that the change should be a medicine, not a penalty. They ordered and compelled all prostitutes to marry; they transformed harlots into wives, fulfilling the word and command of the apostle that every woman should have her husband and every man his wife,[52] that

---

[52] I Corinthians 7. 2.

since incontinence cannot be restrained without some permissible indulgence of the flesh, sexual desire might have this legitimate outlet without sinful lust. In this, indeed, provision was made not only that women who could not live without husbands should have them, but also that through their domestic guardians those who did not know how to protect themselves should be safe. While the marriage bond constantly bound them, even if the customary unchastity of their former lives enticed them to sin, their husbands' guardianship should keep them from going astray. The Vandals also added severe requirements of chastity to prevent lust, coercing lewdness by the sword with the obvious purpose of preserving the chastity of both sexes by conjugal affection at home, and the fear of the laws in public. Thus purity should rest on a double basis of love at home and fear abroad. Moreover, the laws they possessed were not at all like those enactments that removed a part of the wickedness without preventing all of its obscenity, or like those Roman decrees that cut off adulterers from other men's wives but left them free access to single women, forbidding adultery while encouraging houses of ill fame.[53] These seem to have feared that men would be too chaste and pure if sexual vice were entirely forbidden. Not such are those of whom we speak, who have forbidden loose living as well as adultery, who wish women to be women only to their husbands and men to exercise their male functions only with their wives; who do not permit sexual desires to stray beyond the marriage bed, but order their laws after the pattern of the divine law, so that they think nothing permissible to them in this matter that God did not wish to permit. So they did not think any man should be given license by them to do anything that is not permitted to all by the divine power.

23. I know that what I say may seem to some intolerable, but

---

[53] Note the phrasing in Cod. Theod. IX. 7. 1 (A.D. 326): " . . . those women, the vileness of whose lives has proved them unworthy of the protection of the law."

I must treat these matters in the light of reason, not of personal prejudices.[54] Let anyone who is angry at what I say tell me this, has not Socrates always been considered the wisest of all men, and that too on the testimony of the Delphic demon, who might be called the prince of philosophers, as he was the prince of demons? Let us then consider what laws Socrates decreed as to chastity and what those men of whom we have been speaking have ordained about it.

Socrates said: "Let no man have a wife of his own, for marriage should be common to all; for so there will be greater harmony among the states, if all men have intercourse indiscriminately with all women, and all women with all men, and if all men become husbands of all women, and all women wives of all men."[55] Have we ever known any madman, or any possessed or driven out of his senses by any sort of insanity, say such a thing as this? You say, O chief of philosophers, that by the terms of this ordinance all men will be the husbands of all women, and all women the wives of all men, and all their children the offspring of all parents. But I maintain that no man would then be any woman's husband, no woman the wife of any man, and no child the offspring of any parents, for where all is promiscuous and confused, no one can claim anything as his own. And some men say that it was not sufficient for the wisest of philosophers to teach others such ideas, but he must needs carry them out for himself, handing his wife over to another man, as indeed the Roman Cato, that second Socrates of Italian birth, actually did.[56] See then the examples given us by the Roman and Attic wisdom; as far as in them lay, they made all husbands

---

[54] With this chapter compare Lactantius *Inst. div.* III. 21.

[55] The ultimate source of this passage is of course Plato *Republic* V. 457; it is not clear through what channel Salvian derived it. He does not appear to have read Greek, and the Latin of the paragraph does not suggest Cicero's *De re publica* as a direct source. It was, however, a well-known topic, and may have been the subject of rhetorical exercises in the schools.

[56] The *locus classicus* for this is Lucan *De bello civili* II. 329-333, from which Augustine (*Bon. coniug.* 21) clearly drew his example of the Younger

panders of their wives. Yet Socrates outdid the rest, for he wrote books on the subject, and handed his shameful ideas down to posterity.[57] So he had the more reason to glory in his teachings; as far as his principles were concerned, he made a brothel of the world. He is said to have been unjustly condemned by the judges. That is true, for it would have been better for the whole human race to condemn a man for preaching such doctrines. Without doubt it has condemned him. Since, indeed, as far as this theory goes all have repudiated his doctrines, all have condemned him not only by the authority of the sentence passed at his trial, but even more by their choice of a way of life, and rightly too.

Let us now compare with his statutes those of the men whom God has recently ordered to rule in Africa. Socrates decreed that no one should have a wife of his own, they that no one should have one not his own. He wished every woman to be subject to all men, they that no woman should know any man but her husband. He wished a mixed and promiscuous generation, they one purely born and regulated. He ordained that all houses should be of evil reputation, and they that there should be none such. He tried to build evil resorts in every dwelling, they removed them even from entire cities. He wished to prostitute all maidens, they made the prostitutes chaste.

Would that Socrates' error had been his alone, and not that of many, or even the majority of Romans! These follow Socrates' precepts in this matter even if they accept his teachings in nothing else, for many men have more than one wife apiece, and countless women have many husbands each. Are not all our cities full of dens of vice, and reeking with houses of ill fame? When I said all, I meant of course the noblest and loftiest, for such is the preroga-

---

Cato, handing his wife Marcia to a friend "to fill another's house with sons." See Souter, *Classical Review*, XIV (1900), 164. This was a popular *exemplum*, especially among Christian writers, as is shown by R. Kohl, *De scholasticarum declamationum argumentis ex historia petitis* (Paderborn, 1915), p. 104.

[57] Salvian here confused Socrates with the "Socratic dialogues" of Plato.

tive of dignity and honor in our great cities that they excel others as much in indecency as they do in size.

What hope, I ask you, can there be for the Roman state when barbarians are more chaste and pure than the Romans? What I say is all too little: what hope of life or pardon, I ask, can we have in the sight of God when we see chastity in the barbarians and even so are not willing to be chaste ourselves? Should we not feel shame and confusion at this? Already among the Goths you will find none impure except the Romans, none unchaste among the Vandals except the Romans. So much has the desire for chastity accomplished for the barbarians, so much has the severity of their moral code gained, that not only are they themselves chaste, but — though it is so new and strange an event as to be almost incredible — they have even made some Romans chaste.

If my human frailty permitted, I should wish to shout beyond my strength, to make my voice ring through the whole world: Be ashamed, ye Roman people everywhere, be ashamed of the lives you lead. No cities are free of evil haunts, no cities anywhere are free from indecency, except those in which barbarians have begun to live. Do we then wonder that we are wretched who are so impure, that we are conquered by the enemy who are outdone by them in honor, that they possess our properties who abjure our wickedness? It is neither the natural strength of their bodies that makes them conquer nor the weakness of our nature that makes us subject to defeat. Let no one think or persuade himself otherwise — it is our vicious lives alone that have conquered us.[58]

---

[58] Compare Augustine *Sermo de tempore barbarico* (Migne, PL, XL, col. 703): "Neither by the enemy, nor by the barbarians, but by their own action are all men slain in their souls by seeing, consenting and not preventing. We have all abided in quiet, and as long as we do not wish the perverse peace of our state disturbed, we do not receive the true peace that we deserve. We scorn to preserve the peace of a good life, and so the peace of our times has come to an end."

THE EIGHTH BOOK

1. I think, nay, I am certain, that the great length of my argument will arouse distaste in many, especially since it upbraids our vicious lives. For most men wish praise, and no one enjoys censure. Worse than this, however evil a man is, however profligate, he would rather be falsely praised than rightly reproved, and prefers to be deceived by the mockery of false praise than healed by the most salutary admonitions. Since this is true, what are we to do? Must we accede to the will of wicked men? Or if they wish even empty praise conferred on them, is it fitting to proffer silly and meaningless eulogies? Surely we must consider that, as men of honor should not mock even those who wish to make themselves ridiculous, so they should not laud in lying phrases those who yearn to be adorned by praise, however false.[1] We must not take into account the preferences of individuals, but rather what is fitting for us to say, especially since the prophet said: "Woe unto them that put bitter for sweet and sweet for bitter."[2]

We must by every means hold fast to the truth, so that what a thing is in fact, it may also be in words, and those that contain sweetness be called sweet, and those that contain bitterness, bitter. This is the more obligatory in the present discussion of a sacred matter, when our iniquities are made by many a cause of wrath against God, and men try to avoid seeming themselves worthy of

---

[1] Compare Sidonius *Ep.* VIII. 10: "If you had had any consideration for my modesty you would have kept in mind the saying of Symmachus: 'as true praise adorns, so false praise reproves.'" The saying is not found in Symmachus' writings, but Grégoire and Collombet cite it as used by Caesarius of Arles in his 25th homily to the monks of Lérins, which I have been unable to trace, and by Pope Pelagius I in a letter to Sapaudus, bishop of Arles, as the saying of a *vir doctissimus.*

[2] Isaiah 5. 20.

accusation by first accusing him. When they blasphemously call
him careless and neglectful of human affairs, and say that he does
not govern according to justice, or even that he does not govern
at all, what else are they doing but accusing God of laziness and
abuse and injustice? Alas for the blindness of human folly! for
the madness of insane audacity! It is God, O man, that you call
careless and neglectful. If you injured any freeborn man with such
slanders, you would be accused at law of malicious abuse; if you
so attacked any illustrious or eminent man you would be sentenced
in the courts. Such slanders are chiefly hurled at prodigal wards;
it is the special byword for profligate youths, to call them wastrels
and careless and negligent about their property. What sacrilegious
words! what profane impudence! We use such terms of God as we
would not employ of any men except those of the most abandoned
sort. Yet this is not all the abuse given him: as I said before, men
even brand him as unjust. If we claim that we do not deserve our
sufferings and are unworthy to endure our present misfortunes,
surely we are calling God, who bids us endure undeserved evils,
unjust. You say, however, that he does not bid, but merely permits
us to endure them. Suppose we grant this point, still I ask how far
he is from ordering what he permits? For he who knows we endure
such woes and can prevent our suffering them, proves beyond a
doubt that we ought to endure whatever he permits. From this it
is manifest that his acquiescence is part of his judgment, and that
we are enduring a sentence from heaven. As all things are subject
to sacred authority and the will of God rules everything, whatever
evils and whatever punishments we bear daily are the censure of
his divine hand, which censure, indeed, we constantly arouse and
kindle by our sins. We kindle the fire of the celestial wrath and
arouse the flames by which we are burned, so that the words of the
prophet may rightly be used against us as often as we endure such
ills: ''Make your way into the flames of the fire that you have

kindled."[3] From this we see that according to the sacred sentence each sinner is preparing for himself the suffering that he endures. None of our misfortunes can be imputed to God; we are the authors of our own misery. For God is gracious and merciful and, as the Scripture says, he wishes no one to perish or be injured. So whatever is done against us is done by our own actions; there is nothing more cruel to us than ourselves; we, I say, are torturing ourselves even against God's will.

But, forsooth, I seem to be contradicting myself; whereas I said before that we are punished by God on account of our sins, now I say that we are punishing ourselves. Both are true; we are indeed punished by God, but we ourselves force him to punish us. Inasmuch as we cause our own punishment, who can doubt that we are chastising ourselves by our crimes? For whoever gives cause for his punishment chastises himself, according to the saying: "Every one is bound by the chains of his sins."[4] If wicked men are bound by the chains of their sins, every sinner doubtless binds himself when he sins.

2. Since I have already spoken at length of the unchastity of Africa, let me now briefly discuss its blasphemies, for the paganism of the majority has had no interruption. They have indeed confined within their own walls their native crime, by which of course I mean that "Celestial" demon of the Africans,[5] to which I suppose the pagans of old gave so fair-sounding a title in order that having no divinity it should at least have a name, and lacking any virtue derived from actual power should gain honor from its designation. Who among them has not been initiated into the worship of that idol? Who has not been dedicated to it by his very family and birth? I am not speaking now of men who are pagans as much by profession and name as in their way of life, and whose name indi-

---

[3] *Ibid.* 50. 11.

[4] See Proverbs 5. 22.

[5] That is, the goddess Tanit, frequently called *Dea Caelestis* by Latin authors.

cates their heathen error. Paganism is certainly more tolerable and less evil in men avowedly pagan; the more deadly peril lies in the fact that many who have made their vows to Christ continue to give their real devotion to idols. For did not those who were called Christians turn from the worship of Christ to that of the "Celestial deity," or — which is far worse — worship her even before they paid their devotions to him? Who among them did not cross the Lord's threshold redolent of the odor of demoniacal sacrifices and go up to the altar of Christ reeking with the foulness of very demons, so that it would be less monstrous not to come at all to the Lord's temple than to come in such a fashion? For a Christian who does not come to church is guilty of neglect, but one who comes in such a way is guilty of sacrilege. It is less difficult to atone for failure to honor God than for direct insult to him. So we see that any who have acted thus have not given honor to God, but have taken it away from him. They have even in a way given the attention due to the church of God to an idol, because that to which priority is accorded gains in honor from that which is relegated to second place. See then the faith of the Africans, and especially of the noblest among them! See what their religion and their Christianity have been! It was in scorn of Christ that men called them Christians. Though the apostle cries: "Ye cannot drink the cup of the Lord and the cup of devils; ye cannot be partakers of the Lord's table and of the table of devils," [6] it was not enough for them to drink the cup of the Lord with the cup of devils, but they must take the latter first. It was not enough for them to match the table of devils with the Lord's table, unless they came to the temple of God fresh from the worship of infamous superstitions and breathed on the holy altars of Christ the foul miasma of the diabolical spirit itself.

3. But, you say, they do not all do these things — only the highest and most powerful are guilty of these wrongs. Suppose

---

[6] I Corinthians 10. 21.

I agree to this. Still, since the greater part of a city is made up of the richest and most powerful households, you see that the whole city was polluted by the sacrilegious superstition of a few great men. No one indeed can doubt that all the households are either like the masters who rule them, or worse, and usually worse! Therefore, since even good masters as a general rule have bad slaves, it is easy to decide what sort of households all of these were, in which servile minds, already disposed to evil, were made more vicious by the wickedness of their masters.

Suppose for the sake of the argument that what we said was true only of all the most powerful and noble. Were the vices that were common to noble and ignoble alike less serious? I mean the hatred and abuse of all holy men, for surely it is a sort of sacrilege to hate those who worship God. Just as the man who injures our slaves thereby harms us, and the man who flogs another's sons tortures the father's affection by his children's suffering, so anyone who injures a servant of God violates the divine majesty, as the Lord said to his apostle: "He that receiveth you, receiveth me, and he that despiseth you, despiseth me."[7] Our most gracious and loving Lord shared his honor and disgrace alike with his servants, to the end that no one who injured a servant of God should think that the man alone was hurt by his action, since injury to God would undoubtedly be mingled with the harm inflicted on his followers. Of this God gave us proof, according to his most indulgent love, in these words: "For he that toucheth you toucheth the pupil of my eye."[8] To express the tenderness of his love he used the most tender part of the body, that we might clearly understand that God is injured by a contempt of his saints as slight as the touch required to injure the eyesight. So the people of Africa injured and hated the servants of God and God himself in them.

4. But perhaps the question will be asked: "In what ways was

---

[7] Matthew 10. 40; Luke 10. 16.
[8] Zechariah 2. 8.

their hatred manifested?'' In the same manner, of course, in which
also the Jews' hatred of Christ was declared when they said to him:
''Thou art a Samaritan and hast a devil,'' [9] when they mocked and
cursed him, when they breathed into his face and gnashed their
teeth over his head. Whence also the Savior himself says in the
Psalms: ''All they that saw me laughed me to scorn; they shot
out their lips and shook their heads.'' [10] And elsewhere he says:
''They have tempted me and laughed me to scorn, they gnashed
upon me with their teeth.'' [11] So is the hatred of the Africans for
the monks — that is, for the servants of God — proved, because they
mocked at and cursed them, because they attacked and execrated
them, because they did practically everything against them that
the wickedness of the Jews contrived against our Savior before they
actually shed his divine blood. But they, you say, did not kill the
saints, while we read that the Jews did.

Whether they killed or not, I do not know; I make no claims of
that, but yet how great a defence is it that the only element of
pagan persecution lacking was the very end of persecution? Let us
assume that the saints were not killed there; what then shall we
make of the fact that they are not far from killing who hate with
the desire to kill, especially as the Lord himself says: ''Whosoever
hateth his brother without a cause is a murderer?'' [12]

Yet it was not without cause that they persecuted the servants
of God. For who can say that it was without a cause, seeing that
these men differed from them in all the characteristics of their life
and habits, that in them they saw nothing that was theirs, since
all was God's? The greatest cause of discord is diversity of interests, because it is nearly or quite impossible that a man should
love in another that with which he himself is at variance. So it was

---

[9] John 8. 48.
[10] Psalms 22. 7.
[11] Jeremiah 20. 7; Psalms 35. 16.
[12] I John 3. 15.

not without cause, as I said, that they hated those in whom they saw everything hostile and inimical to them. For they lived in constant wickedness, but the saints in constant innocence; they lived in lust, these in chastity; they in evil dens, these in monasteries; they almost constantly with the devil, and these incessantly with Christ. It was not without cause that within the cities of Africa, and especially within the walls of Carthage, a people as unhappy as they were unfaithful could scarcely look without reviling and curses at a man pale and in monkish garb, his flowing locks cut even to the shaved skin. And if ever any servant of God from the monasteries of Egypt or the sacred places of Jerusalem or the holy and venerable retreats of the desert came to that city in performance of his sacred mission, as soon as he appeared to the people, he met with contumely, sacrilege and curses. Nor was this all, he was flayed by the vile derision of dissolute men and hissing mockery of the coarsest sort; so that if any man uninformed of these things witnessed the scene, he would not think that a man was being mocked, but that some strange and unheard-of monster was being expelled from the city.

5. Consider the faith of the Africans and especially the people of Carthage. It was safer for the apostles of old to enter the cities of the pagans, and those wild and barbarous assemblies had less hatred of their arrival and presence. The holy vessel of election, Paul the apostle, spoke of the worship and majesty of one God, and the people of the Athenians, most superstitious though they were, heard him patiently.[13] The Lycaonians also so marvelled at the apostles that, seeing their divine strength, they thought they were not men.[14] But in Carthage the servants of God were scarcely allowed to appear in the streets and public squares without mockery and cursing. Certain men think that this was not persecution be-

---

[13] Acts 17. 16-34. One scarcely expects to find the Athenian Ecclesia cited as an example of a wild and barbarous assembly.

[14] Acts 14.

cause they were not actually killed. You know that brigands have a proverb that those they spare owe their lives to them.[15] But in Carthage this benefit was due less to the men than to the laws, for the laws of the Twelve Tables forbade a man to be put to death without a trial. Hence we see that the power of the Lord's religion was indeed great in a place where his servants were only permitted to escape death at the hands of Christians because they were defended by pagan law. Yet we wonder that such Christians are now suffering at the hands of the barbarians, when they themselves inflicted barbarous treatment on the saints.

So God is just and his judgments are righteous, for, as the Scripture says: "What men have sowed, that shall they also reap." [16] God seems to have referred to the wickedness of the people of Africa, when he said: "Recompense her according to her work; according to all that she hath done do unto her; for she hath been proud against the Lord." [17] Let us [18] then be surprised and angry that they now endure some few trials at the hands of men! Their conduct toward God has been far worse than any treatment they have received, especially if one compares their sufferings and their misdeeds with due consideration of the distinction between the persons concerned.[19]

---

[15] See Cicero *Or. Philippica* II. 3. 5.

[16] Galatians 6. 7.

[17] Jeremiah 50. 29.

[18] Here Pauly inserted the negative *minime*, for which the MSS give no authority. I have omitted it as unnecessary; without it the sentence furnishes a characteristic example of Salvian's irony. See H. K. Messenger, *op. cit.*, sec. 48.

[19] Here ends the text as it is preserved in the MSS. Whether the succeeding chapters have been lost, or the author left his work unfinished, cannot now be determined. In view, however, of the many years between the composition of the book and Salvian's death, the former alternative seems the more probable.

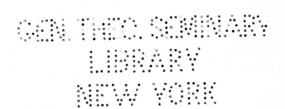

BIBLIOGRAPHY [1]

BRAKMAN, C. J. "Observationes grammaticae et criticae in Salvianum: accedit appendix de Gennadii capite lxviii," *Mnemosyne*, LII (1924), 113-185.

BRAKMAN, C. J. *Opstellen over Onderwerpen uit de Latijnsche Letterkunde*, II, ch. 17. Leyden, 1926.

BRUNI, G. *Un apologista della Provvidenza fra le invasioni barbariche del sec. V d. C.* Rome, 1925.

CEILLIER, R. *Histoire générale des auteurs sacrés et ecclésiastiques*, XV (Paris, 1748), 46-81.

COOPER-MARSDIN, A. C. *The History of the Islands of the Lérins.* Cambridge, 1913.

GEFFCKEN, J. "Stimmungen im untergehenden Weströmerreich," *Neue Jahrbücher für das klassische Altertum*, XXIII (1920), 256-269.

GIRAUD, I. *De Salviano dissertatio.* Montpellier, 1849.

HAEMMERLE, ALOIS. *Studia Salviana.* Landshut and Neuberg, 1891-1899.

---

[1] For the chief editions and translations of Salvian's works see Introduction, pp. 29 ff. and note 57. I have included in this bibliography only books and articles relating especially to Salvian. A fuller list will be found in Bruni, *Un apologista della Provvidenza* (Rome, 1925), 79-82, which includes some studies not accessible to me. General discussions of conditions in the Roman world in the fifth century are too numerous and too well-known to require listing here. For readers desiring an initial acquaintance with the subject, however, the following brief list may be of service:

BURY, J. B. *The Invasion of Europe by the Barbarians*, New York, 1928.

Cambridge Medieval History, I: *The Christian Roman Empire and the Founding of the Teutonic Kingdoms.* Cambridge, 1911.

DILL, SAMUEL. *Roman Society in the Last Century of the Western Empire*, 2d ed. Cambridge, 1898.

HALPHEN, LOUIS. *Les Barbares, des grandes invasions aux conquêtes turques du Xe siècle.* Paris, 1926.

HODGKIN, THOMAS. *Italy and Her Invaders*, I, 2d ed. Oxford, 1892.

LOT, FERDINAND. *La Fin du monde antique et le début du moyen âge.* Paris, 1927.

In references in the footnotes, Migne, PL refers to the *Patrologia Latina*, CSEL to the Vienna *Corpus Scriptorum Ecclesiasticorum Latinorum*, MGH to the *Monumenta Germaniae Historica*.

HALM, K. "Über die handschriftliche Überlieferung des Salvianus," *Sitzungsberichte der Münchener Akademie der Wissenschaften, Phil.-hist. Klasse*, 1876, 390-412.

HIRNER, F. X. *Commentatio de Salviano eiusque libellis*. Freising, 1869.

Histoire littéraire de la France, II (1735), 517-535.

MÉRY, L. *Étude sur Salvien, prêtre de Marseille*. Marseille, 1849.

MESSENGER, H. K. *De temporum et modorum apud Salvianum usu*, unpublished dissertation in the Harvard College Library, 1924. Summary published in *Harvard Studies in Classical Philology*, XXXVI (1925), 180-182.

MORICCA, U. "Salviano e la data del *De gubernatione Dei*," *Rivista di filologia classica*, XLVI (1918), 241-255.

PAULY, Fr. "Die handschriftliche Überlieferung des Salvianus," *Sitzungsberichte der Wiener Akademie der Wissenschaften, Phil.-hist. Klasse*, XCVIII (1881), 3-41.

SCHMALZ, J. H. "Zu Salvian," *Berliner philologische Wochenschrift*, XXXV (1915), cols. 1041-1047.

STERNBERG, G. "Das Christentum des fünften Jahrhunderts im Spiegel des Salvianus von Massilia," *Theologische Studien und Kritiken*, LXXXII (1909), 29-78, 163-205.

THOUVENOT, R. "Salvien et la ruine de l'Empire romain," *Mélanges de l'École française de Rome*, XXXVII (1918-1919), 145-163.

VALRAN, G. *Quare Salvianus presbyter Massiliensis magister episcoporum a Gennadio dictus sit*. Paris, 1899.

WALTZING, J. P. "Tertullien et Salvien," *Musée Belge*, XIX-XXIV (1920), 39-43.

WESTON, A. H. *Latin Satirical Writing Subsequent to Juvenal*, Yale dissertation, 1915, 143-154.

WEYMANN, C. "Salvianus und Paulinus von Nola," *Historisches Jahrbuch*, XV (1894), 372-373.

WOLFFLIN, Ed. "Allitteration und Reim bei Salvian," *Archiv für lateinische Lexikographie*, XIII (1902-4), 41-49.

ZSCHIMMER, W. *Salvianus der Presbyter von Massilia und seine Schriften*. Halle, 1875.

INDEX

Aaron, 60, 63
Abel, 50
Abihu, 62
Abiron, 62
Abraham's life as proof of God's judgment, 53 f.
Absalom, 71, 74
Achar, 157, 214
Adam, 50
Aëtius, 22, 201n
Aetna, 210
Africa, 179n; commerce and wealth of, 208; interest of Salvian in, 8; Vandal conquest of, 106, 178, 205 ff.; wickedness of, 207 ff.
Alans, characteristics of, 123, 209
Alaric, 178n
Alemanni, drunkenness of, 123
Allix, Peter, 15
Alps, 155, 160
Amnon, 74
Amphitheaters, 162
Ananias, 158
Animal fights, 160 f.
Anthemius, Emperor, 169n
Aquitanians, wealth and vices of, 191 ff., 204
Arcadius, Emperor, 105n, 109n
Arians, 121n, 136 ff., 178
Arvandus, 105n
Assyrians, 198, 206
Asylum, 150
Athens, 230
Athletes, 162
Attic wisdom, 221
Attila, 140
Augury, 161
Augustine, St., 21, 22, 43; Bon. coniug., 221n; Contra ep. Manichaei, 135n; Sermo de tempore barbarico, 26, 119n, 223n

Ausonius, 10, 23
Auspiciola, daughter of Salvian, 11
Authority of God superior to reason, 24, 78
Avarice, attack of Salvian on, 16; characteristic vice of Romans, 209
Bagaudae, rebellion of, 122 ff.
Baluze, Stephen, 7, 31 f., 82n, 172n, 181n
Baptismal vows, renunciation of spectacles in, 167 f.
Barbarians, chastity of, 196 ff., 223; classification of as heretics and pagans, 121; compared with Romans, 77, 119 ff., 147 f., 191 ff.; invasions of as occasion for denial of God's government, 3; Roman responsibility for heresy of, 138; tribute exacted by, 188; vices of, 122f.
Belgae invaded by Vandals, 204
Bellarmine, 27
Benedad, king of Syria, 198
Blasphemy, punishment for causing, 129-130
Boniface, Roman general, 202n
Bonnet, Père, 27, 32n
Borromeo, St. Carlo, 32n, 160n
Bossuet, 33
Brakman, C. J., 15, 19, 233
Brassicanus, 31, 32
Brouwer, 181n
Bruni, G., 25n, 32n, 233
Bury, J. B., 24n, 140n, 233

Caesarius of Arles, 12, 13, 224n; Ep. ad germanos, 111n; Regula ad monachos, 111n; Vita, 13
Cain, 50 f.
Cambridge Medieval History, 233
Capernaum, 113
Capitatio, 150n

RECORDS OF CIVILIZATION
SOURCES AND STUDIES

FORTHCOMING VOLUMES

Calendar Reform in the Thirteenth Century. By Mary C. Welborn, Instructor in History, Florida State College for Women.

The Council of Constance. By Louise Ropes Loomis, Professor of History, Wells College.

Epics from the Peasant Life of Medieval Germany: Wernher der Gartenaere's Meier Helmbrecht and Hartman von Aue's Der arme Heinrich. By Clair Hayden Bell, Professor of German, University of California.

Helmold: Slavic Chronicle. By Francis J. Tschan, Associate Professor of History, Pennsylvania State College.

The History of Constantinople, by Gunther, the German. By M. R. Gutsch, Professor of History, University of Texas.

Marcus Porcius Cato's Book on Farming. By Dr. Ernest Brehaut.

Medieval Universities and Intellectual Life. By Lynn Thorndike, Professor of History, Columbia University.

Old Norwegian Law: The Gulathing Law and the Frostathing Law. By Laurence M. Larson, Professor of History, University of Illinois.

Orosius: Seven Books of History against the Pagans. By Irving W. Raymond, Assistant Professor of History, Columbia University.

Pierre Dubois: On the Recovery of the Holy Land. By W. I. Brandt, Associate Professor of History, College of the City of New York.

The Sources for the Early History of Ireland. Volume Two: Secular. By Dr. James F. Kenney.

Tracts on Liberty, 1649-1669. By William Haller, Associate Professor of English, Columbia University.

William of Tyre: History of Things Done in the Lands beyond the Sea. By Mrs. Emily Atwater Babcock, Instructor in Latin, and A. C. Krey, Professor of History, University of Minnesota.

Zabara: Book of Delight. By Moses Hadas, Instructor in Classics, Columbia University.

COLUMBIA UNIVERSITY PRESS
COLUMBIA UNIVERSITY
NEW YORK

FOREIGN AGENT
OXFORD UNIVERSITY PRESS
HUMPHREY MILFORD
AMEN HOUSE, LONDON, E. C.

RECORDS OF CIVILIZATION
SOURCES AND STUDIES

Edited under the auspices of the

Department of History, Columbia University

A series of volumes containing documents in translation, commentaries and interpretations, and bibliographical guides. (Uniform in size and binding, octavo, cloth, stamped in gold.)

PREVIOUSLY PUBLISHED

Hellenic Civilization. By G. W. Botsford and E. G. Sihler. pp. xiii + 719. $4.50.

History of the Franks, by Gregory, Bishop of Tours. Selections, translated with notes by Ernest Brehaut. pp. xxi + 284, map. $3.50.

The Book of the Popes (Liber Pontificalis). Translated with an introduction by Louise Ropes Loomis. pp. xxii + 169. $3.00.

An Introduction to the History of History. By James T. Shotwell. pp. xii + 339. $4.50.

The Literature of the Old Testament in Its Historical Development. By Julius A. Bewer. pp. xiv + 452. $3.00.

A Guide to the Printed Materials for English Social and Economic History, 1750-1850. By Judith Blow Williams. Two volumes. pp. xxiii + 535; iv + 653. $10.00.

The See of Peter. By James T. Shotwell and Louise Ropes Loomis. pp. xxvi + 737. $10.00.

The History of Yaballaha III. Translated from the Syriac and annotated by James A. Montgomery. pp. ix + 82. $2.00.

The Two Cities, by Otto, Bishop of Freising. Translated in full with introduction and notes by Charles Christopher Mierow. pp. xv + 523. $10.00.

An Arab-Syrian Gentleman and Warrior in the Period of the Crusades: Memoirs of Usāmah ibn-Munqidh. Translated from the original manuscript by Philip K. Hitti. pp. x + 265. $4.50.

The Sources for the Early History of Ireland. Volume One: Ecclesiastical. By James F. Kenney. pp. xvi + 807. $12.50.

COLUMBIA UNIVERSITY PRESS
COLUMBIA UNIVERSITY
NEW YORK

FOREIGN AGENT
OXFORD UNIVERSITY PRESS
HUMPHREY MILFORD
AMEN HOUSE, LONDON, E. C.